SIX MONTHS AT THE WHITE HOUSE.

SIX MONTHS

AT

THE WHITE HOUSE

WITH

ABRAHAM LINCOLN.

The Story of a Picture.

BY

F. B. CARPENTER.

1866

INTRODUCTION BY

HAROLD HOLZER

2008

The WHITE HOUSE HISTORICAL ASSOCIATION is a nonprofit
organization, chartered on November 3, 1961, to enhance
understanding, appreciation, and enjoyment of the historic
White House. Income from the sale of the association's books
and guides is returned to the publications program
and is used as well to acquire historical
furnishings and memorabilia for the White House.

Address inquiries to: White House Historical Association
740 Jackson Place, N.W., Washington, D.C. 20006
www.whitehousehistory.org

Originally published in 1866 by Hurd and Houghton, New York.
White House Historical Association edition, 2008

ISBN 978-1-931917-03-2
Library of Congress Control Number 2008926984
Printed in the U.S.A.

*Frontispiece: The North Front of the White House during the
Lincoln administration c. 1860.* [Library of Congress]

FOREWORD

In this volume, the White House Historical Association has reset *Six Months at the White House* from the original edition, preserving typographical errors as they were, without comment. We have added an introduction by Lincoln historian Harold Holzer, an album of related photographs, and a new index.

INTRODUCTION

BY HAROLD HOLZER

Francis Bicknell Carpenter—the self-taught artist and influential memoirist who deserves more credit than anyone of his time for conceiving and recording both the public and personal images of Abraham Lincoln—was born in the remote rural village of Homer, New York, on August 6, 1830.

Not unlike Lincoln himself, who ultimately became the primary focus of his artistic and literary careers, Carpenter rose from "humble circumstances," according to his earliest biographer, and "earned his own prosperity and reputation by good conduct and hard work" to forge "a truly American career." The most enduring accomplishments of that career were the creation of iconic portraits of Lincoln as an emancipator and father, as well as authorship of one of the most influential Lincoln reminiscences ever published. The book that has been reprinted in this new edition by the White House Historical Association—notably, the first ever to be illustrated with Carpenter's own Lincoln art—reflects its author's own remarkable White House experience as the American equivalent of a court painter, as well as his remarkably perceptive, if unapologetically loving, view of its most famous occupant.

In stark contrast to contemporary Lincoln portrayers like Boston painter Thomas M. Johnston, the son of a famous artist, Carpenter evolved from no established artistic tradition. The story goes that his father was but a "respectable farmer" who not only expressed little interest in the subject, but was paraphrased as confessing, much like George II: "I hate painting, and poetry too."[1]

Yet young "Frank," as he was known, was by the age of eight determinedly drawing on every available surface he could cover with his pictures, beginning with a schoolroom door that he eagerly defaced. With "neither instructions, books, nor models" at his disposal, he practiced on walls, smooth wooden planks, "blank leaves of old account books," and the cheap foolscap paper he purchased with his own scant earnings. The boy's exuberant sketching prompted one neighbor to remark: "Humph! you can't turn over a chip on his father's farm without findin' a pictur' of a chicken or sunthin' on t'other side on't."[2] The rustic observer was not alone in thinking the youth's artistic inclinations somewhat exotic. William O. Stoddard, a future White

1. Fred. B. Perkins, *The Picture and the Men: Being Biographical Sketches of President Lincoln and His Cabinet; Together with an Account of the Life of the Celebrated Artist F. B. Carpenter, Author of the Great National Painting, The First Reading of the Emancipation Proclamation Before the Cabinet of President Lincoln . . .* (New York: A. J. Johnson, 1867), 3.
2. *Ibid.*, 8–9.

House clerk and Lincoln biographer who also grew up in Carpenter's hometown, five years his junior, remembered Frank not only as a "Homer boy" but also "the first artist I ever heard of."[3]

Being a "Homer boy" may have excited no automatic ambitions in the realm of art, but it did involve these youngsters from an early age in both antislavery politics and Protestant piety, a background that profoundly influenced Carpenter's dual careers. Although small, their village boasted thriving Universalist, Methodist, Baptist, and Congregationalist churches, and its children were routinely expected to attend Sunday school and avidly study the Bible.[4] Carpenter was raised in the Congregationalist tradition, and remained a deeply religious man throughout his life, shunning the "Bohemian lifestyle" that most nineteenth-century Americans came to associate with artists.[5] Carpenter's "views on the ethics of Art, as well as his moral and religious sentiments generally," his biographer testified in 1867, told him that "the artist ought of necessity to be of the purest character" and boast a "union of artistic ability and moral excellence."[6]

---

3. Harold Holzer, ed., *Lincoln's White House Secretary: The Adventurous Life of William O. Stoddard* (Carbondale: Southern Illinois University Press, 2007), 63.

4. *Ibid.*, 38, 43.

5. Mark E. Neely, Jr., *The Inner Life of Abraham Lincoln*, orig. pub. 1868 (Lincoln: University of Nebraska Press, 1995), vii.

6. Perkins, *The Picture and the Men*, 17–18.

The local political hero of the day was William H. Seward, who hailed from the nearest big city, Auburn, and became governor of New York when Carpenter was only eight years old. Whigs like Seward believed in free labor and high protective tariffs, and his Central New York supporters, including Carpenter, never forsook these core beliefs. Carpenter's lifelong affection for Seward would later subtly manifest itself in the most famous of his paintings, notwithstanding the fame it achieved as an iconic representation of the man who defeated him to become the Republican candidate for president in 1860: Abraham Lincoln.

Despite the absence of encouragement from his family, Carpenter persisted with his art. Apprenticed to an Ithaca grocer at the age of thirteen, he failed spectacularly enough to be sent back home labeled a "hopeless dunce," with no hope of a prosperous future in the mercantile field. The only professional artistic instruction to which he was exposed at the time came when a young Auburn artist named George L. Clough arrived in Homer in search of commissions. Frank watched him work, and became more determined than ever to master the craft of painting. Though—again, supposedly like Lincoln—he received no sympathy from his father, who complained whenever his son neglected his farm chores to draw or sketch, the precocious Carpenter apparently won him over at last when he made a successful likeness of his mother using a "piece of coat lining" as a canvas. Neighbors who saw the portrait said it was "decidedly better than the works of the wandering artists who had been the only painters there before," the itinerant George Clough, no doubt, included.[7]

Further convinced of his son's talents when Frank executed a companion portrait of himself, the elder Carpenter finally sent the boy off to Syracuse to study under Sanford Thayer, a portrait and genre painter who earlier had been a student of the prominent artist Charles Loring Elliott. In 1846, at the age of sixteen, Frank established a little studio of his own in Homer, and enrolled briefly at the nearby Cortland Academy (whose founding trustees he would later paint). The following year, he visited New York City for the first time in his life, viewed the large portraits of the nation's founders on display at City Hall as well as the paintings on exhibition at the New-York Historical Society, and within months, further inspired, took home a coveted prize for a portrait submitted to the American Art-Union.[8] He was on his way to a full-time career as a painter.

By 1851, Carpenter was an associate of the National Academy of Design with a studio in New York. Just four years

---

7. Perkins, *The Picture and the Men*, 9–11.

8. *Ibid.*, 18–19; Harold Holzer, Gabor S. Boritt, and Mark E. Neely, Jr., "Francis Bicknell Carpenter (1830–1900): Painter of Abraham Lincoln and his Circle," *American Art Journal*, 16 (Spring 1984): 68.

later he opened a temporary studio in Washington, where he completed a life portrait of President Franklin Pierce, who called him "an artist of rare genius & merit."[9] Millard Fillmore had sat for him earlier, so by the time Lincoln became the first Republican in the White House, Carpenter had established himself as a successful painter of presidents. He had also become more ardent in his antislavery views, a friend and correspondent of the young antislavery minister Theodore Thornton Munger, and increasingly convinced that God had ordained the abolition of slavery. Thus it was no real surprise that Lincoln's Emancipation Proclamation, which took effect January 1, 1863, struck Carpenter as "an act unparalleled for moral grandeur in the history of mankind," signaling a "long prayed-for year of jubilee."[10] Carpenter, naturally enough, was inspired to undertake a visual tribute. "Surely," as he wrote later in this very book, *Six Months at the White House*, "Art should unite with Eloquence and Poetry to celebrate such a scene."[11]

The artist's wealthy friend Frederick A. Lane agreed to finance the endeavor, and reached out to influential

---

9. *The Home Journal*, February 9, 1856; Franklin Pierce to Lewis Cass, February 5, 1855, Hildene, the [Robert Todd] Lincoln Family Home, Manchester Vermont, preserved and donated by Clara Scherer and A. George Scherer, descendants of the artist. The author is grateful to Hildene curator Brian Knight for bringing these letters to his attention, and to historian Jason Emerson for sharing the files.

10. Francis B. Carpenter, *Six Months at the White House: The Story of a Picture* (New York: Hurd & Houghton, 1866), 12.

11. *Ibid.*

Republicans like newspaperman Samuel Sinclair and Indiana Congressman Schuyler Colfax, both of whom urged Lincoln to pose. "I wish to paint this picture now," Carpenter impatiently emphasized to Illinois Congressman Owen Lovejoy, an old friend of Lincoln's, "while all the actors in the scene are living and while they are still in the discharge of the duties of their several high offices—I wish to make it the standard authority for the portrait of each and all especially Mr. Lincoln as it is the great act of his life by which he will be remembered through all generations." From the outset, as Carpenter confidently assured Lovejoy and others, he planned to have the result exhibited in all of America's large cities and engraved in the highest style.[12]

Convinced that the project was worth supporting, Lovejoy helped arrange for Carpenter to set up a studio inside the White House to accomplish his goal. To his disappointment, the artist was not permitted to move into the mansion, as he hoped: the president's son was due home soon, and there were no bedrooms to spare. Still, Carpenter became the closest thing to an artist-in-residence Lincoln ever welcomed, though he never lived in the White House, as the title of his book implied.

---

12. Francis B. Carpenter to Owen Lovejoy, January 5, 1864, location of original unknown; typescript in the Lincoln Museum collection, Fort Wayne, Indiana

"I think the coast is all clear to you any time you choose to come on now," Lovejoy wrote Carpenter once the arrangements had been finalized. "You can make yourself immortal as soon as you choose."[13]

Although the artist believed that the Emancipation Proclamation had elevated Lincoln "to a dignity and glory almost divine," he insisted that it should be portrayed in art not as a "fable," but as "a substantial fact—the immaculate conception of Constitutional Liberty." He maintained that "if honestly and earnestly painted, it need borrow no interest from imaginary curtain or column, gorgeous furniture or allegorical statue" (perhaps a not-so subtle critique of the work of rival painter Edward Dalton Marchant, who a few months earlier had worked in the White House to portray Lincoln as an Emancipator whose signature on his proclamation metaphorically breaks the shackles on a nearby statue marked "Liberty").[14]

Declaring, in contrast, that he "had no more right to depart from the facts, than has the historian in his record," he chose as his own subject not the signing of the final proclamation, but the July 1862 cabinet meeting at which Lincoln first told his ministers that he intended to issue the momentous order. "If I

---

13. Owen Lovejoy to Francis B. Carpenter, January 15, 1864, Hildene Collection, preserved by Clara Scherer, and donated by A. George Scherer.

14. For Marchant's work, see Harold Holzer, *Lincoln Seen and Heard* (Lawrence: University Press of Kansas, 2000), 15.

cannot make the portraiture of the scene itself sufficiently attractive without the false glitter of tapestry hangings, velvet table-cloths, and marble columns," the artist memorably recalled in this book, "then I shall at least have the satisfaction of having failed in the cause of truth."[15] Of course, by the time he wrote these words Carpenter had already enjoyed the advantage of seeing Lincoln's drably furnished office for himself. In his book, he cleverly made a virtue of its plain appearance. But he never quite explained why he decided to portray the moment at which his longtime hero, William Seward, actually objected to issuing the proclamation until it could be sustained by a Union battlefield victory. The most famous painting ever made of the Emancipation Proclamation thus ironically depicted not its enactment but its postponement.

Nevertheless, thanks to the recollections he published in this memoir, we know exactly how the artist went about accomplishing his task. No Lincoln-era icon was ever more meticulously described. As *Six Months at the White House* attests, Carpenter set up his canvas in the State Dining Room of the Executive Mansion and worked there from February through July 1864. He executed model heads of Lincoln and his cabinet officers, and produced a sheaf of sketches of Lincoln's office. He also commissioned a number of photographs showing Lincoln

---

15. Carpenter, *Six Months at the White House*, 11–12, 26, 29.

standing and sitting inside his dimly lit White House office—
these the only photographs of Lincoln in the mansion—and
ordered an additional portfolio of photographs made at
Mathew Brady's gallery on Pennsylvania Avenue. Only then
did he chalk out and commence painting his nine-foot by four-
teen-and-a-half foot canvas. Lincoln gave him unprecedented
access to meetings and frequent opportunities to sketch and
paint, sometimes to the annoyance of other visitors.

At the end of "six months' incessant labor" on July 22,
Carpenter led the cabinet into the State Dining Room to
inspect the final work, where the president "expressed his
'unschooled opinion'" that it was a success, Carpenter recalled
with pride, "in terms which could not but have afforded the
deepest gratification to any artist." Ordering that it go on public view in the East Room, Lincoln told Carpenter: "In my
judgment, it is as good a piece of work as the subject will admit
of . . . and I am right glad you have done it."[16] So, for the longest
time, were the American people. The following March, the
painting went on exhibition in the Capitol rotunda—which,
even then, the artist hoped would become its permanent home.
The temporary display was timed to the president's re-inaugu-
ration, and one guard remembered once seeing a sunbeam burst

16. Carpenter, *Six Months at the White House*, 64–65; Carpenter, "Anecdotes and
Reminiscences," in Henry G. Raymond, *Life, Public Services, and State Papers of Abraham
Lincoln* (New York: Derby & Miller, 1865), 763–764.

through the windows from atop the dome to illuminate Lincoln's face, an omen that inspired him to declare: "Look! that is as it should be. God bless him! May the sun shine on his head forever!"[17]

But the picture did not remain in the Capitol for long. Instead, it went off on its promised national tour, where it earned high praise, even though Carpenter unaccountably began repainting the Lincoln portrait—"retouching some injuries and remedying some defects in minor details," in the words of one sympathetic observer, all but destroying it in the view of others.[18] "I saw it many years afterwards," the president's son Robert Lincoln commented in 1903, "and it seemed to me that during those years he had kept tinkering at it until he had, in my opinion, nearly ruined it."[19]

Carpenter's transformation from ambitious and well-connected artist to best-selling writer occurred right after Lincoln's assassination in 1865. The tragedy spiked public interest in both artistic and literary tributes to the martyred leader, and with his grand work on tour, and the print adaptation in the hands of an engraver, its appearance as a print likely to be

17. *Ibid.*, 42–43.

18. Perkins, *The Picture and the Men*, 47.

19. Robert T. Lincoln to Warren C. Crane, December 15, 1903, Abraham Lincoln Presidential Library and Museum, Springfield, Illinois, Robert Todd Lincoln Letter File, Reel 62. I thank Robert Lincoln biographer Jason Emerson for bringing this letter to my attention.

delayed, Carpenter was no doubt eager to take advantage of his experience as a first-hand observer of the great man. Two weeks after the assassination, he published his "Personal Impressions of Mr. Lincoln" in the anti-slavery New York weekly, *The Independent*, staking a unique claim to intimacy with the martyr by stressing: "As an occupant of the White House" he had "enjoyed the freedom of his office at almost all hours." Carpenter went on to produce a series of Lincoln recollections in that newspaper. In June he published another article on the late president in the magazine *Hours at Home*, based on what he similarly called his "six months familiar intercourse with him under the same roof."[20]

"The truth is," he confided, "I had no idea of writing a book at the time of painting my picture . . . . When I wrote my first sketch in the *Independent* I had no thought of writing a record.—The intense interest of the public, in every thing relating to Lincoln was the occasion of the continuation of the series." Explaining how he managed to remember so many details of his White House experience," Carpenter admitted, "I did not even keep a record of incidents, but simply a pocket diary of my work from day to day." Evidently it proved sufficient, though the surviving diary, which this writer has person-

20. Francis B. Carpenter, "Personal Impressions of Mr. Lincoln," *The* [New York] *Independent*, "April 27, 1865; Carpenter, "In Memoriam," *Hours at Home*, June 1865, 158.

ally examined, contains little detail. "By referring to this however," the artist nonetheless insisted, "various incidents would
return to me[.]"[21] The logical next step was to combine and edit
all his articles for a book.

Carpenter might have been well served to see also to the
more expeditious engraved adaptation of his monumental history painting. The noted engraver Alexander H. Ritchie had
contracted to undertake the adaptation in 1864, and Derby &
Miller of New York arranged to publish it. Critics like journal-
ist Noah Brooks, who complained of the painting's "rawness,
lack of finish, and commonplaceness," believed its "chief faults"
would be "remedied in the engraving." Brooks went so far as to
predict—accurately as it turned out—that it would be "prized in
every liberty-loving household" as "a perpetual remembrance of
the noblest event in American history."[22] Ever cooperative,
Lincoln himself signed on as the first subscriber to a $50 signed
artist's proof of the eagerly anticipated result. But the print was
not issued until 1866 (by which time Lincoln was dead), and

21. Francis B. Carpenter to William H. Herndon, December 4, 1866, in Douglas L.
Wilson and Rodney O. Davis, eds., *Herndon's Informants: Letters, Interviews, and
Statements about Abraham Lincoln* (Urbana: University of Illinois Press, 1966), 495.

22. Noah Brooks dispatch, July 25, 1864, in P. J. Staudenraus, ed., *Mr. Lincoln's Washington:
Selections from the Writings of Noah Brooks, Civil War Correspondent* (New York: Thomas
Yoseloff, 1967), 361, 363.

while it certainly went on to achieve huge popularity (some 30,000 copies were made from the Ritchie plate over the next twenty years),[23] and earned a reputation as the standard portrait of Lincoln the emancipator, it was not available when the furor of demand for Lincoln imagery first manifested itself at the time of his murder.

Carpenter had even worse luck with a carefully planned portrait of the Lincoln family. Based on his lengthy work experience and extraordinary access to the White House, no artist ever had a better opportunity to portray all the Lincolns together. None possessed a deeper understanding of the potential impact of such imagery on public memory. Though he chose to ignore it, for example, Carpenter well knew the irascible side of Lincoln's youngest son, Tad, and Lincoln's extraordinary forbearance in dealing with his difficult child. On the day the crew of Brady camera operators came to the White House to photograph Lincoln in his office—Carpenter had commissioned the pictures to serve as models for his Emancipation painting—the cameramen retreated to a nearby closet to develop their plates.

Believing that he had exclusive rights to the closet, an infuriated Tad burst into his father's office and lectured Carpenter

---

23. J. C. Derby, *Fifty Years Among Authors, Books, and Publishers* (New York: Derby & Miller, 1884), 489. The New York *Independent* reported on February 2, 1871 that it had purchased the plate for $8,000 and was selling prints for $10 as a premium for subscriptions to the newspaper.

that he "had no right to use his room, and that the men should not go in even to get their things." What was more, he had locked the door and hidden the key. Patiently, the president ordered the boy to unlock the closet, and when he later learned that his "great pet" had failed to comply, compressed his lips, strode out of the room, and returned a few minutes later key in hand. But he was all tenderness. "Tad," he apologized, "is a peculiar child. He was violently excited when I went to him. I said, 'Tad, do you know you are making your father a great deal of trouble?' He burst into tears, instantly giving me up the key."[24]

To Carpenter, this brief glimpse into the home life of the president, though "trifling in itself," offered the "gauge of his entire domestic character." He made sure to insert the tale into his book, along with W. D. Kelly's recollection that "The President never seemed grander in my sight than when, stealing upon him in the evening, I would find him with a book open before him, as he is represented in the popular photograph, with little Tad beside him."[25]

Carpenter must have related that anecdote with particular pride, because he had personally escorted Lincoln to Mathew Brady's gallery on February 9, 1864, the day Brady took the pic-

---

24. Carpenter, *Six Months at the White House*, 91–92.

25. *Ibid.*, 92–93.

ture Kelly described. What was more, Carpenter likely had a direct hand in arranging the pose. Understandably, he felt a proprietary ownership of the resulting likeness of Lincoln and Tad studying an oversize, Bible-like volume (it was, in fact, a Brady sample photo album). But famous as it later became, it did not see the light of day until after the assassination, when it was belatedly published in *Harper's Weekly*, nearly a year after its appearance might have done the living Lincoln much good by softening the image of the commander-in-chief whose enemies routinely accused him of heartlessly trampling on civil liberties.

Carpenter himself may have suppressed it. Until 1865, it seems entirely plausible that the artist kept it for his exclusive use as a model for his own planned picture of the Lincolns. After all, it was Carpenter, under whose guidance the image of the tender father had been born. The assassination, however, made the picture too hot a property to withhold any longer, and the Brady gallery released it as a photographic collectible. Quickly, the pose inspired countless other artists and printmakers, who copied it for crude Lincoln family pictures of their own. Since the Lincolns had never posed together for the cameras as a family, the Carpenter-inspired Brady photograph of

Lincoln and Tad emerged as the central image in every composite.[26]

Meanwhile, Carpenter, as usual, became absorbed in his own family portrait project, and thus lost the immediate credit he deserved for creating the image of the beleaguered politician who somehow made time for his family however much the reality of Lincoln's busy presidential life suggested quite the opposite. The artist did paint a tiny oil on copper of Lincoln and Tad reading in 1864, but it was neither exhibited nor reproduced at the time. His beautiful companion portraits of the President and his wife, and a painting that showed Mary wearing a brooch containing a young likeness of her husband also remained sadly unknown to the public.

Carpenter's large oil of the entire family—with the Brady photograph faithfully reproduced and the photographic models for the other family members meticulously suggested by Mary Todd Lincoln herself—was not adapted in mezzotint by J. C. Buttre until 1867, by which time the market had been saturated with inferior Lincoln family prints. In fact, Buttre took so long to produce the adaptation that the engraver was compelled to add a moustache to Carpenter's original portrait of

---

26. For examples, see Harold Holzer, Gabor S. Boritt, and Mark E. Neely, Jr., *The Lincoln Image: Abraham Lincoln and the Popular Print* (New York: Charles Scribner's Sons, 1984), 160–188. The photograph of Lincoln and Tad first appeared in *Harper's Weekly*, May 6, 1865.

eldest son Robert, who had taken to sporting facial hair during the long interval between Carpenter's plan and Buttre's publication.[27] Robert dismissed the result as "amusing," pointing out four decades later that he had "never sat to him for a picture," and complaining that Carpenter painted him "as 16 or 18 years old in '64," when "I was then 21."[28] In fact, Robert had entirely missed the point of the Carpenter composition. The canvas showed the Lincolns not in 1864, but in 1861, before war and the death of middle son Willie plunged the family into what Mary called a "fiery furnace of affliction."[29] Carpenter was right and Robert was wrong: the so-called "Prince of Rails" was indeed eighteen years old at the time.

This second long delay in bringing one of his projects to the public may well have influenced the artist to focus on his literary work. Theoretically, Carpenter may have become so frustrated by print publishing delays beyond his direct control that he took to writing as a way to stake his claim as an eyewitness to history. But it is equally likely that there was a direct confluence at work between publishers of books and publishers of

---

27. For the genesis of the project see Mark E. Neely, Jr. and Harold Holzer, *The Lincoln Family Album: Photographs from the Personal Collection of a Historic American Family*, orig. pub. 1990, rev. ed. (Carbondale: Southern Illinois University Press, 2006), 86–89.

28. Robert T. Lincoln to Warren C. Crane, December 15, 1903.

29. Mary Lincoln to Hannah Shearer, November 20, 1864, in Justin G. Turner and Linda Levitt Turner, *Mary Todd Lincoln: Her Life and Letters* (New York: Alfred A. Knopf, 1972), 189.

portraits: work in one field could be made to benefit work in the other.

In 1865, for example, *New York Times* editor Henry J. Raymond issued one of the first full-length, post-assassination biographies of Abraham Lincoln. It was published by Derby & Miller, the same firm that had contracted to issue A. H. Ritchie's eagerly anticipated engraving of Carpenter's painting, *First Reading of the Emancipation Proclamation Before the Cabinet*. In an example of skillful mutual marketing, Raymond's book concluded with a forty-one-page long appendix by none other than Francis B. Carpenter, detailing his six months' work in Lincoln's White House.[30]

In his "chapter of anecdotes," as Carpenter modestly called it, he "endeavored to embrace only those which bear the marks of authenticity," establishing criteria that would guide the rest of his literary career. He would use either stories "I myself heard the President relate," or others "communicated to me by persons who either heard or took part in them."[31] One may argue with his decision to include these supposedly authoritative second-hand stories, but the recollections established the artist as a uniquely positioned memoirist as well as a passionate advocate of Lincoln's growing reputation as a "Great Emancipator."

---

30. Carpenter, "Anecdotes and Reminiscences," in Raymond, *Abraham Lincoln*, 725–766.
31. *Ibid.*, 725.

And Derby & Miller undoubtedly anticipated that the epilogue would boost sales of the print, whenever it appeared.

Carpenter's epilogue also contributed to Lincoln's image as a man of God, even though the president had conspicuously declined to join any church congregation during his years in Illinois and Washington. In the artist-turned-memoirist's view, "a sincerer *Christian* never lived." Carpenter cited as evidence Lincoln's "constitutional tendency to dwell upon sacred things" and an emotional nature which finds ready expression in religious conversation and revival meetings." The writer was perhaps on firmer ground when he insisted: "I believe no man had a more abiding sense of his dependence upon God, or faith in the Divine government, and in the power of Truth and Right in the world."[32]

By now it was only a matter of time before Carpenter expanded his *Independent* articles and the Henry J. Raymond essay into a book of his own. *Six Months at the White House: The Story of a Picture* appeared in its first edition in 1866. Carpenter introduced it by candidly, yet endearingly, admitting that it was written "in a spirit of enthusiasm and affection, which there has been no effort to disguise." The author further described his work as "a simple matter-of-fact record of daily experience and observation, fragmentary, but true, in all essential particulars,"

---

32. *Ibid.*, 731.

an effort "to portray the man as he was revealed to me, without any attempt at idealization."[33] In truth, he padded the book with stories from other sources, somewhat diminishing its reliability as a first-hand source—though Carpenter was always careful to ascribe to others the incidents he had not witnessed on his own.

However flawed, the format clicked with the public. The artist's own biographer accurately judged the result "a singularly full collection of the most graphic and entertaining anecdotes and reminiscences."[34] It proved a commercial triumph. An 1867 advertisement for the volume hailed it as the "great success of the year," adding: "one million persons have read, are now reading, or are about to read Carpenter's book . . . 20 thousand already sold . . . merchants, farmers . . . everybody needs this book."[35] Elegant new editions appeared in blue, green, and brown bindings, and an 1879 reprint claimed 27,000 copies sold to date.[36] Most of these editions usefully concluded with endpapers promoting the engraved adaptation of "Carpenter's Great National Picture," replete with glowing testimonials from the cabinet officers it portrayed (Salmon Chase, for one,

---

33. Carpenter, *Six Months at the White House*, v.

34. Perkins, *The Picture and the Men*, iv.

35. *The Independent*, July 4, 1867.

36. F. B. Carpenter, *The Inner Life of Abraham Lincoln. Six Months at the White House* (Boston: Houghton, Osgood & Co., 1879), title page.

pronounced it "a complete success;" William Seward called it "admirable;" and Edward Bates praised it as "a manifest success"). Thus his publishers wisely used Carpenter's writings to promote his art.

The book's reputation has hardly wavered since. For nearly a century-and-a-half, Lincoln biographers have regarded it as perhaps the best source ever written about Lincoln's day to day life in the White House. Historian Mark E. Neely Jr., for example, called it "a valuable source for Lincoln's activities in the decisive year of his reelection," featuring "numerous anecdotes which are widely quoted by biographers and are available in no other source."[37] Not every scholar has agreed. In rebuttal, Don E. Fehrenbacher argued that Carpenter "probably exaggerated the extent of his intimacy with Lincoln and, if Mary Lincoln can be believed, eventually wore out his welcome with presumptuous intrusions upon the president's time. Carpenter's recollected works are a mixture of what he himself heard and what he heard secondhand from others, and it is not always easy to tell the difference."[38] True, much of what appeared in the final 150 pages of the book recycled anecdotes first introduced by others—many of the tales spurious or exaggerated—but in

---

37. Mark E. Neely Jr., *The Abraham Lincoln Encyclopedia* (New York: McGraw-Hill, 1982), 47.

38. Don E. Fehrenbacher and Virginia Fehrenbacher, *Recollected Words of Lincoln* (Stanford, Cal.: Stanford University Press, 1996), 79.

its first-hand accounts of Lincoln at work, it surpassed every other account of its day. Even noting "the absence of corroborating material," a scholar of the new generation, Matthew Pinsker, hailed Carpenter as a "credible witness" to Lincoln's life in the first half of 1864.[39]

Significantly, as Neely has pointed out with both admiration and astonishment, Carpenter was apparently the only observer of his time ever to ask Lincoln directly about how and why he issued the Emancipation Proclamation—a remarkable accomplishment perhaps most easily explained by the expectation by other writers of the day that they would have ample time to inquire about the historic act after Lincoln's anticipated retirement.[40] Instead, thanks to Carpenter alone, we have Lincoln's stunning admission that he would not affix his name to the document on January 1, 1863, until he was sure his hand had stopped throbbing after hours spent greeting visitors at a White House New Year's reception. He did not want future generations to regard a quaking signature and imagine that "he hesitated."[41]

Francis B. Carpenter made brilliant use of his extraordinary access to the president and his family, but eventually fell out of

---

39. Matthew Pinsker, *Lincoln's Sanctuary: Abraham Lincoln and the Soldiers' Home* (New York: Oxford University Press, 2003), 65.

40. Neely, *Inner Life*, v.

41. Carpenter, *Six Months at the White House*, 269.

favor with its survivors. For a time, however, the mercurial Mary granted him as much access as did her husband. Following the assassination, she wrote an extraordinary letter to the artist revealing what she remembered of her final conversations with him on a carriage ride they took through Washington before returning to the White House to dress for their fateful visit to Ford's Theatre ("I never saw him so supremely cheerful").[42] After Lincoln's death, Mary gave Carpenter what she clearly considered a sacred relic: a "very plain cane," which had been "handled by *him*."[43] When the artist brought out yet another print adaptation, Frederick D. Halpin's line-and-stipple engraving of his model head of Lincoln, Mary praised it lavishly as the "most perfect likeness of my husband, that I have ever seen."[44] And then when Carpenter embarked on the effort to paint the definitive portrait of the Lincoln family, Mary sent him photographs she believed were worthy of adaptation, and shared her frank admission that she disliked most of her own camera images. Unfortunately for the artist turned memoirist, these revelations arrived too late to be included in his earliest articles for the

---

42. Mary Lincoln to Francis B. Carpenter, November 15, 1865, Turner and Turner, *Mary Todd Lincoln: Her Life and Letters*, 284–285.

43. Mary Lincoln to Francis B. Carpenter, December 25, 1866, *ibid.*, 403–404.

44. *Ibid.*

Independent. He never violated the widow's confidences in his subsequent writings.[45]

That did not prevent his relations with Mary from exploding in 1868, when the artist—or his publisher—decided to give his book *Six Months at the White House* a new life by re-issuing it with a presumptuous new title: *The Inner Life of Abraham Lincoln*. The suggestion of intimacy sent the still-grieving widow into a fury. "I can scarcely express to you," she told one of her husband's old friends, "how indignant I feel, when such men, mere adventurers, with whom my husband had scarcely the least acquaintance, write & publish such false statements about him." Mary made it seem as if she objected merely to Carpenter's claim that Lincoln and Seward had met back in 1848 (a claim that had appeared unchallenged in his first edition). More likely, it was the new title that outraged Mary, painfully reminding her of a recent lecture by Lincoln's former law partner, which suggested that the late president had loved his tragic onetime fiancée Ann Rutledge more than his wife. Mary took out her anger on the artist:

> This man Carpenter, never had a dozen interviews
> with the late president and the latter complained
> more than once to me, that C. presumed upon the
> privilege he had given C. to have the use of the

45. Mary Lincoln to Francis B. Carpenter, November 15, 1865, *ibid.*, 283–285.

State dining room, for a short time, whilst he was executing his painting. This as only done, in consequence of the rumor we had heard of his indigent circumstances. He is a second edition of Mr L's crazy drinking law partner, Herndon, endeavouring to write himself into notice, leaving truth, far, far, in the distance. C. intruded frequently into Mr L's office, when time was too precious to be idled. Of this fact, I am well aware. To think of this stranger, silly adventurer, daring to write a work, entitled, "The inner life of Abraham Lincoln." Each scribbling writer, almost strangers to Mr L., subscribe themselves, his most intimate friend![46]

In truth, Carpenter fully understood the limits of his association with Abraham Lincoln, even if he occasionally crossed the line: "I loved him heart and soul," he confessed in 1867, "but he cared little for me, perhaps would never have thought of me a half dozen times had he lived."[47] Of course, many of his closest intimates said much the same thing about Lincoln. They got little back save for the opportunity to serve and observe him. Carpenter made more of his opportunity than most, in both visual and written terms.

---

46. Mary Lincoln to Henry C. Deming, December 16, 1867, *Ibid.*, 463–464.

47. Francis B. Carpenter to William H. Herndon, January 16, 1867, Herndon-Weik Collection, Library of Congress.

In 1878, with help from Lincoln's onetime White House secretary John G. Nicolay, along with Carpenter's old Homer friend, William O. Stoddard, Congress finally acquired his painting *The First Reading of the Emancipation Proclamation*. A "pale" and "nervous" Carpenter proudly attended the dedication ceremonies, and basking at last in the success he fully believed he deserved, seemed oblivious to the ironic fact that the principal orators that day emphasized Lincoln's epochal work in preserving the Union, not in issuing the document Carpenter had hoped to immortalize with his painting.[48]

Thereafter, Carpenter's artistic reputation plummeted. He earned several important commissions, but produced nothing as notable as *First Reading*. An effort to recreate its success and style resulted in a large canvas called *International Arbitration*, which depicted the joint American-British commission meeting in Washington in 1871 to settle the Civil War-era *Alabama* claims. But once again, Carpenter dithered, taking some twenty years to complete the large group portrait—again showing men gathered around a conference table—before donating it to

---

48. *New York Times*, February 13, 1878. The nation did not directly acquire the painting, as Carpenter hoped. But philanthropist Elizabeth Thompson was persuaded to pay the artist $25,000 to purchase it, then donated it to Congress. It hangs today over the west staircase in the Senate wing. See William Kloss and Diane K. Skvarla, *United States Senate: Catalogue of Fine Art*, ed. Jane R. McGoldrick (Washington: U. S. Government Printing Office, 2002), 121.

Queen Victoria. Today, the canvas is lost; the royal art collection can no longer even explain what became of it.

During his half-year stint at the White House, Carpenter had created several additional, important Lincoln works (including an intriguing picture of Lincoln without his famous beard, commissioned by an old friend), and these deserve far wider circulation than they have achieved. But Carpenter ill-advisedly persisted in painting the president long after his talents had faded. His final Lincoln portraits are little more than caricatured daubs, and it remains extremely difficult to know precisely when he produced them. Carpenter stubbornly dated all his subsequent Lincoln work with the year of his six months at the White House: 1864.[49]

Largely forgotten by the time of his death on May 23, 1900, was his peerless contribution to Lincoln memory (one obituary even misrepresented his most famous work as a painting of the "signing," rather than the first reading, of the Emancipation Proclamation).[50] Yet by the turn of the new century, thanks in large measure to the artist-writer's visionary effort on canvas and in print, Lincoln was widely regarded as the Great

---

49. For an example of this later work, see Holzer, Boritt, and Neely, "Francis Bicknell Carpenter," 86–87. Carpenter admirer Bartlett Cowdrey admitted that one of the final works was so crude it looked like a forgery. Bartlett Cowdrey to Paul M. Angle, June 19, 1937, copy in the Carpenter Papers, Cortland County Historical Society, Cortland, New York.

50. *New York Times*, May 24, 1900.

Emancipator—as well as a loving father figure—images that Francis Bicknell Carpenter had conceived and captured.

Fortunately for his reputation, Carpenter's book has endured far longer than the fashion for the kind of static history paintings and formal portraiture in which he specialized as an artist. "I have felt that I had no business to make a book, and indeed this was the last thing in my thought to do so," he once admitted in an unusual burst of self-effacement. "I had little or no training for literary work[.] My schooling was all at a country district school, with one term of twelve weeks, at the village academy.—I know little of the classics, or in fact of anything—speak no language and know no language but English and poor at that."

But of his "little book," he proudly acknowledged, "like Topsy 'it grew,'" adding with rare understatement: "I believe some incidents therein throw light on the character of the man."[51] Even the relentlessly ambitious Francis B. Carpenter would be surprised to know that his little volume has "grown" into an indispensable resource: the most vivid mirror ever held to the White House life of Abraham Lincoln.

---

51. Francis B. Carpenter to William H. Herndon, December 24, 1866, Wilson and Davis, eds., *Herndon's Informants*, 521–522.

PREFACE TO THE FIRST EDITION.

——————————

IN offering this volume to the public I shall attempt no apology for its shortcomings, other than to say that its production is the result of the unexpected popularity of the series of articles, relating to the illustrious subject of whom it mainly treats, which were commenced in the New York "Independent" soon after the assassination.

Written in a spirit of enthusiasm and affection, which there has been no effort to disguise, the book is, nevertheless, a simple matter-of-fact record of daily experience and observation, fragmentary, but *true*, in all essential particulars. There has been no disposition to select from, embellish, or suppress, any portion of the material in my possession. The incidents given were not in any sense isolated exceptions to the daily routine of Mr. Lincoln's life. My aim has been throughout these pages to portray *the man* as he was revealed to me, without any attempt at idealization.

In addition to my own reminiscences, I have woven into the book various personal incidents, published and unpublished, which bear intrinsic evidence of genuineness,—attaching in these instances, where it seemed necessary and proper, the sources of such contributions.

I am not one of those inclined to believe that Mr. Lincoln, in the closing months of his career, reached the full measure of his greatness. Man may not read the future: but it is my firm conviction, that, had he lived through his second term, he would have continued to grow, as he had grown, in the estimation and confidence of his countrymen; rising to a grander moral height with every emergency, careful always to weigh every argument opposed to his convictions, but, once mounted upon those convictions, grounded in righteousness, as immovable as one of the giant ranges of our own Rocky Mountains!

Aspiring in no sense to the dignity of a biography, this volume will fulfil its object if it helps to any better knowledge of one, who, apart from the reverence with which he ever will be regarded for his connection with the cause of human Freedom, was the best product and exemplar which the world has yet seen of American soil and institutions; the study of whose character, illustrating as it did the highest form of statesmanship, founded upon truth, justice, and solid integrity, combining the deepest wisdom with a child-like freshness and simplicity,—will be of perpetual interest and value.

F. B. C.

96 *West 45th Street,* New York.

SIX MONTHS AT THE WHITE HOUSE

◆

I.

I LEAVE to other and abler pens the proper estimate of ABRAHAM LINCOLN as a ruler and statesman,—his work and place in history. Favored during the year 1864 with several months of personal intercourse with him, I shall attempt in these pages to write the story of that association; not for any value which the record will have in itself, but for the glimpses it may afford of the person and character of the man,—every detail of whose life is now invested with enduring interest for the American people.

II.

That Art should aim to embody and express the spirit and best thought of its own age seems self-evident. If it fails to do this, whatever else it may accomplish, it falls short of its highest object. It cannot dwell always among classic forms, nor clothe its conceptions in the imagery of an old and worn-out world. It must move on, if it is to keep pace with that "increasing purpose which through the ages runs," and its ideals must be wrought out of the strife of a living humanity.

It has been well said by a recent writer: "The record of the human family to the advent of Christ, was the preparation of the photographic plate for its image. All subsequent history is the bringing out of the divine ideal of true manhood." Slowly, but surely, through the centuries, is this purpose being accomplished. Human slavery has been the material type or expression of spiritual bondage. On the lowest or physical plane, it has symbolized the captivity and degradation of our higher nature; with the breaking in of new light, and the inspiration of a deeper life, it is inevitably doomed. That man, to attain the full development of the faculties implanted in him, must be in spiritual and physical freedom, is a principle which lies at the foundation of all government; and the enfranchisement of a race to-day thus becomes the assertion and promise of a true and coming Emancipation for all men.

III.

When ABRAHAM LINCOLN, called from the humblest rank in life to preside over the nation during the most momentous period of its history, uttered his Proclamation of Freedom,—shattering forever the chains which bound four millions of human beings in slavery; an act unparalleled for moral grandeur in the history of mankind,—it was evident to all who sought beneath the surface for the cause of the war that the crisis was past,—that so surely as Heaven is on the side of Right and

Justice, the North would triumph in the great struggle which had assumed the form of a direct issue between Freedom and Slavery.

In common with many others, I had from the beginning of the war believed that the government would not be successful in putting down a rebellion based upon slavery as its avowed corner-stone, without striking a death-blow at the institution itself. As the months went on, and disappointment and disaster succeeded one another, this conviction deepened into certainty. When at length, in obedience to what seemed the very voice of God, the thunderbolt was launched, and, like the first gun at Concord, "was heard around the world," all the enthusiasm of my nature was kindled. The "beast" Secession, offspring of the "dragon" Slavery, drawing in his train a third part of our national stars, was pierced with the deadly wound which could not be healed. It was the combat between Michael and Satan of Apocalyptic vision, reënacted before the eyes of the nineteenth century.

IV.

To paint a picture which should commemorate this new epoch in the history of Liberty, was a dream which took form and shape in my mind towards the close of the year 1863,— the year made memorable in its dawn by the issue of the final decree. With little experience to adapt me for the execution of such a work, there had nevertheless come to me at times glowing conceptions of the true purpose and character of Art, and an intense desire to do something expressive of appreciation of the great issues involved in the war. The painters of old had delighted in representations of the birth from the ocean of Venus, the goddess of love. Ninety years ago upon this Western continent had been witnessed—no dream of fable, but a substantial fact—the immaculate conception of Constitutional Liberty; and at length through great travail its consummation had been reached. The long-prayed-for year of jubilee had come; the bonds of the oppressed were loosed; the prison doors were opened. "Behold," said a voice, "how a Man may be exalted to a dignity and glory almost divine, and give freedom to a race. Surely Art should unite with Eloquence and Poetry to celebrate such a theme."

I conceived of that band of men, upon whom the eyes of the world centred as never before upon ministers of state, gathered in council, depressed, perhaps disheartened at the vain efforts of many months to restore the supremacy of the government. I saw, in thought, the head of the nation, bowed down with his weight of care and responsibility, solemnly announcing, as he unfolded the prepared draft of the Proclamation, that the time for the inauguration of this policy had arrived; I endeavored to imagine the conflicting emotions of satisfaction, doubt, and distrust with which such an announcement would be received by men of the varied characteristics of the assembled councillors.

For several weeks the design of the picture was slowly maturing, during which time, however, no line was drawn upon paper or canvas. Late one evening, absorbed in thought upon the subject, I took up an unframed photograph lying carelessly in my room; and upon the blank side of this, roughly and hastily sketched, was embodied the central idea of the composition as it had shaped itself in my mind.

To one disposed to look for coincidences in daily life, and regard its events as no mere succession of accidents, there must often come those which wear a deep significance. In seeking a point of unity or action for the picture, I was impressed with the conviction that important modifications followed the reading of the Proclamation at the suggestion of the Secretary of State, and I determined upon such an incident as the moment of time to be represented. I was subsequently surprised and gratified when Mr. Lincoln himself, reciting the history of the Proclamation to me, dwelt particularly upon the fact that not only was the time of its issue decided by Secretary Seward's advice, but that one of the most important words in the document was added through his strenuous representations.

The central thought of the picture once decided upon and embodied, the rest naturally followed; one after another the seven figures surrounding the President dropped into their places.

Those supposed to have held the purpose of the Proclamation as their long conviction, were placed prominently in the foreground in attitudes which indicated their support of the measure; the others were represented in varying moods of discussion or silent deliberation.

A few evenings after the completion of the design I went to see a friend who I knew was intimate with the Hon. Schuyler Colfax and Hon. Owen Lovejoy, through whom I hoped to obtain Mr. Lincoln's assent to my plan. I revealed to him my purpose, and asked his assistance in carrying it into effect. During the following week he went to Washington, and in company with Mr. Colfax called upon the President, and laid before him my project. He kindly listened to the details, and then said: "In short, if I understand you, you wish me to consent to sit to this artist for the picture?" My friends acknowledged this to be the object of their errand. Mr. Lincoln at once, with his accustomed kindness, promised his coöperation.

The last day of the year the Hon. Mr. Lovejoy, whom I had never met, but who had become warmly interested in the execution of the work, being in New York, called at my studio with the wife of my friend, who had been my earnest advocate. At the close of the interview he remarked, in his quaint way, taking me by the hand, "In the words of Scripture, my good friend, I can say now I believe, not on account of the saying of the woman, but because I have seen for myself."

V.

Impracticable as my scheme had at first seemed, the way was thus opened for its execution. When fairly committed to the purpose, however, the want of means and the magnitude of the undertaking almost disheartened me. My original plan embraced a canvas sufficiently large for a life-size group of the President and entire Cabinet; to paint such a picture would consume many months, perhaps years. Enthusiasm alone would never accomplish the work. The few friends to whom I should have felt at liberty to apply for help were not wealthy. Who outside of these could be persuaded that a work of the character and proportions contemplated, undertaken by an artist of no experience in historical studies, would not end in utter failure?

I had left my home at the usual hour one morning, pondering the difficulty which, like Bunyan's lions, seemed now to block the way. As one alternative after another presented itself to my mind and was rejected, the prospect appeared less and less hopeful. I at length found myself in Broadway at the foot of the stairs leading up to my studio. A gentleman at this moment attracted my attention, standing with his back towards me, looking at some pictures exposed in the window of the shop below. Detecting, as I thought, something familiar in his air and manner, I waited until he turned his face, and then found I was not mistaken; it was an old acquaintance who five years before lived near me in Brooklyn, engaged in a similar struggle for a livelihood with myself, though his profession was law instead of art.

We had both changed our residences and had not met for years. After a cordial greeting, he accepted my invitation to ascend to the studio. I had heard that he had been successful in some business ventures, but the matter made but little impression upon me, and had been forgotten. Suddenly there seemed to come into my mind the words: "This man has been sent to you." Full of the singular impression, I laid before him my conception. He heard me through, and then asked if I was sure of President Lincoln's consent and coöperation. I informed him of the pledge which had been given me. "Then," said he, "you shall paint the picture. Take plenty of time,—make it the great work of your life,—and draw upon me for whatever funds you will require to the end."*

VI.

On the evening of February 4th, 1864, I went to Washington. Shortly after noon of the following day, I rang the bell at

---

*To Mr. SAMUEL SINCLAIR, of the *New York Tribune,* for the introduction to Mr. Lincoln, and to FREDERICK A. LANE, Esq., of New York, for the generous aid thus extended, I shall ever be indebted for the accomplishment of my work.

Mr. Lovejoy's residence on Fifteenth Street. To my sorrow, I found him very ill; but it was hoped by his friends that he was then improving. Though very feeble, he insisted upon seeing me, and calling for writing materials, sat up in bed to indite a note introducing me to the President. This, handed to me open, I read. One expression I have not forgotten, it was so like Mr. Lincoln himself, as I afterward came to know him. "I am gaining very slowly.—It is hard work drawing the sled up-hill." And this suggests the similarity there was between these men. Lovejoy had much more of the agitator, the reformer, in his nature, but both drew the inspiration of their lives from the same source, and it was founded in sterling honesty. Their modes of thought and illustration were remarkably alike. It is not strange that they should have been bosom friends. The President called repeatedly to see him during his illness; and it was on one of these occasions that he said to him, "This war is eating my life out; I have a strong impression that I shall not live to see the end." Mr. Lovejoy's health subsequently improved, and for a change he went to Brooklyn, N.Y., where, it will be remembered, he had a relapse, and died, universally mourned as one of the truest and most faithful of our statesmen. Mr. Lincoln did not hear from him directly after he left Washington. Through a friend I learned by letter that he was lying at the point of death. This intelligence I communicated to the President the same evening, in the vestibule of the White House,—meeting him on his way to the War Department. He was deeply affected by it. His only words were, "Lovejoy was the best friend I had in Congress."

To return from this pardonable digression,—I took the note of introduction at once to the White House; but no opportunity was afforded me of presenting it during the day. The following morning passed with the same result, and I then resolved to avail myself of Mrs. Lincoln's Saturday afternoon reception—at which, I was told, the President would be present—to make myself known to him. Two o'clock found me one of the throng pressing toward the centre of attraction, the "blue" room. From the threshold of the "crimson" parlor as I passed, I had a glimpse of the gaunt figure of Mr. Lincoln in the distance, haggard-looking, dressed in black, relieved only by the prescribed white gloves; standing, it seemed to me, solitary and alone, though surrounded by the crowd, bending low now and then in the process of hand-shaking, and responding half abstractedly to the well-meant greetings of the miscellaneous assemblage. Never shall I forget the electric thrill which went through my whole being at this instant. I seemed to see lines radiating from every part of the globe, converging to a focus at the point where that plain, awkward-looking man stood, and to hear in spirit a million prayers, "as the sound of many waters," ascending in his behalf. Mingled with supplication I could discern a clear symphony of triumph and blessing, swelling with an ever-increasing volume. It was the voice of those who had been bondmen and bondwomen, and the grand diapason swept up from the coming ages.

It was soon my privilege, in the regular succession, to take that honored hand. Accompanying the act, my name and profession were announced to him in a low tone by one of the assistant private secretaries, who stood by his side. Retaining my hand, he looked at me inquiringly for an instant, and said, "Oh yes; I know; this is the painter." Then straightening himself to his full height, with a twinkle of the eye, he added, playfully, "Do you think, Mr. C—, that you can make a handsome picture of *me*?" emphasizing strongly the last word. Somewhat confused at this point-blank shot, uttered in a tone so loud as to attract the attention of those in immediate proximity, I made a random reply, and took the occasion to ask if I could see him in his study at the close of the reception. To this he responded in the peculiar vernacular of the West, "I reckon," resuming meanwhile the mechanical and traditional exercise of the hand which no President has ever yet been able to avoid, and which, severe as is the ordeal, is likely to attach to the position, so long as the Republic endures.

VII.

The appointed hour found me at the well-remembered door of the official chamber,—that door watched daily, with so many conflicting emotions of hope and fear, by the anxious throng regularly gathered there. The President had preceded me, and was already deep in Acts of Congress, with which the writing-desk was strewed, awaiting his signature. He received me pleasantly, giving me a seat near his own arm-chair; and after having read Mr. Lovejoy's note, he took off his spectacles, and said, "Well, Mr. C—, we will turn you in loose here, and try to give you a good chance to work out your idea." Then, without paying much attention to the enthusiastic expression of my ambitious desire and purpose, he proceeded to give me a detailed account of the history and issue of the great proclamation.

"It had got to be," said he, "midsummer, 1862. Things had gone on from bad to worse, until I felt that we had reached the end of our rope on the plan of operations we had been pursuing; that we had about played our last card, and must change our tactics, or lose the game! I now determined upon the adoption of the emancipation policy; and, without consultation with, or the knowledge of the Cabinet, I prepared the original draft of the proclamation, and, after much anxious thought, called a Cabinet meeting upon the subject. This was the last of July, or the first part of the month of August, 1862." (The exact date he did not remember.) "This Cabinet meeting took place, I think, upon a Saturday. All were present, excepting Mr. Blair, the Postmaster-General, who was absent at the opening of the discussion, but came in subsequently. I said to the

Cabinet that I had resolved upon this step, and had not called them together to ask their advice, but to lay the subject-matter of a proclamation before them; suggestions as to which would be in order, after they had heard it read. Mr. Lovejoy," said he, "was in error when he informed you that it excited no comment, excepting on the part of Secretary Seward. Various suggestions were offered. Secretary Chase wished the language stronger in reference to the arming of the blacks. Mr. Blair, after he came in, deprecated the policy, on the ground that it would cost the Administration the fall elections. Nothing, however, was offered that I had not already fully anticipated and settled in my own mind, until Secretary Seward spoke. He said in substance: 'Mr. President, I approve of the proclamation, but I question the expediency of its issue at this juncture. The depression of the public mind, consequent upon our repeated reverses, is so great that I fear the effect of so important a step. It may be viewed as the last measure of an exhausted government, a cry for help; the government stretching forth its hands to Ethiopia, instead of Ethiopia stretching forth her hands to the government.' His idea," said the President, "was that it would be considered our last *shriek*, on the retreat". (This was his *precise* expression.) "'Now,' continued Mr. Seward, 'while I approve the measure, I suggest, sir, that you postpone its issue, until you can give it to the country supported by military success, instead of issuing it, as would be the case now, upon the greatest disasters of the war?'" Mr. Lincoln continued: "The wisdom of the view of the Secretary of State struck me with very great force. It was an aspect of the case that, in all my thought upon the subject, I had entirely overlooked. The result was that I put the draft of the proclamation aside, as you do your sketch for a picture, waiting for a victory. From time to time I added or changed a line, touching it up here and there, anxiously watching the progress of events. Well, the next news we had was of Pope's disaster, at Bull Run. Things looked darker than ever. Finally, came the week of the battle of Antietam. I determined to wait no longer. The news came, I think, on Wednesday, that the advantage was on our side. I was then staying at the Soldiers' Home, (three miles out of Washington.) Here I finished writing the second draft of the preliminary proclamation; came up on Saturday; called the Cabinet together to hear it, and it was published the following Monday."

At the final meeting of September 20th, another interesting incident occurred in connection with Secretary Seward. The President had written the important part of the proclamation in these words:—

"That, on the first day of January, in the year of our Lord one thousand eight hundred and sixty-three, all persons held as slaves within any State or designated part of a State, the people whereof shall then be in rebellion against the United

States, shall be then, thenceforward, and forever FREE; and the Executive Government of the United States, including the military and naval authority thereof, will *recognize* the freedom of such persons, and will do no act or acts to repress such persons, or any of them, in any efforts they may make for their actual freedom." "When I finished reading this paragraph," resumed Mr. Lincoln, "Mr. Seward stopped me, and said, 'I think, Mr. President, that you should insert after the word "*recognize*," in that sentence, the words "*and maintain.*"' I replied that I had already fully considered the import of that expression in this connection, but I had not introduced it, because it was not my way to promise what I was not entirely *sure* that I could perform, and I was not prepared to say that I thought we were exactly able to 'maintain' this."

"But," said he, "Seward insisted that we ought to take this ground; and the words finally went in!"

"It is a somewhat remarkable fact," he subsequently remarked, "that there were just one hundred days between the dates of the two proclamation issued upon the 22d of September and the 1st of January. I had not made the calculation at the time."

Having concluded this interesting statement, the President then proceeded to show me the various positions occupied by himself and the different members of the Cabinet, on the occasion of the first meeting. "As nearly as I remember," said he, "I

sat near the head of the table; the Secretary of the Treasury and
the Secretary of War were here, at my right hand; the others
were grouped at the left."

At this point, I exhibited to him a pencil sketch of the composition as I had conceived it, with no knowledge of the facts or
details. The leading idea of this I found, as I have stated on a
previous page, to be entirely consistent with the account I had
just heard. I saw, however, that I should have to reverse the picture, placing the President at the other end of the table, to
make it accord with his description. I had resolved to discard
all appliances and tricks of picture-making, and endeavor, as
faithfully as possible, to represent the scene as it actually transpired; room, furniture, accessories, all were to be painted from
the actualities. It was a scene second only in historical importance and interest to that of the Declaration of Independence;
and I felt assured, that, if honestly and earnestly painted, it
need borrow no interest from imaginary curtain or column,
gorgeous furniture or allegorical statue. Assenting heartily to
what is called the "realistic" school of art, when applied to the
illustration of historic events, I felt in this case, that I had no
more right to depart from the facts, than has the historian in
his record.

When friends said to me, as they frequently did, "Your picture will be bald and barren," my reply was, "If I cannot make
the portraiture of the scene itself sufficiently attractive without

the false glitter of tapestry hangings, velvet table-cloths, and marble columns, then I shall at least have the satisfaction of having failed in the cause of truth." I reasoned in this way: The most important document submitted to a cabinet during our existence as a nation is under discussion. A spectator permitted to look in upon that scene would give little thought and small heed to the mere accessories and adjuncts of the occasion. His mind would centre upon the immortal document,—its anxious author, conscious of his solemn responsibility, announcing his matured and inflexible purpose to his assembled councillors. He would listen with unparalleled eagerness to the momentous sentences uttered for the first time in the ears of men, and to the discussion upon them, impatient of mere formalities and technicalities. Should a thought be sprung of important bearing, or an overlooked contingency be brought forward, how intently would its effect be watched. What varying emotions, consequent upon peculiarities of temperament and character, would be expressed in the countenances of the different individuals composing the group. How each in turn would be scanned. Above all, the issues involved:—the salvation of the Republic—the freedom of a Race. "Surely," I said, "such a scene may be painted, and abiding if not absorbing interest secured, without the aid of conventional trappings. The republican simplicity of the room and furniture, with its thronging associations, will more than counterbalance the lack of splendor, and the artistic mania for effect. I will depend solely for my success upon the interest of the subject, and its truthfulness of representation." And this purpose I carried with me to the end.

VIII.

The first sketch of the composition, as it was afterward placed upon the canvas, was matured, I believe, the same afternoon, or the following Monday after the interview recorded above, upon the back of a visiting card; my pockets affording evidence of the employment of all loose material at hand in leisure moments, in the study of the work. The final arrangement of the figures was the result of much thought and many combinations, though the original conception as to the moment of time and incident of action was preserved throughout. The general arrangement of the group, as described by the President, was fortunately entirely consistent with my purpose, which was to give that prominence to the different individuals which belonged to them respectively in the Administration. There was a curious mingling of fact and allegory in my mind, as I assigned to each his place on the canvas. There were two elements in the Cabinet, the radical and the conservative. Mr. Lincoln was placed at the head of the official table, between two groups, nearest that representing the radical, but the uniting point of both. The chief powers of a government are War and Finance: the ministers of these were at his right,—the Secretary of War, symbolizing the great struggle, in the immediate foreground; the Secretary of the Treasury, actively supporting the new policy, standing by the President's side. The Army being the right hand, the Navy may very properly be styled the left hand of the government. The place for the Secretary of the Navy seemed, therefore, very naturally to be on Mr. Lincoln's left, at the rear of the table. To the Secretary of State, as the great expounder of the principles of the Republican party, the profound and sagacious statesman, would the attention of all at such a time be given. Entitled to precedence in discussion by his position in the Cabinet, he would necessarily form one of the central figures of the group. The four chief officers of the government were thus brought, in accordance with their relations to the Administration, nearest the person of the President, who, with the manuscript proclamation in hand, which he had just read, was represented leaning forward, listening to, and intently considering the views presented by the Secretary of State. The Attorney-General, absorbed in the constitutional questions involved, with folded arms, was placed at the foot of the table opposite the President. The Secretary of the Interior and the Postmaster-General, occupying the less conspicuous positions of the Cabinet, seemed to take their proper places in the background of the picture.

When, at length, the conception as thus described was sketched upon the large canvas, and Mr. Lincoln came in to see it, his gratifying remark, often subsequently repeated, was, "It is as good as it can be made."

IX.

I have thus revealed, step by step, the mental process by which the picture of which I write came into being. Whether the story bears any analogy to that by which the works of others have been produced, or the composition conforms to established rules and precedents in art or not, is to me a matter of indifference. I was true to my intuitions, and endeavored to adhere as faithfully as practicable to the facts.

It is not my purpose to follow in detail the progress, thenceforward, of the work. As the thread upon which are strung my memories of the late President, allusions to it will be unavoidable throughout these pages; but hereafter I intend that they shall be subordinate and incidental to matters of more general interest. It is not too much to say that the enthusiasm in which the work was conceived, flagged not to the end. The days were too short for labor upon it. Lighting at nightfall the great chandelier of the state dining-room, which was finally assigned me for a studio instead of the library, where the windows were shaded by the portico, the morning light frequently broke in upon me still standing pencil or palette in hand, before the immense canvas, unable to break the spell which bound me to it.

X.

"We will turn you in loose here," proved an "open sesame" to me during the subsequent months of my occupation at the White House. My access to the official chamber was made nearly as free as that of the private secretaries, unless special business was being transacted. Sometimes a stranger, approaching the President with a low tone, would turn an inquiring eye toward the place where I sat, absorbed frequently in a pencil sketch of some object in the room. This would be met by the hearty tones of Mr. Lincoln,—I can hear them yet ringing in my ears,—"Oh, you need not mind him; he is but a painter." There was a satisfaction to me, differing from that of any other experience, in simply sitting with him. Absorbed in his papers, he would become unconscious of my presence, while I intently studied every line and shade of expression in that furrowed face. In repose, it was the saddest face I ever knew. There were days when I could scarcely look into it without crying. During the first week of the battles of the Wilderness he scarcely slept at all. Passing through the main hall of the domestic apartment on one of these days, I met him, clad in a long morning wrapper, pacing back and forth a narrow passage leading to one of the windows, his hands behind him, great black rings under his eyes, his head bent forward upon his breast,—altogether such a picture of the effects of sorrow, care, and anxiety as would have melted the hearts of the worst of his adversaries, who so mistakenly applied to him the epithets of tyrant and usurper. With a sorrow almost divine, he, too, could have said of the rebellious States, "How often would I have gathered you together, even as a hen gathereth her chickens under her wings, *and ye would not!*" Like another Jeremiah, he wept over the desolations of the nation; "he mourned the slain of the daughter of his people."

Surely, ruler never manifested so much sympathy, and tenderness, and charity. How like the last words of the Divine one himself, "Father, forgive them, for they know not what they do," will the closing sentences of his last inaugural address resound in solemn cadence through the coming centuries. Truly and well says the London "Spectator" of that address: "We cannot read it without a renewed conviction that it is the noblest political document known to history, and should have for the nation and the statesmen he left behind him something of a sacred and almost prophetic character. Surely, none was ever written under a stronger sense of the reality of God's government. And certainly none written in a period of passionate conflict ever so completely excluded the partiality of victorious faction, and breathed so pure a strain of mingled justice and mercy."

XI.

The following Tuesday I spent with Mr. Lincoln in his study. The morning was devoted to the Judge-Advocate-

General, who had a large number of court-martial cases to submit to the President. Never had I realized what it was to have power, as on this occasion. As case after case was presented to Mr. Lincoln, one stroke of his pen confirmed or commuted the sentence of death. In several instances Judge Holt referred to extenuating circumstances,—extreme youth, previous good conduct, or recommendations to mercy. Every excuse of this kind, having a foundation in fact, was instantly seized upon by the President, who, taking the document containing the sentence, would write upon the back of it the lightest penalty consistent with any degree of justice. As he added the date to one of these papers, he remarked casually, varying the subject of conversation, "Does your mind, Judge Holt, associate events with dates? Every time this morning that I have had occasion to write the day of the month, the thought has come up, 'This was General Harrison's birthday.'" One of the cases brought forward at this time I recollect distinctly. The man's name was Burroughs; he had been a notorious spy; convicted and sentenced to death, a strong effort had been made in his behalf by powerful friends. It was an aggravated case, but an impression had evidently been made upon the President by the strength and pertinacity of the appeal. As Judge Holt opened the record, he stated that a short time previous Burroughs had attempted to escape from confinement, and was shot dead in the act by the sentinel on guard. With an expression of relief, Mr. Lincoln rejoined, "I ought to be obliged to him for taking his fate into his own hands; he has saved *me* a deal of trouble."

During a brief absence of the President, Judge Holt told me that the atrocities of some of the criminals condemned, surpassed belief. "A guerilla leader in Missouri," said he, "by the name of Nichols, was in the habit of filling the ears of wounded Unionists who fell into his hands with gunpowder, setting fire to it, and blowing their heads to pieces. When captured, a number of human *ears* were found upon his person." Referring to Mr. Lincoln's disposition to pardon or commute the majority of the death sentences, he remarked, "The President is without exception the most tender-hearted man I ever knew."

Judge Holt, it will be remembered, was called into Mr. Buchanan's cabinet towards the close of his administration. Glancing around the room,—incidentally referring to my errand there,—he said, "This room was the theatre of some very exciting scenes during the last months of Mr. Buchanan's term." He spoke warmly of the courage and fearlessness of Stanton, on those occasions, who did not hesitate to call *traitors* and *treason* by their right names.

When the clock struck twelve, Mr. Lincoln drew back from the table, and with a stretch of his long arms, remarked, "I guess we will go no farther with these cases to-day; I am a little tired, and the Cabinet will be coming in soon." "I believe, by the by," he added, "that I have not yet had my breakfast,—this business has been so absorbing that it has crowded everything else out of my mind."

And so ended the work of one morning; simple in its detail, but pregnant with hope and joy, darkness and death, to many human beings.

XII.

As the different members of the Cabinet came in, the President introduced me, adding in several instances,—"He has an idea of painting a picture of us all together." This, of course, started conversation on the topic of art. Presently a reference was made by some one to Jones, the sculptor, whose bust of Mr. Lincoln was in the crimson parlor below. The President, I think, was writing at this instant. Looking up, he said, "Jones tells a good story of General Scott, of whom he once made a bust. Having a fine subject to start with, he succeeded in giving great satisfaction. At the closing sitting he attempted to define and elaborate the lines and markings of the face. The General sat patiently; but when he came to see the result, his countenance indicated decided displeasure. 'Why, Jones, what have you been doing?' he asked. 'Oh,' rejoined the sculptor, 'not much, I confess, General; I have been working out the details of the face a little more, this morning.' 'Details?' exclaimed the General, warmly; '——the details! Why, my man, you are spoiling the bust!'"

At three o'clock the President was to accompany me, by appointment, to Brady's photographic galleries on Pennsylvania Avenue. The carriage had been ordered, and Mrs. Lincoln, who was to accompany us, had come down at the appointed hour, dressed for the ride, when one of those vexations, incident to all households, occurred. Neither carriage or coachman was to be seen. The President and myself stood upon the threshold of the door under the portico, awaiting the result of the inquiry for the coachman, when a letter was put into his hand. While he was reading this, people were passing, as is customary, up and down the promenade, which leads through the grounds to the War Department, crossing, of course, the portico. My attention was attracted to an approaching party, apparently a countryman, plainly dressed, with his wife and two little boys, who had evidently been straying about, looking at the places of public interest in the city. As they reached the portico, the father, who was in advance, caught sight of the tall figure of Mr. Lincoln, absorbed in his letter. His wife and the little boys were ascending the steps. The man stopped suddenly, put out his hand with a "hush" to his family, and, after a moment's gaze, he bent down and whispered to them,—"There is the President!" Then leaving them, he slowly made a half circuit around Mr. Lincoln, watching him intently all the while. At this point, having finished his letter, the President turned to me, and said: "Well, we will not wait any longer for the carriage; it won't hurt you and me to walk down." The country-man here approached very diffidently, and asked if he might be allowed to take the President by the hand; after which, "Would he extend the same privilege to his wife and little boys?" Mr. Lincoln good-naturedly approached the latter, who had remained where they were stopped, and, reaching down, said a kind word to the bashful little fellows, who shrank close up to their mother, and did not reply. This simple act filled the father's cup full. "The Lord is with you, Mr. President," he said reverently; and then, hesitating a moment, he added, with strong emphasis, "and the people too, sir; and the people too!"

The walk, of a mile or more, was made very agreeable and interesting to me by a variety of stories, of which Mr. Lincoln's mind was so prolific. Something was said soon after we started about the penalty which attached to high positions in a demo-cratic government—the tribute those filling them were com-pelled to pay to the public. "Great men," said Mr. Lincoln, "have various estimates. When Daniel Webster made his tour through the West years ago, he visited Springfield among other places, where great preparations had been made to receive him. As the procession was going through the town, a barefooted little darkey boy pulled the sleeve of a man named T., and asked,—'What the folks were all doing down the street?' 'Why, Jack,' was the reply, 'the biggest man in the world is coming.' Now, there lived in Springfield a man by the name of G.,—a very corpulent man. Jack darted off down the street, but presently returned, with a very disappointed air. 'Well, did you see him?' inquired T. 'Yees,' returned Jack; 'but laws—he ain't half as big as old G.'"

Shortly afterward, he spoke of Mr. Ewing, who was in both President Harrison's and President Taylor's cabinet. "Those men," said he, "were, you know, when elected, both of advanced years,—sages. Ewing had received, in some way, the nickname of 'Old Solitude.' Soon after the formation of Taylor's cabinet, Webster and Ewing happened to meet at an evening party. As they approached each other, Webster, who was in fine spirits, uttered, in his deepest bass tones, the well-known lines,—

"'O Solitude, where are the charms
That sages have seen in thy face?'"

The evening of Tuesday I dined with Mr. Chase, the Secretary of the Treasury, of whom I painted a portrait in 1855, upon the close of his term as United States Senator. He said during the dinner, that, shortly after the dedication of the cemetery at Gettysburg, the President told this story at a cabinet meeting. "Thad. Stevens was asked by some one, the morning of the day appointed for that ceremony, where the President and Mr. Seward were going. 'To Gettysburg,' was the reply. 'But where are Stanton and Chase?' continued the questioner. 'At home, at work,' was the surly answer; 'let the dead bury the dead.'" This was some months previous to the Baltimore Convention, when it was thought by some of the leaders of the party, that Mr. Lincoln's chances for a re-nomination were somewhat dubious.

Levee night occurring weekly, during the regular season, was always a trying one to the President. Whenever sympathy was expressed for him, however, he would turn it off playfully, asserting that the tug at his hand was much easier to bear than that upon his heartstrings for all manner of favors beyond his power to grant, to which he had daily to submit. As I took his hand at the levee, which closed my first day's experiences with him, he said in his homely way, "Well, C., you have seen one day's run;—what is your opinion of it?"

XIII.

Wednesday morning was devoted to the continued examination of the court-martial cases, to the great vexation of a score of political applicants, whom I could hear impatiently pacing the floor of the hall and waiting-room. At one o'clock, however, the doors were thrown open, and the throng admitted and dismissed, as rapidly as possible. I was much amused and interested, later in the day, in a variety of characters who presented themselves. First was an elderly lady, plainly but comfortably dressed, whose son was a prisoner in Baltimore. Her story, spun out to some length, was briefly this: Her son had been serving in the Rebel army. He heard that his sister was lying dead at home, and his mother at the supposed point of death. He determined to see them, and succeeded in getting through our lines undiscovered. He found his mother better. Before he got ready to return, he became very ill himself. She said she hid him in the house until he recovered, and on his way back to his regiment he was captured. He was now anxious to take the oath, and his mother assured the President that he should henceforth "have nothing to do with the Rebels." Mr. Lincoln sat quietly through the story, his face in half shadow. As she finished he said, with some impatience,—"Now this is a pretty story to come to me with, isn't it? Your son came home from fighting against his country; he was sick; you secreted him, nursed him up, and when cured, started him off again to help destroy some more of our boys. Taken prisoner, trying to get through our lines, you now want me to let him off upon his oath." "Yes," said the woman, not in the least disconcerted, "and I give you my word, Mr. President, he shall never have anything more to do with the Rebels—never—I was always opposed to his joining them." "Your word," rejoined Mr. Lincoln dryly, "what do I know about your word?" He finally took the application, and writing something upon the back of it, returned it to her with the words, "Now, I want you to understand that I have done this just to get rid of you!" "Oh," said she, "Mr. President, I have always heard that you were such a kind-hearted man, and now I know it is true." And so, with much apparent satisfaction, she withdrew.

The party that followed consisted of a lady and two gentlemen. She had come to ask that her husband, who was also a prisoner of war, might be permitted to take the oath and be released from confinement. To secure a degree of interest on the part of the President, one of the gentlemen claimed to be an acquaintance of Mrs. Lincoln; this, however, received but little attention, and the President proceeded to ask what position the lady's husband held in the Rebel service. "Oh," said she, "he was a captain." "A *captain!*" rejoined Mr. Lincoln, "indeed!— rather too big a fish to set free simply upon his taking the oath. If he was an officer, it is proof positive that he has been a zealous rebel; I cannot release him." Here the lady's friend reiterated the assertion of his acquaintance with Mrs. Lincoln. Instantly the President's hand was upon the bell-rope. The usher in attendance answered the summons. "Cornelius, take this man's name to Mrs. Lincoln, and ask her what she knows of him." The boy presently returned, with the reply that "*the Madam*" (as she was called by the servants) knew nothing of him whatever. The man said it was very strange. "Well, it is just as I suspected," said the President. The party made one more attempt to enlist his sympathy, but without effect. "It is of no use," was the reply; "I cannot release him;" and the trio withdrew, the lady in high displeasure.

Next came a Methodist minister by the name of "G.," claiming to be the son of the inventor of iron-clad gunboats. He had understood that the President appointed the hospital chaplains, and he greatly desired such a place. Mr. Lincoln replied rather curtly, that he could do nothing for him. "But I was told, sir, that these appointments were made by the President," said the gentleman, very respectfully. "I will just tell you how that is," was the answer; "when there are vacancies I appoint, not without." The clergyman here alluded to his having left with the private secretary a war-sermon which he had lately preached. Stepping out, he returned with the pamphlet, saying, as he handed it to the President, "I suppose, sir, you have little time to read anything of this kind; but I shall be very glad to leave it with you." Upon this he bowed himself out, and the sermon was carelessly tossed aside, never to be thought of again by Mr. Lincoln.

Subsequently the sermon fell into my hands. The only thing I remember about it was the practical application of a professional incident. The clergyman one day fell in with two soldiers fighting. One had the other down, and was severely handling him. Rebuking the men, the one underneath responded very heartily, "Plase your *riverince*, I am willing to give up this minute, solely out of respect for your *riverince*." And so the preacher thought the South should be made to say "in regard to the Constitution."

XIV.

The examples given of the observations of two days, are fair illustrations of the usual White House routine, varied of course by official or diplomatic business, and a greater or less pressure of visitors, some of whom would linger in the ante-room day after day, waiting admission. The incidents of no two days could of course be alike. I shall never cease to regret that an additional private secretary could not have been appointed, whose exclusive duty it should have been to look after and keep a record of all cases appealing to executive clemency. It would have afforded full employment for one man, at least; and such a volume would now be beyond all price.

Just before leaving for Washington, I met a brother artist, who, upon learning of my proposed purpose, laid before me the details of an interesting case, concerning his only son, begging me to bring the circumstances to the President's knowledge. When the war broke out the young man in question was living at the South. Eventually driven into the Rebel service, he was improving his first opportunity to go over to the Union lines, when he was taken prisoner. His story was disbelieved, and he had been in prison for more than a year at Alton, Illinois. His father had spent many months in the endeavor to have him released, without success. So many formalities and technicalities were in the way that he became completely discouraged, and appealed to me as his last hope. The boy was very ill, and he feared if not speedily released, would soon die. Promising the father that I would bear the case in mind, I improved an opportunity, as soon as I felt sure of having found favor with the President, to speak to him about it. I believe it was on the private staircase, that, meeting him one evening, I ventured to introduce the subject. I assured him of the entire good faith and loyalty of both father and son. Of course he had never heard of the case before. Considering the subject a moment, he said, "Come up-stairs by-and-by, and I guess we can fix it up."

An hour later I entered his room, and gave him very briefly the particulars of the case; reading one or two letters from the young man to his father. "That will do," said the President, putting on his spectacles, and taking the letter out of my hand, he turned it over and wrote on the back of it, "Release this man upon his taking the oath. A. LINCOLN." "There," said he, "you can take that over to the War Department yourself, if you choose. You will find it all right."

XV.

Wednesday night, February 10th, was an exciting one at the White House, the stables belonging to the mansion being burned to the ground. The loss most severely felt was of the two ponies, one of which had belonged to Willie Lincoln, the President's second son, who died in 1862, and the other to Tad, the youngest, and pet of his father, who in his infancy nicknamed him Tadpole, subsequently abbreviated to Taddie, and then Tad. His real name is Thomas, named for the father of Mr. Lincoln. Upon "Tad's" learning of the loss, he threw himself at full length upon the floor, and could not be comforted. The only allusion I ever heard the President make to Willie was on this occasion, in connection with the loss of his pony. John Hay, the assistant private secretary, told me that he was rarely known to speak of his lost son.

The morning following the fire, Robert Lincoln came into his father's office, and said he had a point of law which he wished to submit. It appeared that one of the coachmen had two or three hundred dollars in greenbacks in his room over the stables, which were consumed. Robert said that he and John Hay had been having an argument as to the liability of the government for its notes, where it could be shown that they had been burned, or otherwise destroyed. The President turned the matter over in his mind for a moment, and said, "The payment of a note presupposes its presentation to the maker of it. It is the sign or symbol of value received; it is not *value* itself, that is clear. At the same time the production of the note seems a necessary warrant for the demand; and while the moral obligation is as strong without this, governments and banking institutions do not recognize any principle beyond the strictly legal. It is an established rule that the citizen cannot sue the government; therefore, I don't see but that it is a dead loss for Jehu."

About this time a couple of Kentucky gentlemen called. As they rose to take leave, one of them, who may have noticed little Tad,—as he usually spent much time in his father's office,—said to the President: "General Crittenden told me an interesting incident about his son, eight or nine years old, a few days since. A day or two after the battle of Chickamauga, the little fellow came into camp. The General rode during the battle a horse which went by the name of John Jay, a great favorite with his son. Manifesting his delight upon again seeing his father, by covering him with caresses, the child at length said, 'Papa, where is John Jay?' 'Oh,' said his father, 'your horse behaved very badly during the fight; he insisted, very cowardly, upon taking me to the rear.' The little fellow's eyes sparkled. 'Papa,' said he, 'I know John Jay would never have done that of his own will. It must have been *your* work.'"

Montgomery Blair told me that when the convention which nominated Mr. Lincoln met at Chicago, there was a hideous painting in the hall which was brought forward subsequently as a likeness of the nominee. Most of the delegates having never seen the original, the effect upon them was indescribable. I replied to Mr. Blair that my friend Brady, the photographer, insisted that his photograph of Mr. Lincoln, taken the morning

of the day he made his Cooper Institute speech in New York,—
much the best portrait, by the way, in circulation of him during
the campaign,—was the means of his election. That it helped
largely to this end I do not doubt. The effect of such influences,
though silent, is powerful. Fremont once said to me, that the
villanous wood-cut published by the New York "Tribune," the
next day after his nomination, lost him twenty-five votes in
one township, to his certain knowledge.

On one of the last days of February, I called, with my friend
W——, of New York, upon Mr. Lovejoy, who was supposed
to be convalescent. He thought himself nearly well again, and
was in fine spirits. Indications of an organized movement to
bring forward Fremont, as an opposition candidate to Mr. Lincoln, had recently appeared. Mr. Lovejoy was very severe upon
it; he said, "Any attempt to divide the party at such a time was
criminal in the last degree." I remember observing that many of
the extreme anti-slavery men appeared to distrust the President.
This drew out his indignant condemnation. "I tell you," said he,
"Mr. Lincoln is at heart as strong an anti-slavery man as any of
them, but he is compelled to *feel* his way. He has a responsibility in this matter which many men do not seem to be able to
comprehend. I say to you frankly, that I believe his course to be
right. His mind acts slowly, but when he moves, it is *forward*.
You will never find him receding from a position once taken. It
is of no use talking, or getting up conventions against him. He

is going to be the candidate of the Baltimore Convention, and is sure to be reëlected. 'It was foreordained from the foundation of the world.' I have no sympathy or patience with those who are trying to manufacture issues against him; but they will not succeed; he is too strong with the masses. For my part," he concluded, "I am not only willing to take Mr. Lincoln for another term, but the same cabinet, right straight through."

XVI.

Wednesday, March 2d, I had an unusually long and interesting sitting from the President. I invited Mr. Samuel Sinclair, of New York, who was in Washington, to be present. The news had recently been received of the disaster under General Seymour in Florida. Many newspapers openly charged the President with having sent the expedition with primary reference to restoring the State in season to secure its vote at the forthcoming Baltimore Convention. Mr. Lincoln was deeply wounded by these charges. He referred to them during the sitting; and gave a simple and truthful statement of the affair, which was planned, if I remember rightly, by General Gillmore. A few days afterward, an editorial appeared in the New York "Tribune," which was known not to favor Mr. Lincoln's renomination, entirely exonerating him from all blame. I took the article to him in his study, and he expressed much gratification at its candor. It was, perhaps, in connection with the news-

paper attacks, that he told, during the sitting, this story.—"A
traveller on the frontier found himself out of his reckoning one
night in a most inhospitable region. A terrific thunder-storm
came up, to add to his trouble. He floundered along until his
horse at length gave out. The lightning afforded him the only
clew to his way, but the peals of thunder were frightful. One
bolt, which seemed to crash the earth beneath him, brought
him to his knees. By no means a praying man, his petition was
short and to the point,—"O Lord, if it is all the same to you,
give us a little more light and a little less noise!"

Presently the conversation turned upon Shakspeare, of
whom it is well known Mr. Lincoln was very fond. He once remarked, "It matters not to me whether Shakspeare be well or ill
acted; with him the thought suffices." Edwin Booth was playing an engagement at this time at Grover's Theatre. He had
been announced for the coming evening in his famous part of
Hamlet. The President had never witnessed his representation
of this character, and he proposed being present. The mention
of this play, which I afterward learned had at all times a peculiar charm for Mr. Lincoln's mind, waked up a train of thought
I was not prepared for. Said he,—and his words have often returned to me with a sad interest since his own assassination,—
"There is one passage of the play of "Hamlet" which is very apt
to be slurred over by the actor, or omitted altogether, which
seems to me the choicest part of the play. It is the soliloquy of

the king, after the murder. It always struck me as one of the finest touches of nature in the world."

Then, throwing himself into the very spirit of the scene, he took up the words:—

"O my offence is rank, it smells to heaven;
It hath the primal eldest curse upon 't,
A brother's murder!—Pray can I not,
Though inclination be as sharp as will;
My stronger guilt defeats my strong intent;
And, like a man to double business bound,
I stand in pause where I shall first begin,
And both neglect. What if this cursed hand
Were thicker than itself with brother's blood?
Is there not rain enough in the sweet heavens
To wash it white as snow? Whereto serves mercy
But to confront the visage of offence;
And what's in prayer but this twofold force—
To be forestalled ere we come to fall,
Or pardoned, being down? Then I'll look up;
My fault is past. But O what form of prayer
Can serve my turn? Forgive me my foul murder?—
That cannot be; since I am still possessed
Of those effects for which I did the murder,—
My crown, my own ambition, and my queen.

May one be pardoned and retain the offence?
In the corrupted currents of this world,
Offence's gilded hand may shove by justice,
And oft 't is seen the wicked prize itself
Buys out the law; but 't is not so *above*.
There is no shuffling; there the action lies
In its true nature; and we ourselves compelled,
Even to the teeth and forehead of our faults,
To give in evidence. What then? what rests?
Try what repentance can; what can it not?
Yet what can it when one cannot repent?

O wretched state! O bosom black as death!
O bruised soul that, struggling to be free,
Art more engaged! Help, angels, make assay!
Bow, stubborn knees! And heart with strings of steel,
Be soft as sinews of the new-born babe;
All may be well!"

He repeated this entire passage from memory, with a feeling and appreciation unsurpassed by anything I ever witnessed upon the stage. Remaining in thought for a few moments, he continued:—

"The opening of the play of 'King Richard the Third' seems to me often entirely misapprehended. It is quite common for an actor to come upon the stage, and, in a sophomoric style, to begin with a flourish:—

   "'Now is the winter of our discontent
     Made glorious summer by this sun of York,
     And all the clouds that lowered upon our house,
     In the deep bosom of the ocean buried!'

Now," said he, "this is all wrong. Richard, you remember, had been, and was then, plotting the destruction of his brothers, to make room for himself. Outwardly, the most loyal to the newly crowned king, secretly he could scarcely contain his impatience at the obstacles still in the way of his own elevation. He appears upon the stage, just after the crowning of Edward, burning with repressed hate and jealousy. The prologue is the utterance of the most intense bitterness and satire."

Then, unconsciously assuming the character, Mr. Lincoln repeated, also from memory, Richard's soliloquy, rendering it with a degree of force and power that made it seem like a new creation to me. Though familiar with the passage from boyhood, I can truly say that never till that moment had I fully appreciated its spirit. I could not refrain from laying down my palette and brushes, and applauding heartily, upon his conclusion, saying, at the same time, half in earnest, that I was not sure but that he had made a mistake in the choice of a profession, considerably, as may be imagined, to his amusement. Mr. Sinclair has since repeatedly said to me that he never heard these choice passages of Shakspeare rendered with more effect by the most famous of modern actors.

Mr. Lincoln's memory was very remarkable. With the multitude of visitors whom he saw daily, I was often amazed at the readiness with which he recalled faces and events and even names. At one of the afternoon receptions, a stranger shook hands with him, and, as he did so, remarked, casually, that he was elected to Congress about the time Mr. Lincoln's term as representative expired. "Yes," said the President, "you are from——," mentioning the State. "I remember reading of your election in a newspaper one morning on a steamboat going down to Mount Vernon." At another time a gentleman addressed him, saying, "I presume, Mr. President, that you have forgotten me?" "No," was the prompt reply; "your name is Flood. I saw you last, twelve years ago, at——," naming the place and the occasion. "I am glad to see," he continued, "that the *Flood* flows on." Subsequent to his reëlection a deputation of bankers from various sections were introduced one day by the Secretary of the Treasury. After a few moment's general conversation, Mr. Lincoln turned to one of them, and said: "Your district did not give me so strong a vote at the last election as it did in 1860." "I think, sir, that you must be mistaken," replied the banker. "I have the impression that your majority was considerably increased at the last election." "No," rejoined the President, "you fell off about six hundred votes." Then taking down from the bookcase the official canvass of 1860 and 1864, he referred to the vote of the district named, and proved to be quite right in his assertion.

During this interview,—related to me by one of the party, Mr. P——, of Chelsea, Mass.,—a member of the delegation referred to the severity of the tax laid by Congress upon the State Banks. "Now," said Mr. Lincoln, "that reminds me of a circumstance that took place in a neighborhood where I lived when I was a boy. In the spring of the year the farmers were very fond of the dish which they called greens, though the fashionable name for it nowadays is spinach, I believe. One day after dinner, a large family were taken very ill. The doctor was called in, who attributed it to the greens, of which all had freely partaken. Living in the family was a half-witted boy named Jake. On a subsequent occasion, when greens had been gathered for dinner, the head of the house said: 'Now, boys, before running any further risk in this thing, we will first try them on Jake. If he stands it, we are all right.' And just so, I suppose," said Mr. Lincoln, "Congress thought of the State Banks!"

XVII.

While sitting one day, Secretary Stanton—whom I usually found quite taciturn—referred to the meeting of the Buchanan

Cabinet called upon receipt of the news that Colonel Anderson had evacuated Moultrie, and gone into Fort Sumter. "This little incident," said Stanton, "was the crisis of our history,— the pivot upon which everything turned. Had he remained in Fort Moultrie, a very different combination of circumstances would have arisen. The attack on Sumter—commenced by the South—united the North, and made the success of the Confederacy impossible. I shall never forget," he continued, "our coming together by special summons that night. Buchanan sat in his arm-chair in a corner of the room, white as a sheet, with the stump of a cigar in his mouth. The despatches were laid before us; and so much violence ensued, that he had to turn us all out-of-doors."

The day following, by special permission of Mr. Lincoln, I was present at the regular Cabinet meeting. Judge Bates came in first, and, taking a package out of his pocket, said, "You may not be aware, Mr. President, that you have a formidable rival in the field. I received this through the mail to-day." He unfolded an immense placard, on which was printed in large letters,—"I introduce for President of the United States, Mr. T. W. Smith [I think this was the name], of Philadelphia." The bill then went on to enumerate the qualifications of the candidate, which were of a stunning order; and the whole was signed "George Bates," which the Attorney-General said might be a relative of his, for aught he knew. This decidedly original document was pinned up in a conspicuous place in the council-chamber, where it hung for several days, of course attracting the attention of all visitors, and creating much amusement.

The disaster on the Red River was the subject of official consultation. The positions of the respective forces were traced on the war maps, and various suggestions and opinions offered. The Secretary of the Interior, looking over to where the Secretary of War sat, said he had a young friend whom he wished to have appointed a paymaster in the army. "How old is he?" asked Stanton, gruffly. "About twenty-one, I believe," answered the Secretary of the Interior; "he is of good family and excellent character." "Usher," was the reply, "I would not appoint the Angel Gabriel a paymaster, if he was only twenty-one."

Judge Bates, who was to have a sitting after the adjournment, here beckoned to me, signifying that he was ready for the appointment. And so ended my brief glimpse of a cabinet in session.

XVIII.

General Grant reached Washington, after his nomination to the Lieutenant-Generalship, the evening of March 8th, 1864. His reception at Willard's Hotel, unaccompanied by staff or escort, was an event never to be forgotten by those who witnessed it. Later in the evening he attended the Presidential levee, entering the reception-room unannounced. He was recognized and welcomed by the President with the utmost cordiality, and the distinguished stranger was soon nearly overwhelmed by the pressure of the crowd upon him. Secretary Seward at length mounting a sofa, pulled the modest hero up by his side, where he stood for some time, bowing his acknowledgments to the tumultuous assemblage. He subsequently remarked that this was "his warmest campaign during the war."

The next day at one o'clock he was formally presented by the President with his commission as Lieutenant-General. The ceremony took place in the presence of the Cabinet, the Hon. Mr. Lovejoy, and several officers of the army, and was very brief and simple, as became the character of each of the illustrious chief actors.

On the day following General Grant visited the Army of the Potomac, and upon his return to Washington he made preparations to leave immediately for the West. At the close of a consultation with the President and Secretary of War, he was informed that Mrs. Lincoln expected his presence the same evening at a military dinner she proposed to give in his honor. The General at once responded that it would be impossible for him to remain over,—he "must be in Tennessee at a given time." "But we can't excuse you," returned the President. "It would be the play of 'Hamlet' with *Hamlet* left out, over again. Twelve distinguished officers, now in the city, have been invited to meet you." "I appreciate fully the honor Mrs. Lincoln would do me," replied the General, hesitatingly, knocking the ashes off the end of his cigar; "but—time is very precious just now—and—really, Mr. President, I believe I have had enough of the '*show*' business!"

The dinner was given; the twelve officers did full justice to it; but it is needless to add, the Lieutenant-General was not one of the number.

XIX.

The evening of March 25th was an intensely interesting one to me. It was passed with the President alone in his study, marked by no interruptions. Busy with pen and papers when I entered, he presently threw them aside, and commenced talking again about Shakspeare. Little Tad coming in, he sent him to the library for a copy of the plays, from which he read aloud several of his favorite passages. Relapsing into a sadder strain, he laid the book aside, and leaning back in his chair, said, "There is a poem that has been a great favorite with me for years, to which my attention was first called when a young man, by a friend, and which I afterward saw and cut from a newspaper, and carried in my pocket, till by frequent reading I had it by heart. I would give a great deal," he added, "to know who wrote it, but I never could ascertain." Then, half closing his eyes, he repeated the poem, "Oh! why should the spirit of mortal be proud?" Surprised and delighted, I told him that I should greatly prize a copy of the lines. He replied that he had recently written them out for Mrs. Stanton, but promised that when a favorable opportunity occurred he would give them to me.

Varying the subject, he continued: "There are some quaint, queer verses, written, I think, by Oliver Wendell Holmes, entitled, 'The Last Leaf,' one of which is to me inexpressibly touching. He then repeated these also from memory. The verse he referred to occurs in about the middle of the poem, and is this:—

"The mossy marbles rest
On the lips that he has pressed
    In their bloom;
And the names he loved to hear
Have been carved for many a year
    On the tomb."

As he finished this verse, he said, in his emphatic way, "For pure pathos, in my judgment, there is nothing finer than those six lines in the English language!"

A day or two afterward, he asked me to accompany him to the temporary studio, at the Treasury Department, of Mr. Swayne, the sculptor, who was making a bust of him. While he was sitting, it occurred to me to improve the opportunity to secure the promised poem. Upon mentioning the subject, the sculptor surprised me by saying that he had at his home, in Philadelphia, a printed copy of the verses, taken from a newspaper some years previous. The President inquired if they were published in any connection with his name. Mr. Swayne said that they purported to have been *written* "by Abraham Lincoln." "I have heard of that before, and that is why I asked," returned the President. "But there is no truth in it. The poem was first shown to me by a young man named 'Jason Duncan,' many years ago."

The sculptor was using for a studio the office of the Solicitor of the Treasury Department, an irregular room, packed nearly full of law books. Seating myself, I believe, upon a pile of these at Mr. Lincoln's feet, he kindly repeated the lines, which I wrote down, one by one, as they fell from his lips:—

OH! WHY SHOULD THE SPIRIT OF MORTAL BE PROUD?*

Oh! why should the spirit of mortal be proud?
Like a swift-fleeting meteor, a fast-flying cloud,

---

*The authorship of this poem has been made known since this publication in the *Evening Post*. It was written by William Knox, a young Scotchman, a contemporary of Sir Walter Scott. He died in Edinburgh, in 1825, at the age of 36. The two verses in brackets were not repeated by Mr. Lincoln, but belong to the original poem.

A flash of the lightning, a break of the wave,
He passeth from life to his rest in the grave.

The leaves of the oak and the willow shall fade,
Be scattered around, and together be laid;
And the young and the old, and the low and the high,
Shall moulder to dust, and together shall lie.

The infant a mother attended and loved;
The mother that infant's affection who proved;
The husband, that mother and infant who blest,—
Each, all, are away to their dwellings of rest.

[The maid on whose cheek, on whose brow, in whose eye,
Shone beauty and pleasure,—her triumphs are by;
And the memory of those who loved her and praised,
Are alike from the minds of the living erased.]

The hand of the king that the sceptre hath borne,
The brow of the priest that the mitre hath worn,
The eye of the sage, and the hearth of the brave,
Are hidden and lost in the depths of the grave.

The peasant, whose lot was to sow and to reap,
The herdsman, who climbed with his goats up the steep,
The beggar, who wandered in search of his bread,
Have faded away like the grass that we tread.

[The saint, who enjoyed the communion of Heaven,
The sinner, who dared to remain unforgiven,
The wise and the foolish, the guilty and just,
Have quietly mingled their bones in the dust.]

So the multitude goes—like the flower or the weed
That withers away to let others succeed;
So the multitude comes—even those we behold,
To repeat every tale that has often been told.

For we are the same our fathers have been;
We see the same sights our fathers have seen;
We drink the same stream, we view the same sun,
And run the same course our fathers have run.

The thoughts we are thinking, our fathers would think;
From the death we are shrinking, our fathers would shrink;
To the life we are clinging, they also would cling;—
But it speeds from us all like a bird on the wing.

They loved—but the story we cannot unfold;
They scorned—but the heart of the haughty is cold;
They grieved—but no wail from their slumber will come;
They joyed—but the tongue of their gladness is dumb.

They died—ay, they died;—we things that are now,
That walk on the turf that lies over their brow,

And make in their dwellings a transient abode,
Meet the things that they met on their pilgrimage road.

Yea! hope and despondency, pleasure and pain,
Are mingled together in sunshine and rain;
And the smile and the tear, the song and the dirge,
Still follow each other, like surge upon surge.

'T is the wink of an eye—'t is the draught of a breath—
From the blossom of health to the paleness of death,
From the gilded saloon to the bier and the shroud:—
Oh! why should the spirit of mortal be proud?

XX.

On the way to the sculptor's studio a conversation occurred
of much significance, in view of the terrible tragedy so soon to
paralyze every loyal heart in the nation. A late number of the
New York "Tribune" had contained an account from a correspondent within the Rebel Lines, of an elaborate conspiracy,
matured in Richmond, to abduct, or assassinate—if the first
was not found practicable—the person of the President. A secret organization, composed, it was stated, of five hundred or a
thousand men, had solemnly sworn to accomplish the deed.
Mr. Lincoln had not seen or heard of this account, and at his
request, I gave him the details. Upon the conclusion, he smiled

incredulously, and said: "Well, even if true, I do not see what the Rebels would gain by killing or getting possession of me. I am but a single individual, and it would not help their cause or make the least difference in the progress of the war. Everything would go right on just the same. Soon after I was nominated at Chicago, I began to receive letters threatening my life. The first one or two made me a little uncomfortable, but I came at length to look for a regular instalment of this kind of correspondence in every week's mail, and up to inauguration day I was in constant receipt of such letters. It is no uncommon thing to receive them now; but they have ceased to give me any apprehension." I expressed some surprise at this, but he replied in his peculiar way, "Oh, there is nothing like getting *used* to things!"

In connection with this, Mr. Noah Brooks,—who was to have been Mr. Nicolay's successor as private secretary to the President,—and Colonel Charles G. Halpine, of New York, have referred to personal conversations of exceeding interest, which I transcribe.

In an article contributed to "Harper's Magazine," soon after the assassination, Mr. Brooks says:—

"The simple habits of Mr. Lincoln were so well known that it is a subject for surprise that watchful and malignant treason did not sooner take that precious life which he seemed to hold so lightly. He had an almost morbid dislike for an escort, or guide, and daily exposed himself to the deadly aim of an assassin. One summer morning, passing by the White House at an early hour, I saw the President standing at the gateway, looking anxiously down the street; and, in reply to a salutation, he said, 'Good morning, good morning! I am looking for a newsboy; when you get to that corner, I wish you would start one up this way.' In reply to the remonstrances of friends, who were afraid of his constant exposure to danger, he had but one answer: 'If they kill me, the next man will be just as bad for them; and in a country like this, where our habits are simple, and must be, assassination is always possible, and will come, if they are determined upon it.'"

A cavalry guard was once placed at the gates of the White House for a while, and he said, privately, that "he worried until he got rid of it." While the President's family were at their summer-house, near Washington, he rode into town of a morning, or out at night, attended by a mounted escort; but if he returned to town for a while after dark, he rode in unguarded, and often alone, in his open carriage. On more than one occasion the writer has gone through the streets of Washington at a late hour of the night with the President, without escort, or even the company of a servant, walking all of the way, going and returning.

Considering the many open and secret threats to take his life, it is not surprising that Mr. Lincoln had many thoughts about his coming to a sudden and violent end. He once said that he felt the force of the expression, "To take one's life in his hand;" but that he would not like to face death suddenly. He said that he thought himself a great coward physically, and was sure that he would make a poor soldier, for, unless there was something inspiriting in the excitement of a battle, he was sure that he would drop his gun and run, at the first symptom of danger. That was said sportively, and he added, "Moral cowardice is something which I think I never had."

Colonel Halpine, while serving as a member of General Halleck's staff, had frequently to wait upon the President, both during official hours and at other times. On one of these occasions, Mr. Lincoln concluded some interesting remarks with these words: "It would never do for a President to have guards with drawn sabres at his door, as if he fancied he were, or were trying to be, or were assuming to be, an emperor."

"This expression," writes Colonel Halpine, "called my attention afresh to what I had remarked to myself almost every time I entered the White House, and to which I had very frequently called the attention both of Major Hay and General Halleck— the utterly unprotected condition of the President's person, and the fact that any assassin or maniac, seeking his life, could enter his presence without the interference of a single armed man to hold him back. The entrance-doors, and all doors on the official side of the building, were open at all hours of the day, and very late into the evening; and I have many times entered the mansion, and walked up to the rooms of the two private secretaries, as late as nine or ten o'clock at night, without seeing or being challenged by a single soul. There were, indeed, two attendants,—one for the outer door, and the other for the door of the official chambers; but these—thinking, I suppose, that none would call after office hours save persons who were personally acquainted, or had the right of official entry—were, not unfrequently, somewhat remiss in their duties.

"To this fact I now ventured to call the President's attention, saying that to me—perhaps from my European education—it appeared a deliberate courting of danger, even if the country were in a state of the profoundest peace, for the person at the head of the nation to remain so unprotected.

"'There are two dangers,' I wound up by saying; 'the danger of deliberate political assassination, and the mere brute violence of insanity.'

"Mr. Lincoln heard me through with a smile, his hands locked across his knees, his body rocking back and forth,—the common indication that he was amused.

"'Now, as to political assassination,' he said, 'do you think the Richmond people would like to have Hannibal Hamlin here any better than myself? In that one alternative, I have an insurance on my life worth half the prairie land of Illinois. And beside,'—this more gravely,—'if there were such a plot, and they wanted to get at me, no vigilance could keep them out. We are so mixed up in our affairs, that—no matter what the system established—a conspiracy to assassinate, if such there were, could easily obtain a pass to see me for any one or more of its instruments.

"'To betray fear of this, by placing guards or so forth, would only be to put the idea into their heads, and perhaps lead to the very result it was intended to prevent. As to the crazy folks, Major, why I must only take my chances,—the worst crazy people at present, I fear, being some of my own too zealous adherents. That there may be such dangers as you and many others have suggested to me, is quite possible; but I guess it wouldn't improve things any to publish that we were afraid of them in advance.'

"Upon another occasion I remember his coming over one evening after dinner, to General Halleck's private quarters, to protest—half jocularly, half in earnest—against a small detachment of cavalry which had been detailed without his request, and partly against his will, by the lamented General Wadsworth, as a guard for his carriage in going to and returning from the Soldiers' Home. The burden of his complaint was that he and Mrs. Lincoln 'couldn't hear themselves talk,' for the clatter of their sabres and spurs; and that, as many of them appeared new hands and very awkward, he was more afraid of being shot by the accidental discharge of one of their carbines or revolvers, than of any attempt upon his life or for his capture by the roving squads of Jeb Stuart's cavalry, then hovering all round the exterior works of the city."

XXI.

Judge Bates, the Attorney-General, was one day very severe upon the modern deal school of art, as applied to historic characters and events. He instanced in sculpture, Greenough's "Washington," in the Capitol grounds, which, he said, was a very good illustration of the heathen idea of Jupiter Tonans, but was the farthest possible remove from any American's conception of the Father of his Country. Powell's painting in the Rotunda, "De Soto discovering the Mississippi," and Mills's equestrian statue of Jackson, in front of the President's House, shared in his sarcastic condemnation. He quoted from an old English poet—Creech, I think he said—with much unction:—

"Whatever contradicts my sense
 I hate to see, and can but disbelieve."

"Genius and talent," said he, on another occasion, "are rarely found combined in one individual." I requested his definition of the distinction. "Genius," he replied, "conceives; talent executes."

Referring to Mr. Lincoln's never-failing fund of anecdote, he remarked, "The character of the President's mind is such that his thought habitually takes on this form of illustration, by which the point he wishes to enforce is invariably brought home with a strength and clearness impossible in hours of abstract argument. Mr. Lincoln," he added, "comes very near being a perfect man, according to my ideal of manhood. He lacks but one thing." Looking up from my palette, I asked, musingly, if this was official dignity as President. "No," replied Judge Bates, "that is of little consequence. His deficiency is in the element of *will*. I have sometimes told him, for instance, that he was unfit to be intrusted with the pardoning power. Why, if a man comes to him with a touching story, his judgment is almost certain to be affected by it. Should the applicant be a *woman*, a wife, a mother, or a sister,—in nine cases out of ten, her tears, if nothing else, are sure to prevail."

XXII.

Mr. Seward, whose conversation much of the time, while sitting, was like that of a man soliloquizing aloud, told me on one occasion two or three good stories. Referring to the numerous portraits painted of him at different times, he said, that of all artists whom he had known, Henry Inman was most rapid in execution. For the full-length portrait, painted while he was Governor, for the city of New York, Inman required but two or three sittings of an hour each, with an additional quarter of an hour for the standing figure. This drew out something from me in relation to Elliott's whole length of him, painted at the same period. "My experience with Elliott," he rejoined, "who was then in the beginning of his career, was a very different affair. He seemed to think me like Governor Crittenden's hen." Laughing at the recollection, he lighted a cigar, and continued: "One day the Governor was engaged with his Council, when his little boy, of five or six years, came into the chamber, and said, 'Father, the black hen is *setting*.' 'Go away, my son,' returned the Governor; 'I am very busy.' The child disappeared, but soon returned, and putting his head in at the door, repeated the information. 'Well, well,' replied the Governor, 'you must not bother me now; let her *set*.' The door was shut, but soon afterward again cautiously opened, in the midst of a profound discussion, and the words rang out, 'But father, she is setting on one egg!' The Governor turned around, and looking into the dilated eyes of the excited little fellow, replied dryly, 'Well, my son, I think we will let her *set*. Her time is not *very* precious!'"

Another was of General R——, formerly of the New York State Senate. At the regular session one day, the General gave notice that the following day he would introduce a bill providing a thermometer for every institution of learning in the State. The next morning the clerk was in his private office at the usual hour, reading the bills aloud, and placing them on file for the business of the day. A gentleman who prided himself upon his classical attainments was present, and, as the clerk read the notice given by Senator R——, he was informed that a word borrowed from another language should, according to the rule, always be given its native pronunciation. The original of thermometer, the gentleman said, was a French term, which should be pronounced accordingly. By a process of reasoning the clerk was convinced; and when the bill was announced, he read it according to instructions. General R—— was observed to look up from writing, and fix his eye upon the clerk. The second reading passed, and he rose to his feet, bending forward upon his desk, listening intently, his eyebrows gradually contracting. "Third reading. Senator R—— gave notice of a bill to provide a *thermomètre* for every institution of learning in the State." By this time the attention of the entire house was drawn to the General. "Ther—what?" he demanded, in a stentorian tone. "*Thermomètre*," quietly responded the confident clerk. "Thermometer! thermometer! you——fool; don't you know what a thermometer is?" thundered the enraged Senator, amid roars of laughter.

Speaking once of Henry Clay and Daniel Webster, Mr. Seward remarked, that, as statesmen, they could not well be compared; "they were no more alike than a Grecian temple and a Gothic church,"

I was much interested in an opinion he once expressed of equestrian statues. He said a grand character should never be represented in this form. It was ignoring the divine in human nature to thus link man with an animal, and seemed to him a degradation of true art. "Bucephalus," in marble or bronze was well enough by itself. Place "Alexander" upon his back, and though the animal gained a degree of interest, the *man* lost immeasurably.

XXIII.

Soon after the chalk sketch of my conception had been placed upon the canvas, I attended one of the receptions given by the Secretary of the Navy and Mrs. Welles. While standing as I thought unobserved, near a corner of the room, Mr. Seward approached me, and in a manner of more than usual warmth, said, "I told the President the other day that you were painting your picture upon a false presumption." Looking at him in some surprise, I inquired his meaning. "Oh," he rejoined, "you appear to think in common with many other foolish people, that the great business of this Administration is the destruction of slavery. Now allow me to say you are much mistaken. Slavery was killed years ago. Its death knell was tolled when Abraham Lincoln was elected President. The work of this administration is the suppression of the Rebellion and the preservation of the Union. Abolitionists, like the different religious sects, have been chasing one idea, until they have come to believe that their horizon absolutely bounds the world. Slavery has been in fact but an incident in the history of the nation, inevitably bound to perish in the progress of intelligence. Future generations will scarcely credit the record that such an institution ever existed here; or existing, that it ever lived a day under such a government. But suppose, for one moment, the Republic destroyed. With it is bound up not alone the destiny of a race, but the best hopes of all mankind. With its overthrow the sun of liberty, like the Hebrew dial, would be set back indefinitely. The magnitude of such a calamity is beyond our calculation. The salvation of the nation is, then, of vastly more consequence than the destruction of slavery. Had you consulted me for a subject to paint, I should not have given you the Cabinet Council on Emancipation, but the meeting which took place when the news came of the attack upon Sumter, when the first measures were organized for the restoration of the national authority. That was the crisis in the history of this Administration—not the issue of the Emancipation Proclamation. If I am to be remembered by posterity," he concluded, with much excitement of manner, "let it not be as having loved predominantly white men or black men, but as one who loved his country."

Assenting to much that he had said, I replied, that with all deference, I could not accept his conclusions regarding slavery.

Although more than a year had passed since the issue of the proclamation, the Confederacy, founded upon it, was yet powerful enough to threaten the destruction of the nation, though, for my own part, I did not question the result of the conflict. I looked upon the Declaration of Independence as the *assertion* that all men were created free. Mr. Lincoln's Emancipation Proclamation was the *demonstration* of this great truth. Without slavery the Republic would have been in no danger. That was the canker-worm gnawing away the nation's life. Not until the Administration was ready to strike at the root and cause of the Rebellion, was there any reason to hope for the success of the national cause. Without this step, however grand or high the conception in the minds of men of the Republic, in all probability it would have perished. Therefore, in my judgment, no single act of the Administration could for one moment be compared with that of emancipation. Granting the potential view, the proclamation was necessary, as the sign and seal of the consummation.

"Well," replied Mr. Seward, "you think so, and this generation may agree with you; but posterity will hold a different opinion."

Of course this conversation could not but attract the attention of all in the immediate vicinity. A few moments later, Senator Morgan, referring to the Secretary's assertion that slavery was dead when the Rebellion broke out, told me this characteristic incident of the President, showing that he, at least, did not hold that view. Soon after the issue of the proclamation, having official business, as Governor of New York, which called him to Washington, Mr. Lincoln remarked to him, speaking of his action upon this subject, "We are a good deal like whalers who have been long on a chase. At last we have got our harpoon fairly into the monster; but we must now look how we steer, or with one *flop* of his tail, he will yet send us all into eternity!"

XXIV.

Mr. George Thompson, the English anti-slavery orator, delivered an address in the House of Representatives, to a large audience, April 6th, 1864. Among the distinguished persons present was President Lincoln, who was greatly interested. The following morning, Mr. Thompson and party, consisting of Rev. John Pierpont, Oliver Johnson, formerly President of the Anti-Slavery Society of New York, and the Hon. Lewis Clephane, of Washington, called at the White House. The President was alone when their names were announced, with the exception of myself. Dropping all business, he ordered the party to be immediately admitted. Greeting them very cordially, the gentlemen took seats, and Mr. Thompson commenced conversation by referring to the condition of public sentiment in England in regard to the great conflict the nation was passing through. He said the aristocracy and the "money interest" were desirous of seeing the Union broken up, but that the great heart of the masses beat in sympathy with the North. They instinctively felt that the cause of liberty was bound up with our success in putting down the Rebellion, and the struggle was being watched with the deepest anxiety.

Mr. Lincoln thereupon said: "Mr. Thompson, the people of Great Britain, and of other foreign governments, were in one great error in reference to this conflict. They seemed to think that, the moment I was President, I had the power to abolish slavery, forgetting that, before I could have any power whatever, I had to take the oath to support the Constitution of the United States, and execute the laws as I found them. When the Rebellion broke out, my duty did not admit of a question. That was, first, by all strictly lawful means to endeavor to maintain the integrity of the government. I did not consider that I had a *right* to touch the 'State' institution of 'Slavery' until all other measures for restoring the Union had failed. The paramount idea of the constitution is the preservation of the Union. It may not be specified in so many words, but that this was the idea of its founders is evident; for, without the Union, the constitution would be worthless. It seems clear, then, that in the last extremity, if any local institution threatened the existence of the Union, the Executive could not hesitate as to his duty. In our case, the moment came when I felt that slavery must die that the nation might live! I have sometimes used the illustration in this connection of a man with a diseased limb, and his surgeon. So long as there is a chance of the patient's restoration, the surgeon is solemnly bound to try to save both life *and* limb; but when the crisis comes, and the limb must be sacrificed as the only chance of saving the life, no honest man will hesitate.

"Many of my strongest supporters urged *Emancipation* before I thought it indispensable, and, I may say, before I thought the country ready for it. It was my conviction that, had the proclamation been issued even six months earlier than it was, public sentiment would not have sustained it. Just so, as to the subsequent action in reference to enlisting blacks in the Border States. The step, taken sooner, could not, in my judgment, have been carried out. A man watches his pear-tree day after day, impatient for the ripening of the fruit. Let him attempt to *force* the process, and he may spoil both fruit and tree. But let him patiently *wait*, and the ripe pear at length falls into his lap! We have seen this great revolution in public sentiment slowly but *surely* progressing, so that, when final action came, the opposition was not strong enough to defeat the purpose. I can now solemnly assert," he concluded, "that I have a clear conscience in regard to my action on this momentous question. I have done what no man could have helped doing, standing in my place."

Oliver Johnson, speaking, as he said, for the old Anti-Slavery party, assured the President that they had fully appreciated the difficulties and embarrassments of his position; but when they realized the importance of the grand issue, and observed the conflicting influences that were surging around him, they were in an agony of anxiety lest he should somehow be led to take a false position. If, in the months preceding the issue of the Emancipation Proclamation, they had seemed impatient and distrustful, it was because their knowledge of his character had not been sufficient to assure them that he would be able to stand up manfully against the opposing current. He thanked God that the result had shown that we had a President who was equal to the emergency; and for *his* part he was willing to sink all minor issues in the grand consummation he believed then in sight!

A characteristic incident occurred toward the close of the interview. When the President ceased speaking, the Rev. Mr. Pierpont, impressed with his earnestness, turned to Mr. Thompson, and repeated a Latin quotation from the classics. Mr. Lincoln, leaning forward in his chair, looked from one to the other inquiringly, and then remarked, with a smile, "*Which*, I suppose you are both aware, *I* do not understand."

As the party rose to take leave, the President remarked, motioning toward me, "We have a young man here who is painting a picture down-stairs, which I should be glad to have you see." The gentlemen expressed their acknowledgements of the courtesy, and Mr. Lincoln led the way by the private stair-case to the state dining-room. In the passage through the hall he jocularly remarked to Mr. Thompson, "Your folks made rather sad work of this mansion when they came up the Po-tomac in 1812 [*sic*]. Nothing was left of it but the bare walls." I do not remember the reply to this sally, save that it was given and received in good part. Briefly going over the portraiture and composition of the picture, then in too early a stage for criticism, Mr. Lincoln presently excused himself, and returned to his duties. And thus ended an interview doubtless indelibly stamped upon the memory of each individual privileged in sharing it.

Upon referring to the date of the "Hodges" letter, it will be seen that it was written April 4th, only three days before the visit of Mr. Thompson and party. The coincidence of thought and expression in that statement, and the President's conversa-tion on this occasion, are noticeable; and are explained by the fact, that, with the language of that letter still fresh in his mind, he very naturally fell into a similar vein of illustration.

XXV.

Dr. Holland, in his "Life of Abraham Lincoln," I regret to observe, has thought it worth while to notice the reports, which in one way and another have obtained circulation, that the Pres-ident habitually indulged, in ordinary conversation, in a class of objectionable stories. The biographer, it is true, attempts to palliate this, on the ground that it was no innate love of impurity which prompted such relations, but a keen relish for wit, in any form, the lack of refining influences in early life, and his experience as a lawyer, which necessarily induced professional familiarity with the foulest phases of human nature. The fault is a common one with many men of otherwise unblemished reputation, and cannot be too severely reprehended. The sooner, however, such things can be forgotten, of neighbor, friend, or President, the better. Weaknesses and blemishes are inseparable from common humanity in the present stage of its development; and though, like the spots on the sun, they may serve to inspire in us a feeling of kindred,—let the orb once set, never again to rise on the world, and he who should remember the trifling defects in the universal loss would certainly be considered, if not captious, at least a most inopportune critic.

Mr. Lincoln, I am convinced, has been greatly wronged in this respect. Every foul-mouthed man in the country gave currency to the slime and filth of his own imagination by attributing it to the President. It is but simple justice to his memory that I should state, that during the entire period of my stay in Washington, after witnessing his intercourse with nearly all classes of men, embracing governors, stressors, members of Congress, officers of the army, and intimate friends, I cannot recollect to have heard him relate a circumstance to any one of them, which would have been out of place uttered in a ladies' drawing-room. And this testimony is not unsupported by that of others, well entitled to consideration. Dr. Stone, his family physician, came in one day to see my studies. Sitting in front of that of the President,—with whom he did not sympathize politically,—he remarked, with much feeling, "It is the province of a physician to probe deeply the interior lives of men; and I affirm that Mr. Lincoln is the purest hearted man with whom I ever came in contact." Secretary Seward, who of the Cabinet officers was probably most intimate with the President, expressed the same sentiment in still stronger language. He once said to the Rev. Dr. Bellows: "Mr. Lincoln is the best man I ever knew!"

XXVI.

The 25th of April, Burnside's command marched through Washington, on the way from Annapolis, to reinforce the army of the Potomac. The President reviewed the troops from the top of the eastern portico at Willard's Hotel, standing with uncovered head while the entire thirty thousand men filed through Fourteenth Street. Of course the passage of so large a body of troops through the city—presaging as it did the opening of the campaign—drew out a numerous concourse of spectators, and the coming movement was everywhere the absorbing topic of conversation. Early in the evening, Governor Curtin, of Pennsylvania, with a friend, came into the President's office. As he sat down he referred to the fine appearance of Burnsides's men; saying, with much emphasis, "Mr. President, if there is in the world one man more than another worthy of profound respect, it is the volunteer citizen soldier." To this Mr. Lincoln assented, in a quiet way,—the peculiar dreaminess of expression so remarkable at times, stealing over his face as his mind reverted to the thousands whose lives had been so freely offered upon the altar of their country, and the myriad homes represented by the thronging columns of the day's review, in so many of which there was henceforth to be weary watching and waiting for footsteps which would return no more.

I took this opportunity to get at the truth concerning a newspaper story which went the rounds a year or two previous, purporting to be an account of a meeting of the loyal Governors in Washington, early in the war. It was stated that the President laid the condition of the country before such a council, convened at the White House, and anxiously awaited the result. An oppressive silence followed. Curtin was represented as having been standing, looking out of one of the windows, drumming unconsciously upon a pane of glass. Mr. Lincoln, at length addressing him personally, said: "Andy, what is Pennsylvania going to do?" Turning around, Curtin replied: "She is going to send twenty thousand men to start with, and will double it, if necessary!" "This noble response" [quoted from memory] "overwhelmed the President, and lifted the dead weight which seemed to have paralyzed all present."

I repeated this account substantially as here given; but both parties smiled and shook their heads. "It is a pity to spoil so good a story," returned the President, "but, unfortunately, there is not a word of truth in it. I believe the only convocation of Governors that has taken place during the war," he added, looking at Curtin, "was that at Altoona—was it not?"

Subsequently the two gentlemen proposed to visit my room, and Mr. Lincoln accompanied them. Sitting down under the chandelier on the edge of the long table, which ran the whole length of the apartment, swinging back and forth his long legs, passing his hand occasionally over his brow and through his rough hair (his appearance and manner come back to me most vividly, as I write), he listened abstractedly to my brief explanation of the design of the picture. When I ceased, he took up the record in his own way. "You see, Curtin," said he, "I was brought to the conclusion that there was no dodging this negro question any longer. We had reached the point where it seemed that we must avail ourselves of this element, or in all probability go under." He then went over the circumstances attending the step, in much the same language he had used upon the occasion of my first interview with him. Governor Curtin remarked that the impression prevailed in some quarters that Secretary Seward opposed the policy. "That is not true," replied

Mr. Lincoln; "he advised postponement, at the first meeting, which seemed to me sound. It was Seward's persistence which resulted in the insertion of the word 'maintain,' which I feared under the circumstances was promising more than it was quite probable we could carry out."

The bill empowering the Secretary of the Treasury to sell the surplus gold had recently passed, and Mr. Chase was then in New York, giving his attention personally to the experiment. Governor Curtin referred to this, saying, "I see by the quotations that Chase's movement has already knocked gold down several per cent." This gave occasion for the strongest expression I ever heard fall from the lips of Mr. Lincoln. Knotting his face in the intensity of his feeling, he said, "Curtin, what do you think of those fellows in Wall Street, who are gambling in gold at such a time as this?" "They are a set of sharks," returned Curtin. "For my part," continued the President, bringing his clinched hand down upon the table, "I wish every one of them had his *devilish* head shot off!"

XXVII.

There was one marked element of Mr. Lincoln's character admirably expressed by the Hon. Mr. Colfax, in his oration at Chicago upon his death: "When his judgment, which acted slowly, but which was almost as immovable as the eternal hills when settled, was grasping some subject of importance, the arguments against his own desires seemed uppermost in his mind, and, in conversing upon it, he would present those arguments to see if they could be rebutted."

In illustration of this, it is only necessary to recall the fact that the interview between himself and the Chicago delegation of clergymen, appointed to urge upon him the issue of a proclamation of emancipation, took place September 13, 1862, more than a month after he had declared to the Cabinet his established purpose to take this step. He said to this committee: "I do not want to issue a document that the whole world will see must necessarily be inoperative, like the Pope's bull against the comet!" After drawing out their views upon the subject, he concluded the interview with these memorable words:—

"Do not misunderstand me, because I have mentioned these objections. They indicate the difficulties which have thus far prevented my action in some such way as you desire. I have not decided against a proclamation of liberty to the slaves, but hold the matter under advisement. And I can assure you that the subject is on my mind, by day and night, more than any other. Whatever shall appear to be God's will, I will do! I trust that, in the freedom with which I have canvassed your views, I have not in any respect injured your feelings."

In further evidence of this peculiarity of his mind, I will state that notwithstanding his apparent hesitation in the appointment of a successor to Judge Taney, it is well known to his most intimate friends, that "there had never been a time during his Presidency, when, in the event of the death of Judge Taney, he had not fully intended and expected to nominate Salmon P. Chase for Chief Justice." These were his very words uttered in connection with this subject.

XXVIII.

In Barrett's biography of Mr. Lincoln, it is stated that the first draft of the Emancipation Proclamation was written on board of the steamboat returning from his 8th of July visit to the army at Harrison's Landing. This circumstance was not included in the statement given me, and to others in my presence, at different times; but from the known relations of the author with the President, it is undoubtedly true. The original draft was written upon one side of four half sheets of official foolscap. He flung down upon the table one day for me, several sheets of the same, saying, "There, I believe, is some of the very paper which was used;—if not, it was, at any rate, just like it." The original draft is dated September 22d, 1862, and was presented to the Army Relief Bazaar, at Albany, N.Y., in 1864. It is in the proper handwriting of Mr. Lincoln, excepting two interlineations in pencil, by Secretary Seward, and the formal heading and ending, which were written by the chief clerk of the State Department.

The final Proclamation was signed on New-Year's Day, 1863. The President remarked to Mr. Colfax, the same evening, that the signature appeared somewhat tremulous and uneven. "Not," said he, "because of any uncertainty or hesitation on my part; but it was just after the public reception, and three hours' hand-shaking is not calculated to improve a man's chirography." Then changing his tone, he added: "The South had fair warning, that if they did not return to their duty, I should strike at this pillar of their strength. The promise must now be kept, and I shall never recall one word."

I remember to have asked him, on one occasion, if there was not some opposition manifested on the part of several members of the Cabinet to this policy. He replied, "Nothing more than I have stated to you. Mr. Blair thought we should lose the fall elections, and opposed it on that ground only." "I have understood," said I, "that Secretary Smith was not in favor of your action. Mr. Blair told me that, when the meeting closed, he and the Secretary of the Interior went away together, and that the latter said to him, if the President carried out the policy, he might count on losing *Indiana*, sure!" "He never said anything of the kind to me," returned the President. "And what is Mr. Blair's opinion now?" I asked. "Oh," was the prompt reply, "he proved right in regard to the fall elections, but he is satisfied that we have since gained more than we lost." "I have been told," I added, "that Judge Bates doubted the constitutionality of the proclamation." "He never expressed such an opinion in my hearing," replied Mr. Lincoln. "No member of the Cabinet ever dissented from the policy, in any conversation with me."

XXIX.

It seems necessary at this point that an explanation should be given of a leading article which appeared in the New York "Independent," upon the withdrawal of Mr. Chase from the political canvass of 1864, widely copied by the country press, in which it was stated that the concluding paragraph of the proclamation was from the pen of Secretary Chase. One of Mr. Lincoln's intimate friends, who felt that there was an impropriety in this publication, at that time, for which Mr. Chase was in some degree responsible, went to see the President about it. "Oh," said Mr. Lincoln, with his characteristic simplicity and freedom from all suspicion, "Mr. Chase had nothing to do with it; I think *I* mentioned the circumstance to Mr. Tilton, myself."

The facts in the case are these: While the measure was pending, Mr. Chase submitted to the President a draft of a proclamation embodying his views upon the subject, which closed with the appropriate and solemn words referred to: "And upon this act, sincerely believed to be an act of justice warranted by the Constitution, I invoke the considerate judgment of mankind and the gracious favor of Almighty God!"

Mr. Lincoln adopted this sentence intact, excepting that he inserted after the word "Constitution" the words "upon military necessity."

XXX.

Mr. Chase told me that at the Cabinet meeting, immediately after the battle of Antietam, and just prior to the issue of the September Proclamation, the President entered upon the business before them, by saying that "the time for the annunciation of the emancipation policy could be no longer delayed. Public sentiment," he thought, "would sustain it—many of his warmest friends and supporters demanded it—*and he had promised his God that he would do it!*" The last part of this was uttered in a low tone, and appeared to be heard by no one but Secretary Chase, who was sitting near him. He asked the President if he correctly understood him. Mr. Lincoln replied: "*I made a solemn vow before God, that if General Lee was driven back from Pennsylvania, I would crown the result by the declaration of freedom to the slaves.*"

In February 1865, a few days after the passage of the "Constitutional Amendment," I went to Washington, and was received by Mr. Lincoln with the kindness and familiarity which had characterized our previous intercourse. I said to him at this time that I was very proud to have been the artist to have first conceived of the design of painting a picture commemorative of the Act of Emancipation; that subsequent occurrences had only confirmed my own first judgment of that act as the most sublime moral event in our history. "Yes," said he,—and never do I remember to have noticed in him more earnestness of expression or manner,—"as affairs have turned, *it is the central act of my administration, and the great event of the nineteenth century.*"

XXXI.

The day after the review of Burnside's division, some photographers from Brady's Gallery came up to the White House to make some stereoscopic studies for me of the President's office. They requested a dark closet, in which to develop the pictures; and without a thought that I was infringing upon anybody's rights, I took them to an unoccupied room of which little "Tad" had taken possession a few days before, and with the aid of a couple of the servants, had fitted up as a miniature theatre, with stage, curtains, orchestra, stalls, parquette, and all. Knowing that the use required would interfere with none of his arrangements, I led the way to this apartment.

Everything went on well, and one or two pictures had been taken, when suddenly there was an uproar. The operator came back to the office, and said that "Tad" had taken great offence at the occupation of his room without his consent, and had locked the door, refusing all admission. The chemicals had been taken inside, and there was no way of getting at them, he having carried off the key. In the midst of this conversation, "Tad" burst in, in a fearful passion. He laid all the blame upon me,—said that I had no right to use his room, and that the men should not go in even to get their things. He had locked the door, and they should not go there again—"they had no business in his room!" Mr. Lincoln had been sitting for a photograph, and was still in the chair. He said, very mildly, "Tad, go and unlock the door." Tad went off muttering into his mother's room, refusing to obey. I followed him into the passage, but no coaxing would pacify him. Upon my return to the President, I found him still sitting patiently in the chair, from which he had not risen. He said: "Has not the boy opened that door?" I replied that we could do nothing with him,—he had gone off in a great pet. Mr. Lincoln's lips came together firmly, and then, suddenly rising, he strode across the passage with the air of one bent on punishment, and disappeared in the domestic apartments. Directly he returned with the key to the theatre, which he unlocked himself. "There," said he, "go ahead, it is all right now." He then went back to his office, followed by myself, and resumed his seat. "Tad," said he, half apologetically, "is a peculiar child. He was violently excited when I went to him. I said, 'Tad, do you know you are making your father a great deal of trouble?' He burst into tears, instantly giving me up the key."

This brief glimpse of the home life of the President, though trifling in itself, is the gauge of his entire domestic character. The Hon. W. D. Kelly, of Philadelphia, in an address delivered in that city soon after the assasination, said: "His intercourse with his family was beautiful as that with his friends. I think that father never loved his children more fondly than he. The President never seemed grander in my sight than when, stealing upon him in the evening, I would find him with a book open before him, as he is represented in the popular photograph, with little Tad beside him. There were of course a great many curious books sent to him, and it seemed to be one of the special delights of his life to open those books at such an hour, that his boy could stand beside him, and they could talk as he turned over the pages, the father thus giving to the son a portion of that care and attention of which he was ordinarily deprived by the duties of office pressing upon him."

No matter who was with the President, or how intently he might be absorbed, little Tad was always welcome. At the time of which I write he was eleven years old, and of course rapidly passing from childhood into youth. Suffering much from an infirmity of speech which developed in his infancy, he seemed on this account especially dear to his father. "One touch of nature makes the whole world kin," and it was an impressive and affecting sight to me to see the burdened President lost for the time being in the affectionate parent, as he would take the little fellow in his arms upon the withdrawal of visitors, and caress him with all the fondness of a mother for the babe upon her bosom!

Tad, as he was universally called, almost always accompanied his father upon the various excursions down the Potomac, which he was in the habit of making. Once, on the way to Fortress Monroe, he became very troublesome. The President was much engaged in conversation with the party who accompanied him, and he at length said, "Tad, if you will be a good boy, and not disturb me any more till we get to Fortress Monroe, I will give you a dollar." The hope of reward was effectual for a while in securing silence, but, boy-like, Tad soon forgot his promise, and was as noisy as ever. Upon reaching their destination, however, he said very promptly, "Father, I want my dollar." Mr. Lincoln turned to him with the inquiry: "Tad, do you think you have earned it?" "Yes," was the sturdy reply. Mr. Lincoln looked at him half reproachfully for an instant, and then taking from his pocket-book a dollar note, he said: "Well, my son, at any rate, I will keep *my* part of the bargain."

While paying a visit to Commodore Porter at Fortress Monroe, on one occasion, an incident occurred, subsequently related by Lieutenant Braine, one of the officers on board the flag-ship, to the Rev. Mr. Ewer, of New York. Noticing that the banks of the river were dotted with spring blossoms, the President said, with the manner of one asking a special favor: "Commodore,

Tad is very fond of flowers;—won't you let a couple of your men take a boat and go with him for an hour or two along shore, and gather a few?—it will be a great gratification to him."

There is a lesson in such simple incidents,—abounding as they did in the life of the late President,—which should not be lost upon the young men of this country. The Commander-in-Chief of the Army and Navy of the United States,—with almost unlimited power in his hands,—the meekness and simplicity with which Mr. Lincoln bore the honors of that high position, is a spectacle for all time. How paltry do conceit and vainglory appear in the majesty of such an example.

"Nothing was more marked in Mr. Lincoln's personal demeanor," writes one who knew him well,* "than his utter unconsciousness of his position. It would be difficult, if not impossible, to find another man who would not, upon a sudden transfer from the obscurity of private life in a country town to the dignities and duties of the Presidency, feel it incumbent upon him to assume something of the manner and tone befitting that position. Mr. Lincoln never seemed to be aware that his place or his business were essentially different from those in which he had always been engaged. He brought to every question—the loftiest and most imposing—the same patient inquiry into details, the same eager longing to know and to do exactly

---

*Hon. Henry J. Raymond.

what was just and right, and the same working-day, plodding, laborious devotion, which characterized his management of a client's case at his law office in Springfield. He had duties to perform in both places—in the one case to his country, as to his client in the other. But all duties were alike to him. All called equally upon him for the best service of his mind and heart, and all were alike performed with a conscientious, single-hearted devotion that knew no distinction, but was absolute and perfect in every case."

XXXII.

In the Executive Chamber one evening, there were present a number of gentlemen, among them Mr. Seward.

A point in the conversation suggesting the thought, the President said: "Seward, you never heard, did you, how I earned my first dollar?" "No," rejoined Mr. Seward. "Well," continued Mr. Lincoln, "I was about eighteen years of age. I belonged, you know, to what they call down South, the 'scrubs;' people who do not own slaves are nobody there. But we had succeeded in raising, chiefly by my labor, sufficient produce, as I thought, to justify me in taking it down the river to sell.

"After much persuasion, I got the consent of mother to go, and constructed a little flatboat, large enough to take a barrel or two of things that we had gathered, with myself and little bundle, down to New Orleans. A steamer was coming down the river. We have, you know, no wharves on the Western streams; and the custom was, if passengers were at any of the landings, for them to go out in a boat, the steamer stopping and taking them on board.

"I was contemplating my new flatboat, and wondering whether I could make it stronger or improve it in any particular, when two men came down to the shore in carriages with trunks, and looking at the different boats singled out mine, and asked, 'Who owns this?' I answered, somewhat modestly, 'I do.' 'Will you,' said one of them, 'take us and our trunks out to the steamer?' 'Certainly,' said I. I was very glad to have the chance of earning something. I supposed that each of them would give me two or three bits. The trunks were put on my flatboat, the passengers seated themselves on the trunks, and I sculled them out to the steamboat.

"They got on board, and I lifted up their heavy trunks, and put them on deck. The steamer was about to put on steam again, when I called out that they had forgotten to pay me. Each of them took from his pocket a silver half-dollar, and threw it on the floor of my boat. I could scarcely believe my eyes as I picked up the money. Gentlemen, you may think it was a very little thing, and in these days it seems to me a trifle; but it was a most important incident in my life I could scarcely credit that I, a poor boy, had earned a dollar in less than a day,—that by honest work I had earned a dollar. The world seemed wider and fairer before me. I was a more hopeful and confident being from that time."

XXXIII.

The Hon. Robert Dale Owen was associated in a very interesting interview with Mr. Lincoln, which took place a few weeks prior to the issue of the President's Message for 1863, to which was appended the Proclamation of Amnesty. It had been understood in certain quarters that such a step was at this period in contemplation by the Executive. Being in Washington, Mr. Owen called upon the President on a Saturday morning, and said that he had a matter upon which he had expended considerable thought, which he wished to lay before him. Knowing nothing of the object, Mr. Lincoln replied: "You see how it is this morning; there are many visitors waiting; can't you come up to-morrow morning? I shall be alone then; and, if you have no scruples upon the subject, I can give you as much time as you wish." Mr. Owen assured him of his readiness to come at any hour most convenient, and ten o'clock was named. Punctual to the appointment, the hour found him at the house. A repeated summons at the bell brought no response, and he at length pushed open the door and walked leisurely up the stairs to the reception-room. Neither servant or secretary was to be seen. Presently Mr. Lincoln passed through the hall to his office, and all was still again. Looking vainly for a servant to announce his name, Mr. Owen finally went to the office-door, and knocked.

"Really," said he, "Mr. President, I owe you an apology for coming in upon you in this unceremonious way; but I have for some time been waiting the appearance of a servant."

"Oh," was the good-natured reply, "the boys are all out this morning. I have been expecting you; come in and sit down."

Proceeding directly to the subject he had in hand, at the same time unfolding a manuscript of large proportions, Mr. Owen said:

"I have a paper, here, Mr. President, that I have prepared with some care, which I wish to read to you."

Mr. Lincoln glanced at the formidable document, (really much less voluminous than it appeared, being very coarsely written,) and then, half unconsciously relapsing into an attitude and expression of resignation to what he evidently considered an infliction which could not well be avoided, signified his readiness to listen. The article was a very carefully prepared digest of historical precedents in relation to the subject of amnesty, in connection with treason and rebellion. It analyzed English and continental history, and reviewed elaborately the action of President Washington in reference to Shay's and the subsequent whiskey rebellion.

"I had read but two or three pages," said Mr. Owen, in giving me this account, "when Mr. Lincoln assumed an erect posture, and, fixing his eyes intently upon me, seemed wholly absorbed in the contents of the manuscript. Frequently he would break in with: 'Was that so?' 'Please read that paragraph again,' etc. When at length I came to Washington's proclamation to those engaged in the whiskey rebellion, he interrupted me with: 'What! did Washington issue a proclamation of amnesty?' 'Here it is, sir,' was the reply. 'Well, I never knew that,' he rejoined; and so on through."

Upon the conclusion of the manuscript, Mr. Lincoln said: "Mr. Owen, is that for me?"

"Certainly, sir," said Mr. O., handing him the roll. " I understood that you were considering this subject, and thought a review of this kind might be interesting to you."

"There is a good deal of hard work in that document," continued Mr. Lincoln; "may I ask how long you were preparing it?"

"About three months; but then I have more leisure for such a work than you, Mr. President."

Mr. Lincoln took the manuscript, and, folding it up carefully, arose, and laid it away in the pigeon-hole marked "O," in his desk. Returning to his chair, he said: "Mr. Owen, it is due to you that I should say that you have conferred a very essential service, both upon me and the country, by the preparation of this paper. It contains that which it was exceedingly important that I should know, but which, if left to myself, I never should have known, because I have not the time necessary for such an examination of authorities as a review of this kind involves. And I want to say, secondly, if I had *had* the time, I could not have done the work so well as you have done it."

This frank and generous avowal—so unlike what might be expected, under similar circumstances, from most public men— was exceedingly characteristic of Mr. Lincoln.

XXXIV.

The morning of the last day of April, Mr. Wilkeson, the head of the New York "Tribune" bureau of correspondence in Washington at that period, called upon me with his sister-in-law, Mrs. Elizabeth Cady Stanton, well known for her radical views on political and social questions, who wished an introduction to the President. Later in the day, after the accustomed pressure of visitors had subsided, I knocked at the door of the President's study, and asked if I might bring up two or three New York friends. Mr. Lincoln fortunately was alone, and at once accorded the desired permission. Laying aside his papers, as we entered, he turned around in his chair for a leisurely conversation. One of the party took occasion shortly to endorse very decidedly the Amnesty Proclamation, which had been severely censured by many friends of the Administration. This approval appeared to touch Mr. Lincoln deeply. He said, with a great deal of emphasis, and with an expression of countenance I shall never forget, "When a man is sincerely *penitent* for his misdeeds, and gives satisfactory evidence of the same, he can safely be pardoned, and there is no exception to the rule."

Soon afterward he mentioned having received a visit the night before from Colonel Moody, "the fighting Methodist parson," as he was called in Tennessee, who had come on to attend the Philadelphia Conference. "He told me," said he, "this story of Andy Johnson and General Buel, which interested me intensely. The Colonel happened to be in Nashville the day it was reported that Buel had decided to evacuate the city. The Rebels, strongly reënforced, were said to be within two days' march of the capital. Of course, the city was greatly excited. Moody said he went in search of Johnson, at the edge of the evening, and found him at his office, closeted with two gentlemen, who were walking the floor with him, one on each side. As he entered, they retired, leaving him alone with Johnson, who came up to him, manifesting intense feeling, and said, 'Moody, we are sold out! Buel is a traitor! He is going to evacuate the city, and in forty-eight hours we shall all be in the hands of the Rebels!' Then he commenced pacing the floor again, twisting his hands, and chafing like a caged tiger, utterly insensible to his friend's entreaties to become calm. Suddenly he turned and said, 'Moody, can you pray?' 'That is my business, sir, as a minister of the Gospel,' returned the Colonel. 'Well, Moody, I wish you would pray,' said Johnson; and instantly both went down upon their knees, at opposite sides of the room. As the prayer waxed fervent, Johnson began to respond in true Methodist style. Presently he crawled over on his hands and knees to Moody's side, and put his arm over him, manifesting the deepest emotion. Closing the prayer with a hearty 'Amen' from each, they arose. Johnson took a long breath, and said, with emphasis, 'Moody, I feel better!' Shortly afterwards he asked, 'Will you stand by me?' 'Certainly I will,' was the answer. 'Well, Moody, I can depend upon you; you are one in a hundred thousand!' He then commenced pacing the floor again. Suddenly he wheeled, the current of his thought having changed, and said, 'Oh! Moody, I don't want you to think I have become a religious man because I asked you to pray. I am sorry to say it, but I am not, and have never pretended to be, religious. No one knows this better than you; but, Moody, there is one thing about it—I DO believe in ALMIGHTY GOD! And I believe also in the BIBLE, and I say "d——n" me, if Nashville shall be surrendered!'"

And Nashville was not surrendered.

XXXV.

I have elsewhere intimated that Mr. Lincoln was capable of much dramatic power. It is true this was never exhibited in his

public life, or addresses, but it was shown in his keen appreciation of Shakspeare, and unrivalled faculty of story-telling. The
incident just related, for example, was given with a thrilling effect which mentally placed Johnson, for the time being, along-
side of Luther and Cromwell. Profanity or irreverence was lost
sight of in the fervid utterance of a highly wrought and great-
souled determination, united with a rare exhibition of pathos
and self-abnegation.

A narrative of quite a different character followed closely
upon this, suggested by a remark made by myself. It was an account of how the President and Secretary of War received the
news of the capture of Norfolk, early in the war. "Chase and
Stanton," said Mr. Lincoln, "had accompanied me to Fortress
Monroe. While we were there, an expedition was fitted out for
an attack on Norfolk. Chase and General Wool disappeared
about the time we began to look for tidings of the result, and
after vainly waiting their return till late in the evening, Stanton
and I concluded to retire. My room was on the second floor of
the Commandant's house, and Stanton's was below. The night
was very warm,—the moon shining brightly,—and, too restless
to sleep, I threw off my clothes and sat for some time by the
table, reading. Suddenly hearing footsteps, I looked out of the
window, and saw two persons approaching, whom I knew by
their relative size to be the missing men. They came into the
passage and I heard them rap at Stanton's door and tell him to

get up, and come up-stairs. A moment afterward they entered my room. 'No time for ceremony, Mr. President,' said General Wool; 'Norfolk is ours!' Stanton here burst in, just out of bed, clad in a long nightgown, which nearly swept the floor, his ear catching, as he crossed the threshold, Wool's last words. Perfectly overjoyed, he rushed at the General, whom he hugged most affectionately, fairly lifting him from the floor in his delight. The scene altogether must have been a comical one, though at the time we were all too greatly excited to take much note of mere appearances."

XXXVI.

A great deal has been said of the uniform meekness and kindness of heart of Mr. Lincoln, but there would sometimes be afforded evidence that one grain of sand too much would break even *this* camel's back. Among the callers at the White House one day, was an officer who had been cashiered from the service. He had prepared an elaborate defence of himself, which he consumed much time in reading to the President. When he had finished, Mr. Lincoln replied, that even upon his own statement of the case, the facts would not warrant executive interference. Disappointed, and considerably crestfallen, the man withdrew. A few days afterward he made a second attempt to alter the President's convictions, going over substantially the same ground, and occupying about the same space of time, but without accomplishing his end. The *third* time he succeeded in forcing himself into Mr. Lincoln's presence, who with great forbearance listened to another repetition of the case to its conclusion, but made no reply. Waiting for a moment, the man gathered from the expression of his countenance that his mind was unconvinced. Turning very abruptly, he said: "Well, Mr. President, I see you are fully determined not to do me justice!" This was too aggravating, even for Mr. Lincoln. Manifesting, however, no more feeling than that indicated by a slight compression of the lips, he very quietly arose, laid down a package of papers he held in his hand, and then suddenly seizing the defunct officer by the coat-collar, he marched him forcibly to the door, saying, as he ejected him into the passage: "Sir, I give you fair warning never to show yourself in this room again. I can bear censure, but not insult!" In a whining tone the man begged for his papers, which he had dropped. "Begone, sir," said the President, "your papers will be sent to you. I never wish to see your face again!"

Upon another occasion, as I was going through the passage, the door of the President's office suddenly opened, and two ladies, one of whom seemed in a towering passion, were unceremoniously ushered out by one of the attendants. As they passed me on their way down the stairs, I overheard the elder remonstrating with her companion upon the violence of her expressions. I afterward asked old Daniel what had happened?

"Oh," he replied, "the younger woman was very saucy to the President. She went one step too far; and he told me to show them out of the house?"

Of a similar character is an incident given by "N. C. J.," in a letter to the New York "Times":—

"Among the various applicants, a well-dressed lady came forward, without apparent embarrassment in her air or manner, and addressed the President. Giving her a very close and scrutinizing look, he said, 'Well, madam, what can I do for you?' She proceeded to tell him that she lived in Alexandria; that the church where she worshipped had been taken for a hospital. 'What church, madam?' Mr. Lincoln asked, in a quick, nervous manner. 'The—church,' she replied; 'and as there are only two or three wounded soldiers in it, I came to see if you would not let us have it, as we want it very much to worship God in.' 'Madam, have you been to see the Post Surgeon at Alexandria about this matter?' 'Yes, sir; but we could do nothing with him.' 'Well, we put him there to attend to just such business, and it is reasonable to suppose that he knows better what should be done under the circumstances than I do. See here: you say you live in Alexandria; probably you own property there. How much will you give to assist in building a hospital?'

"'You know, Mr. Lincoln, our property is very much embarrassed by the war;—so, really, I could hardly afford to give much for such a purpose.'

"'Well, madam, I expect we shall have another fight soon; and my candid opinion is, God wants that church for poor wounded Union Soldiers, as much as he does for secesh people to worship in.' Turning to his table, he said, quite abruptly, 'You will excuse me; I can do nothing for you. Good day, madam.'

"I had noticed two other women who stood just back of me. I was fully convinced that I had rightly guessed their errand from their appearance; for one of them, whose wicked eyes shot fire, said to her companion in a spiteful under-tone, 'Oh! the old brute,—there is no use asking for our passes; come, let's go.' And they did go, in evident wrath; leaving the President to perform more pleasant duties."

The same correspondent witnessed also the following scene—

"A couple of aged, plain country people, poorly clad, but with frank open countenances, now came forward. 'Now is your time, dear,' said the husband, as the President dismissed the one preceding them. The lady stepped forward, made a low courtesy, and said, 'Mr. President.'

"Mr. Lincoln, looking over his spectacles, fixed those gray, piercing, yet mild eyes upon her, then lifting his head and extending his hand, he said, in the kindest tones: 'Well, good lady, what can I do for you?'

"'Mr. President,' she resumed, 'I feel so embarrassed I can hardly speak. I never spoke to a President before; but I am a good Union woman down in Maryland, and my son is wounded badly, and in the hospital, and I have been trying to get him out, but somehow couldn't, and they said I had better come right to you. When the war first broke out I gave my son first to God, and then told him he might go fight the Rebels; and now if you will let me take him home I will nurse him up, and just as soon as he gets well enough he shall go right back and help put down the rebellion. He is a good boy, and don't want to shirk the service.'

"I was looking full in Mr. Lincoln's face. I saw the tears gathering in his eyes, and his lips quivered as he replied:

"'Yes, yes, God bless you! you shall have your son. What hospital did you say?' It seemed a relief to him to turn aside and write a few words, which he handed to the woman, saying; 'There, give that to—; and you will get your son, if he is able to go home with you.'

"'God bless you, Mr. President!' said the father, the only words he had uttered; and the mother, making a low courtesy, fairly sobbed: 'O sir, we are so much obliged to you.' 'Yes, yes; all right; and you will find that *that* will bring him,' was spoken in tones so kindly and tender, that they have often since thrilled my memory."

XXXVII.

In the year 1855 or '56, George B. Lincoln, Esq., of Brooklyn, was travelling through the West in connection with a large New York dry-goods establishment. He found himself one night in an insignificant town on the Illinois River, by the name of Naples. The only tavern of the place had evidently been constructed with reference to business on the smallest possible scale. Poor as the prospect seemed, Mr. Lincoln had no alternative but to put up at the place. The supper-room was also used as a lodging-room. After a tolerable supper and a comfortable hour before the fire, Mr. L. told his host that he thought he would "go to bed." "Bed!" echoed the landlord; "there is no bed for you in this house, unless you sleep with that man yonder. He has the only one we have to spare." "Well," returned Mr. Lincoln, "the gentleman has possession, and perhaps would not like a bedfellow." Upon this, a grizzly head appeared out of the pillows, and said, "What is your name?" "They call me Lincoln at home," was the reply. "Lincoln!" repeated the stranger; "any connection of our Illinois Abraham?" "No," replied Mr. L., "I fear not." "Well," said the old man, "I will let any man by the name of 'Lincoln' sleep with me, just for the sake of the name. You have heard of Abe?" he inquired. "Oh yes, very often," replied Mr. Lincoln. "No man could travel far in this State without hearing of *him*, and I would be very glad to claim connection, if I could do so honestly." "Well," said the old gentleman, "my name is Simmons." 'Abe' and I used to live and work together when we were young men. Many a job of wood-cutting and rail-splitting have I done up with him. Abe Lincoln," said he with emphasis, "was the *likeliest* boy in God's world. He would work all day as hard as any of us—and study by firelight in the log-house half the night; and in this way he made himself a thorough practical surveyor. Once, during those days, I was in the upper part of the State, and I met General Ewing, whom President Jackson had sent to the Northwest to make surveys. I told him about Abe Lincoln, what a student he was, and that I wanted he should give him a job. He looked over his memoranda, and, pulling out a paper, said: 'There is—county must be surveyed; if your friend can do the work properly, I shall be glad to have him undertake it—the compensation will be six hundred dollars!' Pleased as I could be, I hastened to Abe, after I got home, with an account of what I had secured for him. He was sitting before the fire in the log-cabin when I told him; and what do you think was his answer? When I finished, he looked up very quietly, and said, 'Mr. Simmons, I thank you very sincerely for your kindness, but I don't think I will undertake the job.' 'In the name of wonder,' said I, 'why? Six hundred dollars does not grow upon every bush out here in Illinois.' 'I know that,' said Abe, 'and I need the money bad enough, Simmons, as you know; but I never have been under obligation to a Democratic administration, and I never intend to be so long as I can get my living another way. General Ewing must find another man to do his work.'"

I related this story to the President one day, and asked him if it was true. "Pollard Simmons!" said he: "well do I remember him. It is correct about our working together; but the old man must have stretched the facts somewhat about the survey of the county. I think I should have been very glad of the job at that time, no matter what administration was in power." Notwithstanding this, however, I am inclined to believe Mr. Simmons was not far out of the way. His statement seems very characteristic of what Abraham Lincoln may be supposed to have been at twenty-three or twenty-five years of age.

Mr. G. B. Lincoln also told me of an amusing circumstance which took place at Springfield soon after Mr. Lincoln's nomination in 1860. A hatter in Brooklyn secretly obtained the size of the future President's head, and made for him a very elegant hat, which he sent by his townsman, Lincoln, to Springfield. About the time it was presented, various other testimonials of a similar character had come in from different sections. Mr. Lincoln took the hat, and after admiring its texture and workmanship, put it on his head and walked up to a looking-glass. Glancing from the reflection to Mrs. Lincoln, he said, with his peculiar twinkle of the eye, "Well, wife, there is one thing likely to come out of this scrape, any how. We are going to have some *new clothes*!"

One afternoon during the summer of 1862, the President accompanied several gentlemen to the Washington Navy-yard, to witness some experiments with a newly-invented gun. Subsequently the party went aboard of one of the steamers lying at the wharf. A discussion was going on as to the merits of the invention, in the midst of which Mr. Lincoln caught sight of some axes hanging up outside of the cabin. Leaving the group, he quietly went forward, and taking one down, returned with it, and said: "Gentlemen, you may talk about your 'Raphael repeaters' and 'eleven-inch Dahlgrens;' but *here* is an institution which I guess I understand better than either of you." With that he held the axe out at arm's length by the end of the handle, or "helve," as the wood-cutters call it—a feat not another person of the party could perform, though all made the attempt. In such acts as this, showing that he neither forgot nor was ashamed of his humble origin, the late President exhibited his true nobility of character. He was a perfect illustration of his favorite poet's words:—

"The rank is but the guinea's stamp,
  The man's the gold, for a' that!"

XXXVIII.

In March, 1864, Edwin Forrest came to Washington to fulfil an engagement at Ford's Theatre. It was announced one day that he was to appear that evening in "Richelieu." I was with the President, when Senator Harris of New York came in. After he had finished his business, which was to secure the remittance of the sentence of one of his constituents, who had been imprisoned on what seemed insufficient grounds, I told the President that Forrest was to play *Richelieu* that evening, and, knowing his tastes, I said it was a play which I thought he would enjoy, for Forrest's representation of it was the most life-like of anything I had ever seen upon the stage. "Who wrote the play?" said he. "Bulwer," I replied. "Ah!" he rejoined; "well, I knew Bulwer wrote novels, but I did not know he was a play-writer also. It may seem somewhat strange to say," he continued, "but I never read an entire novel in my life!" Said Judge Harris, "Is it possible?" "Yes," returned the President, "it is a fact. I once commenced 'Ivanhoe,' but never finished it." This statement, in this age of the world, seems almost incredible—but I give the circumstance as it occurred.

However it may have been with regard to novels, it is very certain—as I have already illustrated—that he found time to read Shakspeare; and that he was also fond of certain kinds of poetry. N. P. Willis once told me, that he was taken quite by surprise, on a certain occasion when he was riding with the President and Mrs. Lincoln, by Mr. Lincoln, of his own accord, referring to, and quoting several lines from his poem entitled "Parrhasius."

In the spring of 1862, the President spent several days at Fortress Monroe, awaiting military operations upon the Peninsula. As a portion of the Cabinet were with him, that was temporarily the seat of government, and he bore with him constantly the burden of public affairs. His favorite diversion was reading Shakspeare. One day (it chanced to be the day before the capture of Norfolk) as he sat reading alone, he called to his aide* in the adjoining room,—"You have been writing long enough, Colonel; come in here; I want to read you a passage in 'Hamlet.'" He read the discussion on ambition between Hamlet and his courtiers, and the soliloquy, in which conscience debates of a future state. This was followed by passages from "Macbeth." Then opening to "King John," he read from the third act the passage in which Constance bewails her imprisoned, lost boy.

Closing the book, and recalling the words,—

"And, father cardinal, I have heard you say
    That we shall see and know our friends in heaven:
    If that be true, I shall see my boy again,"—

Mr. Lincoln said: "Colonel, did you ever dream of a lost friend, and feel that you were holding sweet communion with that

---

*Colonel Le Grand B. Cannon, of General Wool's staff.

friend, and yet have a sad consciousness that it was not a reality?—just so I dream of my boy Willie." Overcome with
emotion, he dropped his head on the table, and sobbed aloud.

XXXIX.

William Wallace Lincoln, I never knew. He died Thursday, February 20th, 1862, nearly two years before my intercourse with the President commenced. He had just entered
upon his twelfth year, and has been described to me as of an
unusually serious and thoughtful disposition. His death was the
most crushing affliction Mr. Lincoln had ever been called upon
to pass through.

After the funeral, the President resumed his official duties,
but mechanically, and with a terrible weight at his heart. The
following Thursday he gave way to his feelings, and shut himself from all society. The second Thursday it was the same; he
would see no one, and seemed a prey to the deepest melancholy. About this time the Rev. Francis Vinton, of Trinity
Church, New York, had occasion to spend a few days in Washington. An acquaintance of Mrs. Lincoln and of her sister,
Mrs. Edwards, of Springfield, he was requested by them to come
up and see the President. The setting apart of Thursday for
the indulgence of his grief had gone on for several weeks, and
Mrs. Lincoln began to be seriously alarmed for the health of her
husband, of which fact Dr. Vinton was apprised. Mr. Lincoln

received him in the parlor, and an opportunity was soon embraced by the clergyman to chide him for showing so rebellious a disposition to the decrees of Providence. He told him plainly that the indulgence of such feelings, though natural, was sinful. It was unworthy [of] one who believed in the Christian religion. He had duties to the living, greater than those of any other man, as the chosen father, and leader of the people, and he was unfitting himself for his responsibilities by thus giving way to his grief. To mourn the departed as *lost* belonged to heathenism—not to Christianity. "Your son," said Dr. Vinton, "is *alive*, in Paradise. Do you remember that passage in the Gospels: 'God is not the God of the *dead* but of the living, for *all* live unto him'?" The President had listened as one in a stupor, until his ear caught the words, "Your son is alive." Starting from the sofa, he exclaimed, "Alive! *alive!* Surely you mock me." "No, sir, believe me," replied Dr. Vinton; "it is a most comforting doctrine of the church, founded upon the words of Christ himself." Mr. Lincoln looked at him a moment, and then, stepping forward, he threw his arm around the clergyman's neck, and, laying his head upon his breast, sobbed aloud. *"Alive? alive?"* he repeated. "My dear sir," said Dr. Vinton, greatly moved, as he twined his own arm around the weeping father, "believe this, for it is God's most precious truth. Seek not your son among the dead; he is not there; he lives to-day in Paradise! Think of the full import of the words I have quoted.

The Sadducees, when they questioned Jesus, had no other conception than that Abraham, Isaac, and Jacob were dead and buried. Mark the reply: 'Now that the dead *are* raised, even Moses showed at the bush when he called the Lord the God of Abraham, the God of Isaac, and the God of Jacob. For he is not the God of the dead, but of the living, *for all live unto him!*' Did not the aged patriarch mourn his sons as dead?—'Joseph is not, and Simeon is not, and ye will take Benjamin also.' But Joseph and Simeon were both living, though he believed it not. Indeed, Joseph being taken from him, was the eventual means of the preservation of the whole family. And so God has called your son into his upper kingdom—a kingdom and an existence as real, more real, than your own. It may be that he too, like Joseph, has gone, in God's good providence, to be the salvation of *his* father's household. It is a part of the Lord's plan for the ultimate happiness of you and yours. Doubt it not. I have a sermon, " continued Dr. Vinton, "upon this subject, which I think might interest you." Mr. Lincoln begged him to send it at an early day—thanking him repeatedly for his cheering and hopeful words. The sermon was sent, and read over and over by the President, who caused a copy to be made for his own private use before it was returned. Through a member of the family, I have been informed that Mr. Lincoln's views in relation to spiritual things seemed changed from that hour. Certain it is, that thenceforth he ceased the observance of the day of the week upon which his son died, and gradually resumed his accustomed cheerfulness.

XL.

Among my visitors in the early part of May was the Hon. Mr. Alley, of Massachusetts, who gave me a deeply interesting inside glimpse of the Chicago Republican Convention in 1860. The popular current had, at first, set very strongly in favor of Mr. Seward, who, many supposed, would be nominated almost by acclamation. The evening before the balloting the excitement was at the highest pitch. Mr. Lincoln was telegraphed at Springfield, that his chances with the Convention depended upon obtaining the votes of two delegations which were named in the despatch; and that, to secure this support, he must pledge himself, if elected, to give places in his Cabinet to the respective heads of those delegations. A reply was immediately returned over the wires, characteristic of the man. It was to this effect:—

"I authorize no bargains, and will be bound by none.
A. LINCOLN."

It is unqestionable that the country was not prepared for the final action of this Convention. In various sections of the Eastern and Middle States, the antecedents and even the name of Mr. Lincoln were entirely unknown. The newspapers announced the nominee as the "Illinois Rail-splitter;" and however popular this title may have been with the masses, it is not to be denied that it seemed to many people a very extraordinary qualification for the Presidency. An acquaintance of mine, who happened to be in Boston on the evening of the day the Convention adjourned, formed one of a large group at his hotel, eagerly discussing the result. Only one or two of the party knew anything whatever of the first name on the "ticket," and what they knew was soon told. Considerable disappointment could be seen in the faces of those composing the circle. One rough-looking sovereign, from Cape Cod, or Nantucket, had listened attentively, but taken no part in the conversation. Turning away at length, with an expression of deep disgust, he muttered: "A set of consummate fools! Nominate a man for the Presidency who has never smelt salt water!"

Some of Mr. Lincoln's immediate neighbors were taken as completely by surprise as those in distant States. An old resident of Springfield told me that there lived within a block or two of his house, in that city, an Englishman, who of course still cherished to some extent the ideas and prejudices of his native land. Upon hearing of the choice at Chicago he could not contain his astonishment.

"What!" said he, "*Abe Lincoln* nominated for President of the United States? Can it be possible! A man that buys a ten-cent beefsteak for his breakfast, and carries it home himself."

A correspondent of the "Portland Press" has given to the public the following account of Mr. Lincoln's reception of the nomination:—

"In June, 1860, a Massachusetts gentleman was induced to take the opportunity, in company with several delegates and others interested in the objects of the Convention, to go to Chicago and spend a few days in visiting that section of our country. In a very few minutes after the final balloting, when Mr. Lincoln was nominated, it happened that a train of cars started upon the Central Railroad, passing through Springfield, and Mr. R. took passage in the same. Arriving at Springfield, he put up at a public house, and, loitering upon the front door-steps, had the curiosity to inquire of the landlord where Mr. Lincoln lived. While giving the necessary directions, the landlord suddenly remarked, 'There is Mr. Lincoln now, coming down the sidewalk; that tall, crooked man, loosely walking this way. If you wish to see him, you will have an opportunity by putting yourself in his track.'

"In a few moments the object of his curiosity reached the point the gentleman occupied, who, advancing, ventured to accost him thus: 'Is this Mr. Lincoln?' 'That, sir, is my name,' was the courteous reply. 'My name is R., from Plymouth County, Massachusetts,' returned the gentleman, and learning that you have to day been made the public property of the United States, I have ventured to introduce myself, with a view to a brief acquaintance, hoping you will pardon such a patriotic curiosity in a stranger.' Mr. Lincoln received his salutations with cordiality, told him no apology was necessary for his introduction, and asked him to accompany him to his residence. He had just come from the telegraph office, where he had learned the fact of his nomination; and was on his return home, when Mr. R. met and accompanied him thither.

"Arriving at Mr. Lincoln's residence, he was introduced to Mrs. Lincoln and the two boys, and entered into conversation in relation to the Lincoln family of the Old Colony,—the Hingham General Lincoln of the Revolutionary army, and the two Worcester Lincolns, brothers, who were governors of Massachusetts and Maine at one and the same time. In reply to Mr. R.'s inquiry, whether he could trace his ancestry to either of those early families of his own name, Mr. Lincoln, with characteristic facetiousness, replied that he could not say that he ever had an ancestor older than his father; and therefore had it not in his power to trace his genealogy to so patriotic a source as old General Lincoln of the Revolution; though he wished he could. After some further pleasant conversation, chiefly relating to the early history of the Pilgrim Fathers, with which he seemed familiar, Mr. R. desired the privilege of writing a letter to be despatched by the next mail. He was very promptly and kindly provided with the necessary means. As he began to write, Mr. Lincoln approached, and tapping him on the shoulder, expressed the hope that he was not a spy who had come thus early to report his faults to the public. 'By no means, sir,' protested Mr. R.; 'I am writing home to my wife, who, I dare say, will hardly credit the fact that I am writing in your house.' 'O, sir,' rejoined Mr. Lincoln, 'if your wife doubts your word, I will cheerfully indorse it, if you will give me permission;' and taking the pen from Mr. R., he wrote the following words in a clear hand upon the blank page of the letter:—

"'I am happy to say that your husband is at the present time a guest in my house, and in due time I trust you will greet his safe return to the bosom of his family.   A. LINCOLN.'

"This gave Mr. R. an excellent autograph of Mr. Lincoln, besides bearing witness to his hospitable and cheerful spirit.

"Whilst thus engaged in pleasant conversation, the cars arrived that brought from Chicago the committee of the Convention appointed to notify Mr. Lincoln of his nomination. He received them at the door, and conducted them to seats in his parlor. On the reception of this committee, Mr. Lincoln appeared somewhat embarrassed, but soon resumed his wonted tranquillity and cheerfulness. At the proper time, Governor Morgan, of New York, chairman of the committee, arose, and, with becoming dignity, informed Mr. Lincoln that he and his fellows appeared in behalf of the Convention in session at Chicago, to inform him that he had that day been unanimously nominated to the office of President of the United States; and asked his permission to report to that body his acceptance of the nomination. Mr. Lincoln, with becoming modesty, but very handsomely, replied that he felt his insufficiency for the vast responsibilities which must devolve upon that office under the impending circumstances of the times; but if God and his country called for his services in that direction, he should shrink from no duty that might be imposed upon him, and therefore he should not decline the nomination.

"After this ceremony had passed, Mr. Lincoln remarked to the company, that as an appropriate conclusion to an interview so important and interesting as that which had just transpired, he supposed good manners would require that he should treat the committee with something to drink; and opening a door that led into a room in the rear, he called out 'Mary! Mary!' A girl responded to the call, to whom Mr. Lincoln spoke a few words in an under-tone, and, closing the door, returned again to converse with his guests. In a few minutes the maiden entered, bearing a large waiter, containing several glass tumblers, and a large pitcher in the midst, and placed it upon the centre-table. Mr. Lincoln arose, and gravely addressing the company, said: 'Gentlemen, we must pledge our mutual healths in the most healthy beverage which God has given to man—it is the only beverage I have ever used or allowed in my family, and I cannot conscientiously depart from it on the present occasion— it is pure Adam's ale from the spring;' and, taking a tumbler, he touched it to his lips, and pledged them his highest respects in a cup of cold water. Of course, all his guests were constrained to admire his consistency, and to join in his example.

"Mr. R., when he went to Chicago, had but little political sympathy with the Republican Convention which nominated Mr. Lincoln; but when he saw, as he did see for himself, his sturdy adherence to a high moral principle, he returned an admirer of the man, and a zealous advocate of his election."

XLI.

In the July following Mr. Lincoln's inauguration, an extra session of Congress was called. In the message then sent in, speaking of secession, and the measures taken by the Southern leaders to bring it about, there occurs the following sentence: "With rebellion thus *sugar-coated*, they have been drugging the public mind of their section for more than thirty years; until, at length, they have brought many good men to a willingness to take up arms against the government," etc. Mr. Defrees, the government printer, told me that, when the message was being printed, he was a good deal disturbed by the use of the term "sugar-coated," and finally went to the President about it. Their relations to each other being of the most intimate character, he told Mr. Lincoln frankly, that he ought to remember that a message to Congress was a different affair from a speech at a mass-meeting in Illinois; that the messages became a part of history, and should be written accordingly.

"What is the matter now?" inquired the President.

"Why," said Mr. Defrees, "you have used an undignified expression in the message;" and then, reading the paragraph aloud, he added, "I would alter the structure of that, if I were you."

"Defrees," replied Mr. Lincoln, "that word expresses precisely my idea, and I am not going to change it. The time will never come in this country when the people won't know exactly what *sugar-coated* means!"

On a subsequent occasion, Mr. Defrees told me, a certain sentence of another message was very awkwardly constructed. Calling the President's attention to it in the proof-copy, the latter acknowledged the force of the objection raised, and said, "Go home, Defrees, and see if you can better it." The next day Mr. Defrees took in to him his amendment. Mr. Lincoln met him by saying: "Seward found the same fault that you did, and he has been rewriting the paragraph also." Then, reading Mr. Defrees's version, he said, "I believe you have beaten Seward; but, 'I jings,' I think I can beat you both." Then, taking up his pen, he wrote the sentence as it was finally printed."

Mr. George E. Baker, Mr. Seward's private secretary, informed me that he was much amused and interested in a phase of Mr. Lincoln's character which came under his own observation. It was Mr. Baker's province to take to the President all public documents from the State Department requiring his signature. During the first few months, Mr. Lincoln would read each paper care fully through, always remarking, "I never sign a document I have not first read." As his cares increased, he at length departed from his habit so far as to say to the messenger, "Won't you read these papers to me?" This went on for a few months, and he then modified this practice by requesting "a synopsis of the contents." His time became more and more curtailed, and for the last year his only expression was, "Show me where you want my name?"

It is not generally known that the speech always made by the President, upon the presentation of a foreign minister, is carefully written for him by the Secretary of State. A clerk in the department ignorant of this custom, was one day sent to the White House by Mr. Seward, with the speech to be delivered upon such an occasion. Mr. Lincoln was writing at his desk, as the clerk entered—a half-dozen senators and representatives occupying the sofa and chairs. Unable to disguise a feeling of delicacy, in the discharge of such an errand, the young man approached, and in a low voice said to the President: "The Secretary has sent the speech you are to make to-day to the Swiss minister." Mr. Lincoln laid down his pen, and, taking the manuscript, said in a loud tone: "Oh, this is a speech Mr. Seward has written for me, is it? I guess I will try it before these gentlemen, and see how it goes." Thereupon he proceeded to read it, in a waggish manner, remarking, as he concluded, with sly humor: "There, I like that. It has the merit of *originality*."

"Within a month after Mr. Lincoln's first accession to office," says the Hon. Mr. Raymond, "when the South was threatening civil war, and armies of office-seekers were besieging him in the Executive Mansion, he said to a friend that he wished he could get time to attend to the Southern question; he thought he knew what was wanted, and believed he could do something towards quieting the rising discontent; but the office-seekers demanded all his time. 'I am,' said he, 'like a man so busy in letting rooms in one end of his house, that he can't stop to put out the fire that is burning the other.' Two or three years later, when the people had made him a candidate for reëlection, the same friend spoke to him of a member of his Cabinet who was a candidate also. Mr. Lincoln said he did not concern himself much about that. It was important to the country that the department over which his rival presided should be administered with vigor and energy, and whatever would stimulate the Secretary to such action would do good. 'R——,' said he, 'you were brought up on a farm, were you not? Then you know what a *chin fly* is. My brother and I,' he added, 'were once ploughing corn on a Kentucky farm, I driving the horse, and he holding the plough. The horse was lazy; but on one occasion rushed across the field so that I, with my long legs, could scarcely keep pace with him. On reaching the end of the furrow, I found an enormous *chin fly* fastened upon him, and knocked him off. My brother asked me what I did that for. I told him I didn't want the old horse bitten in that way "Why," said my brother, "*that's all that made him go!*" Now,' said Mr. Lincoln, 'if Mr. —has a presidential *chin fly* biting him, I'm not going to knock him off, if it will only make his department *go*.'

"On another occasion the President said he was in great distress; he had been to General McClellan's house, and the General did not ask to see him; and as he must talk to somebody, he had sent for General Franklin and myself, to obtain our opinion as to the possibility of soon commencing active operations with the Army of the Potomac. To use his own expression, if something was not soon done, the bottom would fall out of the whole affair, and if General McClellan did not want to use the army, he would like to *borrow it*, provided he could see how it could be made to do something."*

XLII.

One bright morning in May, the Sunday-school children of the city of Washington, marching in procession on anniversary

---

*Raymond's *Life of Lincoln*.

day, passed in review through the portico on the north side of the White House. The President stood at the open window above the door, responding with a smile and a bow to the lusty cheers of the little folks as they passed. Hon. Mr. Odell, of Brooklyn, with one or two other gentlemen, stood by his side as I joined the group. It was a beautiful sight; the rosy-cheeked boys and girls, in their "Sunday's best," with banners and flowers, all intent upon seeing the President, and, as they caught sight of his tall figure, cheering as if their very lives depended upon it. After enjoying the scene for some time, making pleasant remarks about a face that now and then struck him, Mr. Lincoln said: Mrs. Ann S. Stephens told me a story last night about Daniel Webster, when a lad, which was new to me, and it has been running in my head all the morning. When quite young, at school, Daniel was one day guilty of a gross violation of the rules. He was detected in the act, and called up by the teacher for punishment. This was to be the old-fashioned 'feruling' of the hand. His hands happened to be very dirty. Knowing this, on his way to the teacher's desk, he *spit* upon the palm of his *right* hand, wiping it off upon the side of his pantaloons. 'Give me your hand, sir,' said the teacher, very sternly. Out went the right hand, partly cleansed. The teacher looked at it a moment, and said, 'Daniel, if you will find another hand in this school-room as filthy as that, I will let you off this time!' Instantly from behind his back came the *left* hand. 'Here it is, sir,' was the ready reply. 'That will do,' said the teacher, 'for this time; you can take your seat, sir.'"

Mr. Lincoln's heart was always open to children. I shall never forget his coming into the "studio" one day, and finding my own little boy of two summers playing on the floor. A member of the Cabinet was with him, but laying aside all restraint, he took the little fellow at once in his arms, and they were soon on the best of terms.

Old Daniel—alluded to on a previous page—gave me a touching illustration of this element in his character. A poor woman from Philadelphia had been waiting with a baby in her arms for several days to see the President. It appeared by her story, that her husband had furnished a substitute for the army, but sometime afterward, in a state of intoxication, was induced to enlist. Upon reaching the post assigned his regiment, he deserted, thinking the government was not entitled to his services. Returning home, he was arrested, tried, convicted, and sentenced to be shot. The sentence was to be executed on a Saturday. On Monday his wife left her home with her baby, to endeavor to see the President. Said Daniel, "She had been waiting here three days, and there was no chance for her to get in. Late in the afternoon of the third day, the President was going through the passage to his private room to get a cup of tea. On the way he heard the baby cry. He instantly went back to his office and rang the bell. 'Daniel,' said he, 'is there a woman with a baby in the anteroom?' I said there was, and if he would allow me to say it, it was a case he ought to see; for it was a matter of life and death. Said he, 'Send her to me at once.' She went in, told her story, and the President pardoned her husband. As the woman came out from his presence, her eyes were lifted and her lips moving in prayer, the tears streaming down her cheeks." Said Daniel, "I went up to her, and pulling her shawl, said, 'Madam, it was the baby that did it.'"

When Mr. Lincoln visited New York in 1860, he felt a great interest in many of the institutions for reforming criminals and saving the young from a life of crime. Among others, he visited, unattended, the Five Points' House of Industry, and the Superintendent of the Sabbath-school there gave the following account of the event:—

"One Sunday morning, I saw a tall, remarkable-looking man enter the room and take a seat among us. He listened with fixed attention to our exercises, and his countenance expressed such genuine interest that I approached him and suggested that he might be willing to say something to the children. He accepted the invitation with evident pleasure; and, coming forward, began a simple address, which at once fascinated every little hearer and hushed the room into silence. His language was strikingly beautiful, and his tones musical with intense feeling. The little faces would droop into sad conviction as he uttered sentences of warning, and would brighten into sunshine

as he spoke cheerful words of promise. Once or twice he attempted to close his remarks, but the imperative shout of 'Go
on! Oh, do go on!' would compel him to resume. As I looked
upon the gaunt and sinewy frame of the stranger, and marked
his powerful head and determined features, now touched into
softness by the impressions of the moment, I felt an irrepressible curiosity to learn something more about him, and while he
was quietly leaving the room I begged to know his name. He
courteously replied, 'It is Abraham Lincoln, from Illinois.'"

Mr. Nelson Sizer, one of the gallery ushers of Henry Ward
Beecher's church in Brooklyn, told me that about the time of
the Cooper Institute speech, Mr. Lincoln was twice present at
the morning services of that church. On the first occasion, he
was accompanied by his friend, George B. Lincoln, Esq., and
occupied a prominent seat in the centre of the house. On a subsequent Sunday morning, not long afterwards, the church was
packed, as usual, and the services had proceeded to the announcement of the text, when the gallery door at the right of
the organ-loft opened, and the tall figure of Mr. Lincoln
entered, alone. Again in the city over Sunday, he started out
by himself to find the church, which he reached considerably
behind time. Every seat was occupied; but the gentlemanly
usher at once surrendered his own, and, stepping back, became
much interested in watching the effect of the sermon upon the
western orator. As Mr. Beecher developed his line of argument,

Mr. Lincoln's body swayed forward, his lips parted, and he seemed at length entirely unconscious of his surroundings,— frequently giving vent to his satisfaction, at a well-put point or illustration, with a kind of involuntary Indian exclamation,— "*ugh!*"—not audible beyond his immediate presence, but *very* expressive! Mr. Lincoln henceforward had a profound admiration for the talents of the famous pastor of Plymouth Church. He once remarked to the Rev. Henry M. Field, of New York, in my presence, that "he thought there was not upon record, in ancient or modern biography, so *productive* a mind, as had been exhibited in the career of Henry Ward Beecher!"

XLIII.

One of Mr. Lincoln's biographers, speaking of the relations which existed between the President and his Cabinet, says:—

"He always maintained that the proper duty of each Secretary was to direct the details of everything done within his own department, and to tender such suggestions, information, and advice to the President, as he might solicit at his hands. But the duty and responsibility of deciding what line of policy should be pursued, or what steps should be taken in any specific case, in his judgment, belonged exclusively to the President; and he was always willing and ready to assume it."[*]

---

[*]Hon. H. J. Raymond.

The suppression of a portion of Secretary Cameron's official report for 1861, is a case in point. A number of printed copies of the report had left Washington before the "incendiary" passage was observed by Mr. Lincoln. The New York "Tribune" published it as originally written. Late in the evening of the day that these were sent, the government printer took a copy to the President, saying he thought he ought to look it over and see if it was satisfactory. He stated, also, that a number of copies of the report had been already ordered from the printing-office. Mr. Lincoln glanced over the copy placed in his hands, and his eye rested upon the passage in question, which had reference to arming the slaves. Instantly he was aroused. "This will never do!" said he. "Gen. Cameron must take no such responsibility. That is a question which belongs exclusively to me!" Then, with a pencil, he struck out the objectionable clause, and ordered measures to be taken at once to suppress the copies already issued. This decided action created considerable excitement at the time, as the President's policy in reference to slavery had not then been indicated. In the light of subsequent history, it will be regarded as striking evidence of the caution with which he felt his way on this intricate and momentous question. In his own language, in the letter to Col. Hodges, he objected, because the indispensable necessity had not then arrived. To Simon Cameron, however, the honor will ever belong of being the first man connected with the Administration to strike an official blow at the great cause of the war.

Some time after the first battle of Bull Run, General Patterson, who had been severely censured for his action, or want of action, on that occasion, called upon Secretary Cameron, and demanded an investigation of the causes of the failure of the campaign. After listening to his statement, the Secretary said that he would like the President to see the orders and correspondence, and an interview was accordingly arranged for the same evening. The result is given in General Patterson's own words:—

"I called at the hour named, was most kindly received, and read the papers, to which the President attentively listened. When I had finished, Mr. Lincoln said, in substance, 'General, I have never found fault with you nor censured you; I have never been able to see that you could have done anything else than you did do. You obeyed orders, and I am satisfied with your conduct.' This was said with a manner so frank, candid, and manly as to secure my respect, confidence, and good-will. I expressed my gratification with and sincere thanks for his fairness toward me, and his courtesy in hearing my case,—giving me some five hours of his time. I said that so far as he and the War Department were concerned I was satisfied; but that I must have a trial by my peers, to have a public approval, and to stop the abuse daily lavished upon me. The President replied that he would cheerfully accede to any practicable measure to do me justice, but that I need not expect to escape abuse as long as I was of any importance or value to the community; adding that he received infinitely more abuse than I did, but that he had ceased to regard it, and I must learn to do the same."

Although the friendly relations which existed between the President and Secretary Cameron were not interrupted by the retirement of the latter from the War Office, so important a change in the Administration could not of course take place without the irrepressible "story" from Mr. Lincoln. Shortly after this event some gentlemen called upon the President, and expressing much satisfaction at the change, intimated that in their judgment the interests of the country required an entire reconstruction of the Cabinet. Mr. Lincoln heard them through, and then shaking his head dubiously, replied, with his peculiar smile: "Gentlemen, when I was a young man I used to know very well one Joe Wilson, who built himself a log-cabin not far from where I lived. Joe was very fond of eggs and chickens, and he took a good deal of pains in fitting up a poultry shed. Having at length got together a choice lot of young fowls,—of which he was very proud,—he began to be much annoyed by the depredations of those little black and white spotted animals, which it is not necessary to name. One night Joe was awakened by an unusual cackling and fluttering among his chickens. Getting up, he crept out to see what was going on. It was a bright moonlight night, and he soon caught sight of half a dozen of the little pests, which with their dam were running in and out of the shadow of the shed. Very wrathy, Joe put a double charge into his old musket, and thought he would 'clean' out the whole tribe at one shot. Somehow he only killed *one*, and the balance scampered off across the field. In telling the story, Joe would always pause here, and hold his nose. 'Why didn't you follow them up, and kill the rest?' inquired the neighbors. 'Blast it,' said Joe, 'why, it was eleven weeks before I got over killin' *one*. If you want any more skirmishing in that line you can just do it yourselves!'"

XLIV.

The battle of Fair Oaks was fought May 31, 1862; or rather this is the date of the first of the series of battles before Richmond, when, as is now abundantly established, even by Rebel testimony, it would have been an easy matter for McClellan to have captured what proved to be the Sebastopol of the Rebellion. During these terrible battles, many of our wounded men were sent on steamboats and transports to White House landing, upon the estate of Mrs. Fitz Hugh Lee, wife of the Rebel General. Prosper M. Wetmore, of New York city, was, at this juncture, on a visit to the army. Very ill himself while on the Peninsula, his sympathies were greatly excited for the wounded soldiers, confined, during the broiling weather, to the boats, compelled to quench the burning thirst created by their wounds

with the muddy water of the Pamunkey, which caused and aggravated disease in a fearful manner. As a civilian, he was permitted to go on shore, and there found the magnificent lawns
and grounds, including one of the finest springs of water in the
world, all under a protective guard, set over the property by order of the commanding general; and, while civilians like himself were permitted freely to drink at the spring, the suffering
soldiers were prohibited from approaching it! Mr. W.'s indignation was so greatly aroused that, upon reaching Baltimore, on
his return home, he, with two other gentlemen, cognizant of
the facts, determined to go to Washington and lay the case
before the War Department. Upon hearing their statement,
the Secretary of War referred them to Surgeon-General Hammond, saying that a requisition from him, to the effect that
the grounds of the estate were needed for the wounded, would
be instantly responded to by the War Department in the issue
of the necessary order, taking possession. They immediately
waited upon the Surgeon-General, and procured the document
required, upon which Secretary Stanton made out the order,
saying, as he signed it: "Now, gentlemen, you had better see
the President also about this matter, and get his indorsement of
the order." Proceeding to the Executive Mansion, they found,
as usual, the waiting-rooms thronged with visitors; but, representing to the usher in attendance that their business was
extremely urgent, and concerned the wounded of the army,

they were at once shown into Mr. Lincoln's presence. It was late in what had perhaps been a trying or vexatious day. Very briefly, but unceremoniously, the object of their visit was stated. In the language of Mr. W—, "The President listened to the account half impatiently, saying, as the speaker concluded, with an expression of countenance very like a sneer, 'This is another *raid* upon McClellan, I take it!' 'Mr. President,' was the reply, 'we came here to lay these facts before you solely from a sense of duty. Had I the power, sir, I would take possession of the lawns in front of *this* mansion for the benefit or our wounded men, so many of whom are now dying on the Pamunkey, for want of pure air and water. After the sights witnessed upon those seven steamboats now lying at White House, I covet every spot of greensward my eyes rest upon. What I have told you of the actual condition of things at that landing is below the truth, as the gentlemen who accompany me will confirm to your satisfaction. For myself, allow me to say, sir, that I belong to that political organization which opposed your election to the Presidency—the same organization to which General McClellan is presumed to belong. This is no raid upon him or upon you. It is simple justice to the wounded and suffering soldiers that we ask of you.' Entirely convinced by the candor of this reply, Mr. Lincoln then proceeded to a minute questioning in regard to the scenes they had witnessed; and when subsequently told that they had called at Secretary Stanton's request, to secure his approval of the order issued, which embraced only the grounds and spring, 'Not only these,' said he, with emphasis, 'but the order must include the house, and everything else which can in any way contribute to the comfort of the poor boys!' And so the order was made to read before it left Washington."

There is scarcely a parallel in history to the forbearance exhibited by the President toward General McClellan. The incident given above is but one illustration of his impatience with those who preferred charges against the "Commanding General." During the last year of his life, however, in friendly conversation, he could not refrain sometimes from an impromptu sarcasm, nevertheless so blended with wit that it must, one would think, effectually disarm all resentment.

About two weeks after the Chicago Convention, the Rev. J. P. Thompson, of New York, called upon the President, in company with the Assistant Secretary of War, Mr. Dana. In the course of conversation, Dr. T. said: "What do you think, Mr. President, is the reason General McClellan does not reply to the letter from the Chicago Convention?" "Oh!" replied Mr. Lincoln, with a characteristic twinkle of the eye, "*he is intrenching*."

XLV.

One Saturday afternoon, when the lawn in front of the White House was crowded with people listening to the weekly concert of the Marine Band, the President appeared upon the portico. Instantly there was a clapping of hands and clamor for a speech. Bowing his thanks, and excusing himself, he stepped back into the retirement of the circular parlor, remarking to me, with a disappointed air, as he reclined upon the sofa, "I wish they would let me sit out there quietly, and enjoy the music." I state to him on this occasion, that I believed no President, since the days of Washington, ever secured the hearts of the people, and carried them with him as he had done. To this he replied that, in such a crisis as the country was then passing through, it was natural that the people should look more earnestly to their leaders than at other periods. He thought their regard for any man in his position who should sincerely have done his best to save the government from destruction, would have been equally as marked and expressive; to which I did not by any means assent.

I do not recall an instance of Mr. Lincoln's ever referring to any act of his administration with an appearance of complacency or self-satisfaction. I watched him closely during the political excitement previous to the Baltimore Convention, to see if I could discover signs of personal ambition, and I am free to say that, apart from the welfare of the country, there was no evidence to show to my mind that he ever thought of himself. And yet he was very sensitive to the opinions of his friends. A governor of a western State, true and loyal as the best, at a certain juncture conceived himself for some reason aggrieved by Executive action. Having occasion to send in the names of two officers for promotion, he said, in his note to the President, that he hoped whatever feeling he might have against him personally would not prevent his doing justice to the merits of the officers in question. Mr. Lincoln had been utterly unconscious of having given offence, either by lack of appreciation or otherwise, and he seemed greatly touched at the aspersion. He said that, if he had been asked to say which of all the loyal governors had been most active and efficient in raising and equipping troops, if he had made any distinction, where all had done so well, it would have been in favor of the governor in question. At another time, when several conflicting delegations were pressing the claims of different candidates for a position of importance, he said that he had been so troubled about the matter that he had that day refused to see one of the candidates, an old and dear personal friend, lest his judgment should be warped. "If I was less *thin-skinned* about such things," he added, "I should get along much better."

When he had thought profoundly, however, upon certain measures, and felt sure of his ground, criticism, either public or private, did not disturb him. Upon the appearance of what was known as the "Wade and Davis manifesto," subsequent to his renomination, an intimate friend and supporter, who was very indignant that such a document should have been put forth just previous to the presidential election, took occasion to animad-vert very severely upon the course that prompted it. "It is not worth fretting about," said the President; "it reminds me of an old acquaintance, who, having a son of a scientific turn, bought him a microscope. The boy went around, experimenting with his glass upon everything that came in his way. One day, at the dinner-table, his father took up a piece of cheese. 'Don't eat that, father,' said the boy; 'it is full of *wrigglers*.' 'My son,' replied the old gentleman, taking, at the same time, a huge bite, 'let 'em *wriggle*; I can stand it if they can.'"

No President ever manifested such a willingness to receive and act upon advice and suggestions from all sources, as Mr. Lincoln. On a certain occasion a leading officer of the govern-ment, and the governor of the State he represented, had each a candidate for a high State position. The claims of both were urged with great strength. The President was "in a strait betwixt the two." A personal friend from the same State, to whom he mentioned the difficulty of deciding the question without giv-ing offence to one or the other of the parties, suggested that he appoint neither of the candidates, but bestow the office upon a certain officer of the army from that State, who had distin-guished himself, losing an arm or a leg in the service, but who had not solicited in any way the position. Mr. Lincoln instantly fell in with the idea, saying that it seemed to him "just the right thing to do;" and he immediately made out the nomination.

XLVI.

Among the numerous visitors on one of the President's reception days, were a party of Congressmen, among whom was the Hon. Thomas Shannon, of California. Soon after the customary greeting, Mr. Shannon said:—

"Mr. President, I met an old friend of yours in California last summer, Thompson Campbell, who had a good deal to say of your Springfield life." "Ah!" returned Mr. Lincoln, "I am glad to hear of him. Campbell used to be a dry fellow," he continued. "For a time he was Secretary of State. One day, during the legislative vacation, a meek, cadaverous-looking man, with a white neck-cloth, introduced himself to him at his office, and, stating that he had been informed that Mr. C. had the letting of the Assembly Chamber, said that he wished to secure it, if possible, for a course of lectures he desired to deliver in Springfield. 'May I ask,' said the Secretary, 'what is to be the subject of your lectures?' 'Certainly,' was the reply, with a very solemn expression of countenance. 'The course I wish to deliver, is on the Second Coming of our Lord.' 'It is of no use,' said C. 'If you will take my advice, you will not waste your time in this city. It is my private opinion that if the Lord has been in Springfield *once*, He will not come the second time!'"

Representative Shannon, previous to the war, had been an "Old Hunker" Democrat. Converted by the Rebellion, he had

gone to the other extreme, and was one of the radical Abolitionists of the Thirty-Eighth Congress. The last Sunday in
May, the Rev. Dr. Cheever, of New York, delivered one of his
most pungent, denunciatory antislavery discourses, in the Hall
of the House of Representatives. Among the numerous audi-
tors attracted by the name of the preacher, I noticed Mr. Shannon, whose face was not often seen in church. On the way to
my hotel, we fell in together. "Well, S.," said I, "what think you
of that style of preaching?" "It was the first *'Gospel'* sermon I
ever heard in my live!" was the emphatic rejoinder.

One of Mr. Shannon's California colleagues, the Hon.
Mr. Higby, told me that having special business one evening,
which called him to the White House, the President came into
the office, dressed for a state dinner. In the conversation which
followed, holding up his hands, encased in white gloves, he
remarked, with a laugh, that one of his Illinois friends never
could see his hands in that "predicament," without being
reminded of "*canvassed hams!*"

Mr. Lincoln was always ready to join in a laugh at the
expense of his person, concerning which he was very indifferent. Many of his friends will recognize the following story,—
the incident having actually occurred,—which he used to tell
with great glee:—

"In the days when I used to be 'on the circuit,' I was once
accosted in the cars by a stranger, who said, 'Excuse me, sir, but

I have an article in my possession which belongs to you.' 'How is that?' I asked, considerably astonished. The stranger took a jack-knife from his pocket. 'This knife,' said he, 'was placed in my hands some years ago, with the injunction that I was to keep it until I found a man *uglier* than myself. I have carried it from that time to this. Allow me *now* to say, sir, that I think *you* are fairly entitled to the property.'"

XLVII.

I had been engaged in the official chamber until quite late one evening, upon some pencil studies of accessories, necessary to introduce in my picture. The President, Mrs. Lincoln, and the Private Secretaries had gone to the opera, and for the time being I had undisturbed possession. Towards twelve o'clock I heard some persons enter the sleeping apartment occupied by Mr. Nicolay and Major Hay, which was directly opposite the room where I was sitting; and shortly afterward the hearty laugh of Mr. Lincoln broke the stillness, proceeding from the same quarter. Throwing aside my work, I went across the hall to see what had occasioned this outbreak of merriment. The Secretaries had come in and Hay had retired; Mr. Nicolay sat by the table with his boots off, and the President was leaning over the "footboard" of the bed, laughing and talking with the hilarity of a schoolboy. It seemed that Hay, or "John," as the President called him, had met with a singular adventure, which was the subject of the amusement. Glancing through the half-open door, Mr. Lincoln caught sight of me, and the story had to be repeated for my benefit. The incident was trifling in itself, but the President's enjoyment of it was very exhilarating. I never saw him in so frolicsome a mood as on this occasion.

It has been well said by a critic of Shakspeare, that "the spirit which held the woe of 'Lear,' and the tragedy of 'Hamlet,' would have broken, had it not also had the humor of the 'Merry Wives of Windsor,' and the merriment of 'Midsummer Night's dream.'" With equal justice can this profound truth be applied to the late President. The world has had no better illustration of it since the immortal plays were written.

Mr. Lincoln's "laugh" stood by itself. The "neigh" of a wild horse on his native prairie is not more undisguised and hearty. A group of gentlemen, among whom was his old Springfield friend and associate, Hon. Isaac N. Arnold, were one day conversing in the passage near his office, while waiting admission. A congressional delegation had preceded them, and presently an unmistakable voice was heard through the partition, in a burst of mirth. Mr. Arnold remarked, as the sound died away: "That laugh has been the President's life-preserver!"

In a corner of his desk he kept a copy of the latest humorous work; and it was his habit when greatly fatigued, annoyed, or depressed, to take this up and read a chapter, frequently with great relief.

Among the callers in the course of an evening which I well remember, was a party composed of two senators, a representative, an ex-lieutenant-governor of a western State, and several private citizens. They had business of great importance, involving the necessity of the President's examination of voluminous documents. He was at this time, from an unusual pressure of office-seekers, in addition to his other cares, literally worn out. Pushing everything aside, he said to one of the party: "Have you seen the 'Nasby Papers'?" "No, I have not," was the answer; "who is 'Nasby?'" "There is a chap out in Ohio," returned the President, "who has been writing a series of letters in the newspapers over the signature of 'Petroleum V. Nasby.' Some one sent me a pamphlet collection of them the other day. I am going to write to 'Petroleum' to come down here, and I intend to tell him if he will communicate his talent to me, I will *'swap'* places with him." Thereupon he arose, went to a drawer in his desk, and, taking out the "Letters," sat down and read one to the company finding in their enjoyment of it the temporary excitement and relief which another man would have found in a glass of wine. The instant he ceased, the book was thrown aside, his countenance relapsed into its habitual serious expression, and the business before him was entered upon with the utmost earnestness.

During the dark days of '62, the Hon. Mr. Ashley, of Ohio, had occasion to call at the White House early one morning,

just after news of a disaster. Mr. Lincoln commenced some trifling narration, to which the impulsive congressman was in no
mood to listen. He rose to his feet and said: "Mr. President, I
did not come here this morning to hear stories; it is too serious
a time." Instantly the smile faded from Mr. Lincoln's face.
"Ashley," said he, "sit down! I respect you as an earnest, sincere
man. You cannot be more anxious than I have been constantly
since the beginning of the war; and I say to you now, that were
it not for this occasional *vent*, I should die."

XLVIII.

About the first of June I received a call from the Hon.
Horace Greeley, who was temporarily in Washington. Very
near-sighted, his comments upon my work, then about half
completed, were not particularly gratifying. He thought the
steel likenesses in his book, "The American Conflict," were
much better. I called his attention, among other points, to a
newspaper introduced in the foreground of the picture, "symbolizing," I said, "the agency of the 'Press' in bringing about
Emancipation;"—stating, at the same time, that this accessory
was studied from a copy of the "Tribune." Upon this his face
relaxed;—"I would not object," said he, "to your putting in my
letter to the President on that subject."

Knowing that he had not been friendly to the renomination
of Mr. Lincoln, it occurred to me, in my simplicity, that if I

could bring them together, an interview might result in clearing up what was, perhaps, a mutual misunderstanding of relative positions,—though I had never known Mr. Lincoln to mention the name of the editor of the "Tribune," otherwise than with profound respect. Leaving my visitor in front of the picture, I went to the President's office to inform him of the presence of Mr. G. in the house, thinking that he might deem it best, under the circumstances, to receive him below stairs. In this, however, I "reckoned without my host." He looked up quickly, as I mentioned the name, but recovering himself, said, with unusual blandness: "Please say to Mr. Greeley that I shall be *very* happy to see him, *at his leisure*."

I have been repeatedly asked to what extent Mr. Lincoln read the newspapers. It might have dampened the patriotic ardor of many ambitious editors, could they have known that their elaborate disquisitions, sent in such numbers to the White House, were usually appropriated by the servants, and rarely, or never, reached the one they were preëminently intended to enlighten as to his duty and policy. I recollect of but a single instance of newspaper reading on the part of the President, during the entire period of my intercourse with him. One evening, having occasion to go to the Private Secretary's office, supposing the rooms to be vacant, I came upon Mr. Lincoln, seated quietly by himself, for once engaged in looking over the contents of a journal, which he had casually taken up.

The Washington dailies,—the "Chronicle," "Republican," and "Star,"—were usually laid upon his table, and I think he was in the habit of glancing at the telegraphic reports of these; but rarely beyond this. All war news of importance, of course, reached him previous to its publication. He had, therefore, little occasion to consult newspapers on this account. The Private Secretaries, however, usually kept him informed of the principal subjects discussed editorially in the leading organs of the country.

The journals I became most familiar with, in the Secretaries' quarters, besides those mentioned, were the Philadelphia "Press" and "North American;" the Baltimore "American" and "Sun;" the New York "Tribune," "Evening Post," "Independent," "Times," "Herald," and "World;" the Albany "Evening Journal;" the Boston "Advertiser," "Journal," and "Transcript;" the Chicago "Tribune" and "Journal," (the latter valued chiefly for the letters of its war correspondent, B. F. Taylor); the St. Louis "Republican" and "Democrat;" and the Cincinnati "Gazette" and "Commercial."

Violent criticism, attacks, and denunciations, coming either from radicals or conservatives, rarely ruffled the President, if they reached his ears. It must have been in connection with something of this kind, that he once told me this story. "Some years ago," said he, "a couple of 'emigrants,' fresh from the 'Emerald Isle,' seeking labor, were making their way toward the West. Coming suddenly, one evening, upon a pond of water, they were greeted with a grand chorus of bull-frogs,—a kind of music they had never before heard, 'B-a-u-m!'—'B-a-u-m!' Overcome with terror, they clutched their 'shillelahs,' and crept cautiously forward, straining their eyes in every direction, to catch a glimpse of the enemy; but he was not to be found! At last a happy idea seized the foremost one,—he sprang to his companion and exclaimed, 'And sure, Jamie! it is my opinion it's nothing but a "*noise!*"'"

On a certain occasion, the President was induced by a committee of gentlemen to examine a newly invented "repeating" gun; the peculiarity of which was, that it prevented the escape of gas. After due inspection, he said: "Well, I believe this really does what it is represented to do. Now have any of you heard of any machine, or invention, for preventing the escape of 'gas' from newspaper establishments?"

One afternoon he came into the studio, while Mrs. Secretary Welles and a party of friends were viewing the picture. Mrs. Welles said that she "understood from the newspapers that the work was nearly completed; which appeared to be far from the truth." In reply, I made the commonplace remark, that the "papers" were not always "*reliable.*" "That is to say, Mrs. Welles," broke in the President, "they" '*lie,*' and then they '*relie!*'"

At one of the "levees," in the winter of 1864, during a lull in the hand-shaking, Mr. Lincoln was addressed by two lady friends, one of whom is the wife of a gentleman subsequently called into the Cabinet. Turning to them with a weary air, he remarked that it was a relief to have now and then those to talk to who had no favors to ask. The lady referred to is a radical,—a New Yorker by birth, but for many years a resident of the West. She replied, playfully, "Mr. President, I *have* one request to make." "Ah!" said he, at once looking grave. "Well, what is it?" "That you suppress the infamous 'Chicago Times,'" was the rejoinder. After a brief pause, Mr. Lincoln asked her if she had ever tried to imagine how she would have felt, in some former administration to which she was opposed, if her favorite newspaper had been seized by the government, and suppressed. The lady replied that it was not a parallel case; that in circumstances like those then existing, when the nation was struggling for its very life, such utterances as were daily put forth in that journal should be suppressed by the strong hand of authority; that the cause of loyalty and good government demanded it. "I fear you do not fully comprehend," returned the President, "the danger of abridging the *liberties* of the people. Nothing but the very sternest necessity can ever justify it. A government had better go to the very extreme of toleration, than to do aught that could be construed into an interference with, or to jeopardize in any degree, the common rights of its citizens."

XLIX.

A morning or two after the visit of Mr. Greeley, I was called upon by a gentleman, who requested my assistance in securing a brief interview with the President, for the purpose of presenting him with an elaborate pen-and-ink "allegorical, symbolic" representation of the "Emancipation Proclamation;" which, in a massive carved frame, had been purchased at a recent "Sanitary Fair," in one of the large cities, by a committee of gentlemen, expressly for this object. The composition contained a tree, representing Liberty; a portrait of Mr. Lincoln; soldiers, monitors, broken fetters, etc.; together with the text of the proclamation, all executed with a pen. Artistically speaking, such works have no value,—they are simply interesting, as curiosities. Mr. Lincoln kindly accorded the desired opportunity to make the presentation, which occupied but a few moments, and was in the usual form. He accepted the testimonial, he said, not for himself, but in behalf of "the cause in which all were engaged." When the group dispersed, I remained with the President. He returned to his desk; while I examined curiously the pen work, which was exceedingly minute in detail. "This is quite wonderful!" I said, at length. Mr. Lincoln looked up from his papers; "Yes," he rejoined; "it is what I call *ingenious nonsense!*"

The evening following this affair, on entering the President's office, about eleven o'clock, I found him alone, seated at the long table, with a large pile of military commissions before him, which he was signing one by one. As I sat down beside him, he presently remarked, "I do not, as you see, pretend to read over these documents. I see that Stanton has signed them, so I conclude they are all right." Pausing here, he read a portion of one, beginning with the name of the individual. "—is hereby appointed adjutant-general, with the rank of captain, etc. E. M. Stanton, Secretary of War." "There," said he, appending his own signature in the opposite corner; "that *fixes* him out." Thus he went on chatting and writing, until he had finished the lot; then, rising from his chair, he stretched himself, and said, "Well, I have got that job *husked out*; now I guess I will go over to the War Department before I go to bed, and see if there is any news. Walking over with him at his request,—to divert his mind, I repeated a story told me the night previous concerning a 'contraband' who had fallen into the hands of some good pious people, and was being taught by them to read and pray. Going off by himself one day, he was overheard to commence a prayer by the introduction of himself as "Jim Williams—a berry good nigga' to wash windows; 'spec's you know me now?'"

An amusing illustration of the fact that whatever the nature of an incident related to the President, it never failed to remind him of something similar, followed. After a hearty laugh at what he called this "direct way of putting the case," he said: "The story that suggests to me, has no resemblance to it save in the 'washing windows' part. A lady in Philadelphia had a pet poodle dog, which mysteriously disappeared. Rewards were offered for him, and a great ado made without effect. Some weeks passed, and all hope of the favorite's return had been given up, when a servant brought him in one day, in the filthiest condition imaginable. The lady was overjoyed to see her pet again, but horrified at his appearance. 'Where *did* you find him?' she exclaimed. 'Oh,' replied the man, very unconcernedly, 'a negro down the street had him tied to the end of a pole, *swabbing* windows.'"

L.

A day or two previous to the meeting of the Republican Convention, the President read me his letter to the "Owen Lovejoy Monument Association,"—lately written, and not then published,—in which he expressed his appreciation of Mr. Lovejoy in nearly the same language I had heard him use on a former occasion. "Throughout my heavy and perplexing responsibilities here," ran the letter, "to the day of his death, it would scarcely wrong any other to say he was my most generous friend. Let him have the marble monument, along with the well assured and more enduring one in the hearts of those who love liberty unselfishly for all men." A noble tribute, in fitly chosen words!

The evening following the reading of this letter, he said that Mrs. Lincoln and he had promised half an hour to a sort of "artist" who wished to "exhibit" before them in the red-room below. "What kind of an artist?" I inquired. "Oh, not in your line," he answered; "I think he is a sort of mountebank, or comic lecturer, or something of the kind." On my way to my own room, I met in the passage the well-known "Jeems Pipes of Pipesville,"—otherwise Stephen Massett,—whom I at once conjectured to be the individual the President had referred to. The two rooms communicating by double doors, I could not well avoid overhearing a portion of the performance, or more properly lecture, which I think was announced by the title of "Drifting About." Comic imitations of various characters were given, among others that of a stammering man, which appeared greatly to amuse Mr. Lincoln. I could only now and then catch a word of the burlesque, but the voice and ringing laugh of the President were perfectly distinguishable. When the "lecture" ceased, Mr. Lincoln said, "I want to offer a suggestion. I once knew a man who invariably '*whistled*' with his stammering," and he then gave an imitation. "Now," he continued, "if you could get in a touch of nature like that it would be irresistibly ludicrous." "Pipes" applauded the amendment, rehearsing it several times, until he had mastered it to the President's satisfaction; and I dare say the innovation became a part of all subsequent performances.

About this period numerous delegations from various religious bodies and associations thronged the White House. Among the number none met so cordial a reception as that of the "Christian Commission," composed of volunteer clergymen who had just returned from the Wilderness battleground. In the brief address by the chairman of the occasion, he stated that the group before the President embraced those who had been first on the field to offer aid and refreshments to the wounded of that terrible series of battles. In reply Mr. Lincoln expressed his appreciation of the self-denying services rendered by the Commission, in feeling terms. He concluded his response in these words: "And I desire also to add to what I have said, that there is one association whose object and motives I have never heard in any degree impugned or questioned; and that is the 'Christian Commission.' And in 'these days of villany,' as Shakspeare says, that is a record, gentlemen, of which you may justly be proud!" Upon the conclusion of the "ceremony," he added, in a conversational tone, "I believe, however, it is old 'Jack Falstaff' who talks about 'villany,' though of course Shakspeare is responsible."

After the customary hand-shaking, which followed, several gentlemen came forward and asked the President for his autograph. One of them gave his name as "Cruikshank." "That reminds me," said Mr. Lincoln, "of what I used to be called when a young man—'long-shanks.'" Hereupon the rest of the party, emboldened by the success of the few, crowded around the desk, and the President good naturedly wrote his name for each; the scene suggesting forcibly to my mind a country schoolmaster's weekly distribution of "tickets" among his pupils.

LI.

The "Baltimore Convention," which renominated Mr. Lincoln, was convened June 7, 1864. It created comparatively little excitement in Washington or elsewhere, as the action of the various State legislatures and local mass meetings had prepared the public mind for the result.

Toward evening of the 8th,—the day the nominations were made,—Major Hay and myself were alone with the President in his office. He did not seem in any degree exhilarated by the action of the convention; on the contrary, his manner was subdued, if not sad. Upon the lighting of the gas, he told us how he had that afternoon received the news of the nomination for Vice-President before he heard of his own. It appeared that the despatch announcing his renomination had been sent to his office from the War Department while he was at lunch. Afterward, without going back to the official chamber, he proceeded to the War Department. While there, the telegram came in announcing the nomination of Johnson. "What!" said he to the operator, "do they nominate a Vice-President before they do a President?" "Why!" rejoined the astonished official, "have you not heard of your own nomination? It was sent to the White House two hours ago." "It is all right," was the reply; "I shall probably find it on my return."

Laughing pleasantly over this incident, he said, soon afterward,—"A very singular occurrence took place the day I was nominated at Chicago, four years ago, of which I am reminded to-night. In the afternoon of the day, returning home from down town, I went up-stairs to Mrs. Lincoln's sitting-room. Feeling somewhat tired, I lay down upon a couch in the room, directly opposite a bureau upon which was a looking-glass. As I reclined, my eye fell upon the glass, and I saw distinctly *two* images of myself, exactly alike, except that one was a little paler than the other. I arose, and lay down again, with the same result. It made me quite uncomfortable for a few moments, but some friends coming in, the matter passed out of my mind. The next day, while walking in the street, I was suddenly reminded of the circumstance, and the disagreeable sensation produced by it returned. I had never seen anything of the kind before, and did not know what to make of it. I determined to go home and place myself in the same position, and if the same effect was produced, I would make up my mind that it was the natural result of some principle of refraction or optics which I did not understand, and dismiss it. I tried the experiment, with a like result; and, as I had said to myself, accounting for it on some principle unknown to me, it ceased to trouble me. But," said he, "some time ago, I tried to produce the same effect *here*, by arranging a glass and couch in the same position, without success." He did not say, at this time, that either he or Mrs. Lincoln attached any omen to the phenomenon; neither did he say that the double reflection was seen while he was walking about the room. On the contrary, it was only visible in a certain position and at a certain angle; and therefore, he thought, could be accounted for upon scientific principles.*

A little later in the evening, the Hon. Mr. Kelley, of Philadelphia, came in. As he sat down, he took a letter out of his pocket, saying: "Mr. President, while on a visit home, a week or two ago, I took up a number of the "Anti-Slavery Standard," in which there happened to be a communication from Mrs. Caroline H. Dall, of Boston, giving her views of the Fremont movement,

---

*Mr. Lincoln's friend Brooks, of the *Sacramento Union*, has given to the public a somewhat different version of this story, placing its occurrence on the day of the election in 1860. The account, as I have given it, was written before I had seen that by Mr. Brooks, and is very nearly as Hay and myself heard it,—the incident making a powerful impression upon my mind. I am quite confident that Mr. Lincoln said it occurred the day he was first nominated; for he related it to us a few hours after having received intelligence of his renomination, saying, "I am reminded of it to-night." It is possible, however, that I am mistaken in the date. Mr. Brooks's statement that "Mr. Lincoln" was "troubled" about it, regarding it as a "sign that Mr. Lincoln would be reëlected, but would not live through his second term," is undoubtedly correct.

and the situation generally; so admirable in its tone and spirit, that I could not resist the inclination to write to the author, expressing the interest with which I had read the article. The result was a reply, which I hold in my hand, which seems to me so just and able a statement of your position, from the stand-point of a true woman, that I have brought it up to read to you." Mr. Lincoln nodded assent, and listened pensively to the elo-quent tones of the Congressman's voice, who entered into the spirit of the letter with his whole heart,—affirming, as it did, unwavering confidence in the President; the sincerity of his anti-slavery convictions and purposes; and appreciation of the diffi-culties which had environed him,—presenting, in this respect, a marked contrast to the letters and speeches of many of the so-called radicals. Mr. Lincoln said but little, as Judge Kelley con-cluded; but one or two expressions, and the manner accompany-ing them, showed that the sentiments of the writer of the letter were gratefully appreciated.

The day following the adjournment at Baltimore, various political organizations called to pay their respects to the Presi-dent. First came the Convention Committee, embracing one from each State represented,—appointed to announce to him, formally, the nomination. Next came the Ohio delegation, with Menter's Band, of Cincinnati. Following these were the repre-sentatives of the National Union League, to whom he said, in concluding his brief response:—

"I do not allow myself to suppose that either the Convention, or the League, have concluded to decide that I am either the greatest or the best man in America; but, rather, they have concluded that it is not best to *swap* horses while crossing the river, and have further concluded that I am not so poor a horse, but that they might make a *botch* of it in trying to *swap!*"

Another incident, which occurred in the course of the day, created considerable amusement. When the Philadelphia delegation was being presented, the chairman of that body, in introducing one of the members, said: "Mr. President, this is Mr. S——, of the Second District of our State,—a most active and earnest friend of yours and the cause. He has, among other things, been good enough to paint, and present to our League rooms, a most beautiful portrait of yourself." Mr. Lincoln took the gentleman's hand in his, and shaking it cordially, said with a merry voice,—"I presume, sir, in painting your beautiful portrait, you took your idea of me from my principles, and not from my person."

Among the visitors, the same afternoon, were William Lloyd Garrison and Theodore Tilton. In the "Editorial Notes," concerning the convention and nominations, in his newspaper, the New York "Independent," the following week, Mr. Tilton wrote:—

"On his reception day, the President's face wore an expression of satisfaction rather than elation. His reception of

Earliest known photograph of Francis Bicknell Carpenter, produced by Mathew Brady's studio c. 1850–1860.

First Reading of the Emancipation Proclamation by President Lincoln,
by Francis Bicknell Carpenter, oil on canvas, 1864.

Key to the Portrait Group

1. *President Abraham Lincoln*
2. *William H. Seward, Secretary of State*
3. *Salmon P. Chase, Secretary of Treasury*
4. *Edwin M. Stanton, Secretary of War*
5. *Gideon Welles, Secretary of Navy*
6. *Edward Bates, Attorney-General*
7. *Montgomery Blair, Postmaster-General*
8. *Caleb B. Smith, Secretary of Interior*

THE FIRST READING OF THE EMANCIPATION PROCLAMATION BEFORE THE CABINET.

First Reading of the Emancipation Proclamation Before the Cabinet, *engraving by Alexander Hay Ritchie after Francis Bicknell Carpenter, New York, 1866.*

First Reading of the Emancipation Proclamation *by Francis Bicknell Carpenter is currently displayed over the west staircase in the Senate wing of the U.S. Capitol.*

A study of President Lincoln, made by Francis Bicknell Carpenter, in preparation for the First Reading of the Emancipation Proclamation, *oil on canvas, 1864.*

Portrait of Abraham Lincoln, engraving by Frederick W. Halpin
after the study by Francis Bicknell Carpenter, New York, 1866.

This photograph of Lincoln in the White House Cabinet Room was set up by Francis Bicknell Carpenter and taken by Anthony Berger of Mathew Brady's Gallery, April 26, 1864. The legs at right belong to Carpenter himself, posing as he would paint William H. Seward.

Mathew Brady Studio's well-known photograph of President Lincoln with his son Tad was taken by Anthony Berger, but posed under the direction of Francis Bicknell Carpenter on February 9, 1864.

The Lincoln Family, *by Francis Bicknell Carpenter, oil on canvas, c. 1865. From left to right: Mary Todd Lincoln; William Wallace Lincoln, who died in 1862; Robert Todd Lincoln; Thomas "Tad" Lincoln; and the president.*

The Lincoln Family in 1861, *mezzotint by J. C. Buttre after Francis Bicknell Carpenter, 1867, New York.*

Lincoln and Tad *by Francis Bicknell Carpenter, oil on paper-
board, 1873–74. This small painting, just over three inches tall,
was inspired by the 1864 photograph of the president and his son
taken by Anthony Berger in Mathew Brady's studio. Carpenter
painted it after Tad's death at the age of eighteen in 1871.*

Mr. Garrison was an equal honor to host and guest. In alluding to our failure to find the old jail, he said,—'Well, Mr. Garrison, when you first went to Baltimore you couldn't get *out*; but the second time you couldn't get *in!*' When one of us mentioned the great enthusiasm at the convention, after Senator Morgan's proposition to amend the Constitution, abolishing slavery, Mr. Lincoln instantly said,—'It was I who suggested to Mr. Morgan that he should put that idea into his opening speech.' This was the very best word he has said since the proclamation of freedom."

LII.

I have alluded, on a previous page, to the public concerts of the Marine Band,—from the Washington Navy-yard,—given every Saturday afternoon, during the summer, on the grounds in front of the White House; which, on such occasions, were thronged with visitors. The Saturday following the nominations I invited my friend Cropsey, the landscape-painter, from New York,—who, with his wife, was spending a few days in the city,—to come up with Mrs. C. to the studio, which overlooked the pleasure-grounds, and presented a fine opportunity of enjoying both spectacle and music. The invitation was accepted, and the afternoon was devoted to my guests.

Towards the close of the concert the door suddenly opened, and the President came in, as he was in the habit of doing, alone. Mr. and Mrs. Cropsey had been presented to him in the course of the morning; and as he came forward, half hesitatingly, Mrs. C., who held a bunch of beautiful flowers in her hand, tripped forward playfully, and said: "Allow me, Mr. President, to present you with a bouquet!" The situation was momentarily embarrassing; and I was puzzled to know how "His Excellency" would get out of it. With no appearance of discomposure, he stooped down, took the flowers, and, looking from them into the sparkling eyes and radiant face of the lady, said, with a gallantry I was unprepared for,—"Really, madam, if you give them to *me*, and they are *mine*, I think I cannot possibly make so good a *use* of them as to present them to *you*, in return!" Chesterfield could not have extricated himself from the dilemma with more tact and address; and the incident, trifling in itself, may serve to illustrate that there existed in the *ci-devant* "rail-splitter" and "flat-boatman"—uncouth and half-civilized as many supposed him—the essential elements of the true gentleman.

I was always touched by the President's manner of receiving the salute of the guard at the White House. Whenever he appeared in the portico, on his way to or from the War or Treasury Department, or on any excursion down the avenue, the first glimpse of him was, of course, the signal for the sentinel on duty to "present arms." This was always acknowledged by Mr.

Lincoln with a peculiar bow and touch of the hat, no matter how many times it might occur in the course of a day; and it always seemed to me as much a compliment to the devotion of the soldiers, on his part, as it was the sign of duty and deference on the part of the guard.

The Hon. Mr. Odell gave me a deeply interesting incident, which occurred in the winter of 1864, at one of the most crowded of the Presidential levees, illustrating very perfectly Mr. Lincoln's true politeness and delicacy of feeling.

On the occasion referred to, the pressure became so great that the usual ceremony of hand-shaking was, for once, discontinued. The President had been standing for some time, bowing his acknowledgments to the thronging multitude, when his eye fell upon a couple who had entered unobserved,—a wounded soldier, and his plainly dressed mother. Before they could pass out, he made his way to where they stood, and, taking each of them by the hand, with a delicacy and cordiality which brought tears to many eyes, he assured them of his interest and welcome. Governors, senators, diplomats, passed with simply a nod; but that pale young face he might never see again. To him, and to others like him, did the nation owe its life; and Abraham Lincoln was not the man to forget this, even in the crowded and brilliant assembly of the distinguished of the land.

LIII.

The opinion of the Attorney-General, Judge Bates, as to the safety of Mr. Lincoln's being intrusted with the pardoning power, was founded upon an intimate knowledge of the man. A nature of such tenderness and humanity would have been in danger of erring on what many would call the weak side, had it not been balanced by an unusual degree of strong practical good sense and judgment.

The Secretary of War, and generals in command, were frequently much annoyed at being overruled,—the discipline and efficiency of the service being thereby, as they considered, greatly endangered. But there was no going back of the simple signature, "A. LINCOLN," attached to proclamation or reprieve.

The Hon. Mr. Kellogg, representative from Essex County, New York, received a despatch one evening from the army, to the effect that a young townsman, who had been induced to enlist through his instrumentality, had, for a serious misdemeanor, been convicted by a court-martial, and was to be shot the next day. Greatly agitated, Mr. Kellogg went to the Secretary of War, and urged, in the strongest manner, a reprieve. Stanton was inexorable. "To many cases of the kind had been let off," he said; "and it was time an example was made." Exhausting his eloquence in vain, Mr. Kellogg said,—"Well, Mr. Secretary, the boy is not going to be *shot*,—of that I give you fair warning!"

Leaving the War Department, he went directly to the White House, although the hour was late. The sentinel on duty told him that special orders had been issued to admit no one whatever that night. After a long parley, by pledging himself to assume the responsibility of the act, the congressman passed in. The President had retired; but, indifferent to etiquette or ceremony, Judge Kellogg pressed his way through all obstacles to his sleeping apartment. In an excited manner he stated that the despatch announcing the hour of execution had but just reached him. "This man must not be shot, Mr. President," said he. "I can't help what he may have done. Why, he is an old neighbor of mine; I can't allow him to be shot!" Mr. Lincoln had remained in bed, quietly listening to the vehement protestations of his old friend, (they were in Congress together.) He at length said: "Well, I don't believe *shooting* him will do him any good. Give me that pen." And, so saying, "red tape" was unceremoniously cut, and another poor fellow's lease of life was indefinitely extended.

One night Speaker Colfax left all other business to ask the President to respite the son of a constituent, who was sentenced to be shot, at Davenport, for desertion. He heard the story with his usual patience, though he was wearied out with incessant calls, and anxious for rest, and then replied: "some of our generals complain that I impair discipline and subordination in the army by my pardons and respites, but it makes me rested, after a hard day's work, if I can find some good excuse for saving man's life, and I go to bed happy as I think how joyous the signing of my name will make him and his family and his friends."

Mr. Van Alen, of New York, in an account furnished the "Evening Post," wrote: "I well remember the case of a poor woman who sought, with the persistent affection of a mother, for the pardon of her son condemned to death. She was successful in her petition. When she had left the room, Mr. Lincoln turned to me and said: 'Perhaps I have done wrong, but at all events I have made that poor woman happy.'"

The Hon. Thaddeus Stevens told me that on one occasion he called at the White House with an elderly lady, in great trouble, whose son had been in the army, but for some offence had been court-martialled, and sentenced either to death, or imprisonment at hard labor for a long term. There were some extenuating circumstances; and after a full hearing, the President turned to the representative, and said: "Mr. Stevens, do you think this is a case which will warrant my interference?" "With my knowledge of the facts and the parties," was the reply, "I should have no hesitation in granting a pardon." "Then," returned Mr. Lincoln, "I will pardon him," and he proceeded forthwith to execute the paper. The gratitude of the mother was too deep for expression, and not a word was said between her and Mr. Stevens until they were half way down the stairs on their passage out, when she suddenly broke forth in an excited manner with the words, "I knew it was a copperhead lie!" "What do you refer to, madam?" asked Mr. Stevens. "Why, they told me he was an ugly looking man," she replied, with vehemence. "He is the handsomest man I ever saw in my life!" And surely for that mother, and for many another throughout the land, no carved statue of ancient or modern art, in all its symmetry, can have the charm which will for evermore encircle that careworn but gentle face, expressing as lineaments of ruler never expressed before, "Malice towards none—Charity for all."

Though kind-hearted almost to a fault, nevertheless Mr. Lincoln always endeavored to be *just*. The Hon. S. F. Miller, of New York, called upon him one day with the brother of a deserter who had been arrested. The excuse was that the soldier had been home on a sick-furlough, and that he afterwards became partially insane, and had consequently failed to return and report in proper time. He was on his way to his regiment at the front to be tried. The President at once ordered him to be stopped at Alexandria and sent before a board of surgeons for examination as to the question of insanity. "This seemed to me so proper," said the representative, "that I expressed myself satisfied. But on going out, the brother, who was anxious for an immediate discharge, said to me, 'The trouble with your President is, that he is so afraid of doing something wrong.'"

A young man, connected with a New York regiment, had become to all appearance a hardened criminal. He had deserted two or three times, and, when at last detected and imprisoned, had attempted to poison his guards, one of whom subsequently died from the effects of the poison unconsciously taken. Of course, there seemed no defence possible in such a case. But the fact came out that the boy had been of unsound mind. Some friends of his mother took up the matter, and an appeal was made to the Secretary of War. He declined, positively, to listen to it,—the case was too aggravating. The prisoner (scarcely more than a boy) was confined at Elmira, New York. The day for the execution of his sentence had nearly arrived, when his mother made her way to the President. He listened to her story, examined the record, and said that his opinion accorded with that of the Secretary of War; he could do nothing for her. Heart-broken, she was compelled to relinquish her last hope. One of the friends who had become interested, upon learning the result of the application, waited upon Senator Harris. That gentleman said that his engagements utterly precluded his going to see the President upon the subject, until twelve o'clock of the second night following. This brought the time to Wednesday night, and the sentence was to be executed on Thursday. Judge Harris, true to his word, called at the White House at twelve o'clock Wednesday night. The President had retired, but the interview was granted. The point made was that the boy was insane,—thus irresponsible, and his execution would be murder. Pardon was not asked, but a reprieve, until a proper medical examination could be made. This was so reasonable that Mr. Lincoln acquiesced in its justice. He immediately ordered a telegram sent to Elmira, delaying the execution of the sentence. Early the next morning he sent another, by a different line, and, before the hour of execution arrived, he had sent no less than *four* different reprieves, by different lines, to different individuals in Elmira, so fearful was he that the message would fail, or be too late.

This incident suggests another, similar only, however, in the fact that both boys were alleged to be irresponsible. A washerwoman in Troy had a son nearly imbecile as to intellect, yet of good physical proportions. The boy was kidnapped, or inveigled away by some scoundrels, who "enlisted" him, dividing his bounty among themselves. For some time his mother could learn nothing of him. At length she was told that he was in the army. Alone and unfriended she went to Washington to see, in her simplicity, if she could not get his discharge. The gentleman who related the circumstance to me said that she did not even know to which of the New York regiments her son belonged. She could get no chance to speak to the President. At length she watched her opportunity, and intercepted him on his way from the War Department. The result was, that taking down the lad's name and place of residence, this message was written on the back of the card, and sent to the War Department:—

"This poor boy is said to be idiotic. Find him, if possible, and return him to his mother.   A. LINCOLN."

"Calling," says Mr. Colfax, "upon the President one morning in the winter of 1863, I found him looking more than usually pale and careworn, and inquired the reason. He replied, with the bad news he had received at a late hour the previous night, which had not yet been communicated to the press,—he had not closed his eyes or breakfasted; and, with an expression I shall never forget, he exclaimed, 'How willingly would I exchange places to-day with the soldier who sleeps on the ground in the Army of the Potomac.'"

And yet, in the face of such evidence, showing how the great sympathy and sorrow of the late President took hold upon the very roots and springs of his nature, there are not found wanting assertions that he showed a criminal indifference to the sufferings of our prisoners at Libby, Andersonville, and other places; and, in proof of this, it is stated that there is no record of his ever alluding to the subject in any of his public addresses or messages. The questions involved in the suspension of the exchange of prisoners are difficult of decision. Whoever was the cause of this, certainly has fearful responsibility. That it was the President's fault, I do not believe. When the reports, in an authentic form, first reached Washington of the sufferings of the Union prisoners, I know he was greatly excited and overcome by them. He was told that justice demanded a stern retaliation. He said to his friend Mr. Odell, with the deepest emotion: "*I can never, never starve men like that!*" "*Whatever others may say or do, I never can, and I never will, be accessory to such treatment of human beings!*" And although he spoke with the deepest feeling at the Baltimore Fair of the Fort Pillow massacre, and pledged retaliation, yet that pledge was never carried into execution. It was simply impossible for Mr. Lincoln to be cruel or vindictive, no matter what the occasion. In the serene light of history, when party strife and bitterness shall have passed away, it will be seen that, if he erred at all, it was always on the side of mercy and magnanimity.

LIV.

At a private dinner-party at Willard's Hotel, given by Charles Gould, Esq., of New York, I met for the first time the Hon. Hugh McCulloch, then Comptroller of the Currency. An acquaintance commenced, under circumstances calculated to inspire in me a sentiment of profound respect for this gentleman's character and talents. I was much interested, a few days afterward, in an incident in the career of Mr. McCulloch, given me by the Rev. John Pierpont, who was an occasional visitor at the studio, and who, in his hale old age, was occupying one of the subordinate positions in the Department.

The desk at which Dr. Pierpont was occupied was in a room with those of a large number of other clerks, among whom the tall figure and silvery beard of the poet-preacher were very conspicuous. One day, just after Mr. McCulloch had entered upon his duties in Washington, it was announced at the entrance of this room, that the new Comptroller had called to see "Dr. Pierpont." The clerks looked up from their books, and at one another, inquiringly, as Mr. McCulloch took a seat by the poet's desk. "I perceive, Dr. Pierpont," said he, "that you do no remember me?" The venerable preacher looked at him a moment, and replied that he did not think he ever had seen him before. "Oh yes, you have," returned the Comptroller; "I was a member of——Class, in Cambridge, in 1833 and '34, and used to hear you preach. Upon leaving the Law School, purposing to take up my residence at the West, I called upon you and requested one or two letters of introduction to parties in Cincinnati. You gave me two letters, one to a Mr. S——, and the other to a Mr. G——, of that city. Those letters, my dear sir, were the stepping-stones to my fortune. I have not seen you since; but learning that you were in Washington, I told my wife, upon leaving home to take the position offered me here, that the first call I made in Washington should be upon the Rev. John Pierpont." As the Comptroller concluded, Dr. Pierpont put on his spectacles, and looked at him a moment in silence. He at length said:—"Why, Mr. McCulloch, you are the most extraordinary man I ever saw in my life!" "How so?" was the reply. "Why, you have remembered a favor for thirty years."

Dr. Pierpont told me, on another occasion, that in the prosecution of a duty once assigned him in the Department, he had to review a letter-book, containing correspondence with the different officers of the government. Among the letters was a private note, written by Secretary Chase to the Secretary of War, calling his attention to a complaint, made by the colored people of Cincinnati, against certain orders, or officers of the War Department. The letter closed with these words:—

"We cannot afford to lose the support of any part of our people. One poor man, colored though he be, with God on his side, is stronger *against* us than the hosts of the rebellion."

LV.

On the 30th of June, Washington was thrown into a ferment, by the resignation of Mr. Chase as Secretary of the Treasury. The publication, some weeks before, of the "'Pomeroy' secret circular," in the interest of Mr. Chase, as a presidential candidate, had created much talk, and considerable bad feeling in the party. The President, however, took no part in the discussion, or criticism, which followed;—on the contrary, he manifested a sincere desire to preserve pleasant relations, and harmo-

nize existing differences in the Cabinet. In proof of this, I remember his sending one day for Judge Lewis, the Commissioner
of Internal Revenue, and entering into a minute explanation of
a misapprehension, which he conceived the Secretary of the
Treasury to be laboring under; expressing the wish that the
Commissioner would mediate, on his behalf, with Mr. Chase.

Many sincere friends of Secretary Chase considered his
resignation, at this juncture, unfortunate and ill-timed. The
financial situation was more threatening than at any period
during the war. Mr. Chase's administration of the Treasury
Department, amid unparalleled difficulties, had been such as to
secure the confidence and satisfaction of the masses; and his
withdrawal at such a time was regarded as a public calamity,
giving rise to the suspicion that he apprehended national in-
solvency. The resignation, however had been twice tendered
before,—the *third* time it was accepted.

I never saw the President under so much excitement as on
the day following this event. Without consultation or advice, so
far as I ever could learn, he sent to the Senate, the previous
afternoon, the name of Ex-Governor Todd, of Ohio, for the
successorship. This nomination was not popular, and great relief was experienced the next morning, when it was announced
that Governor Todd had declined the position. Mr. Lincoln
passed an anxious night. He received the telegram from Governor Todd, declining the nomination, in the evening. Retiring,

he laid awake some hours, canvassing in his mind the merits of various public men. At length he settled upon the Hon. William P. Fessenden, of Maine; and soon afterward fell asleep. The next morning he went to his office and wrote the nomination. John Hay, the assistant private secretary, had taken it from the President on his way to the Capitol, when he encountered Senator Fessenden upon the threshold of the room. As chairman of the Finance Committee, he also had passed an anxious night, and called thus early to consult with the President, and offer some suggestions. After a few moments' conversation, Mr. Lincoln turned to him with a smile, and said: "I am obliged to you, Fessenden, but the fact is, I have just sent your own name to the Senate for Secretary of the Treasury. Hay had just received the nomination from my hand as you entered." Mr. Fessenden was taken completely by surprise, and, very much agitated, protested his inability to accept the position. The state of his health, he said, if no other consideration, made it impossible. Mr. Lincoln would not accept the refusal as final. He very justly felt that with Mr. Fessenden's experience and known ability at the head of the Finance Committee, his acceptance would go far toward reëstablishing a feeling of security. He said to him, very earnestly, "Fessenden, *the* LORD *has not deserted me thus far, and He is not going to now,*—you must accept!" They separated, the Senator in great anxiety of mind. Throughout the day, Mr. Lincoln urged almost all who called to go and see Mr. Fessenden, and press upon him the duty of accepting. Among these was a delegation of New York bankers, who, in the name of the banking community, expressed their satisfaction at the nomination. This was especially gratifying to the President; and, in the strongest manner, he entreated them to "see Mr. Fessenden and assure him of their support."

I am tempted, just here, to introduce a circumstance which occurred in the course of the day, in which the President and myself were the only actors. In the solitude of the state dining-room, I resumed my work, as usual, that morning; but my mind had been too distracted over night for success. Participating in the general solicitude, I also had been intently revolving the question of a successor to Mr. Chase. Unaccustomed to political currents, and rejecting all considerations of *this* character in a candidate, my thought fastened upon Comptroller McCulloch, as the man for the crisis. His name, at that time, singular as it may seem, had not been suggested by any one, so far as I knew,—certainly no newspaper had advocated his merits or claims. I was at length impelled, by the force of the convictions which engaged my mind, to lay down my palette and brushes, and go upstairs and state them to the President.

Improving the first opportunity when we were left alone, I said, half playfully,—"Mr. President, would you like the opinion of a painter as to who would make a good Secretary of the Treasury?" He looked at me a moment, and said: "Yes, I think I would.

What is your advice?" Said I, "Nominate Hugh McCulloch." "Why," said he, "what do you know of McCulloch?" "Mr. President," I rejoined, "you know painters are thought generally to have very little knowledge of financial matters. I admit that this is true, so far as *I* am concerned; but I do claim to know something of *men*, from the study of character as expressed in *faces*. Now, in my humble judgment, McCulloch is the most suitable man in the community for the position. First; his ability and integrity are unquestionable. Second; as Comptroller of the Currency, he is fully acquainted with the past, present, and proposed future policy of Secretary Chase, and the entire 'machinery' of the Department. Third; he is a practical financier. Having made finance the study of his life, it is obvious he is already educated to the position; whereas, a man taken from the political arena would have everything to learn, and then even, his judgment would be distrusted." Upon this Mr. Lincoln said, with emphasis,—"I believe McCulloch is a very good man!" I think he repeated this once or twice. My errand accomplished, I returned to my labor, satisfied that the instincts of the President could be safely trusted with this, as with other matters; and that, though he might temporarily err, he would ultimately solve the question satisfactorily.

LVI.

Much has been said and written, since Mr. Lincoln's death, in regard to his religious experience and character. Two or three stories have been published, bearing upon this point, which I have never been able to trace to a reliable source; and I feel impelled to state my belief that the facts in the case—if there were such—have received in some way an unwarranted embellishment. Of all men in the world, the late President was the most unaffected and truthful. He rarely or never used language loosely or carelessly, or for the sake of compliment. He was the most indifferent to the effect he was producing, either upon official representatives or the common people, of any man ever in public position.

In the ordinary acceptation of the term, I would scarcely have called Mr. Lincoln a *religious* man,—and yet I believe him to have been a sincere *Christian*. A constitutional tendency to dwell upon sacred things, an emotional nature which finds ready expression in religious conversation and revival meetings, the culture and development of the devotional element till the expression of such thought and experience becomes habitual, were not among his characteristics. Doubtless he felt as deeply upon the great questions of the soul and eternity as any other thoughtful man; but the very tenderness and humility of his nature would not permit the exposure of his inmost convictions, except upon the rarest occasions, and to his most intimate friends. And yet, aside from emotional expression, I believe no man had a more abiding sense of his dependence upon God, or faith in the Divine government, and in the power and ultimate triumph of Truth and Right in the world. The Rev. J. P. Thompson, of New York, in an admirable discourse upon the life and character of the departed President, very justly observed: "It is not necessary to appeal to apocryphal stories— which illustrate as much the assurance of his visitors as the simplicity of his faith—for proof of Mr. Lincoln's Christian character." If his daily life and various public addresses and writings do not show this, surely nothing can demonstrate it.

Fortunately there is sufficient material before the public, upon which to form a judgment in this respect, without resorting to apocryphal resources.

The Rev. Mr. Willets, of Brooklyn, gave me an account of a conversation with Mr. Lincoln, on the part of a lady of his acquaintance, connected with the "Christian Commission," who in the prosecution of her duties had several interviews with him. The President, it seemed, had been much impressed with the devotion and earnestness of purpose manifested by the lady, and on one occasion, after she had discharged the object of her visit, he said to her: "Mrs.——, I have formed a high opinion of your Christian character, and now, as we are alone, I have a mind to ask you to give me, in brief, your idea of what constitutes a true religious experience." The lady replied at some length, stating that, in her judgment, it consisted of a conviction of one's own sinfulness and weakness, and personal need of the Saviour for strength and support; that views of mere doctrine might and would differ, but when one was really brought to feel his need of Divine help, and to seek the aid of the Holy Spirit for strength and guidance, it was satisfactory evidence of his having been born again. This was the substance of her reply. When she had concluded, Mr. Lincoln was very thoughtful for a few moments. He at length said, very earnestly, "If what you have told me is really a correct view of this great subject, I think I can say with sincerity, that I hope I am a Christian. I had lived," he continued, "until my boy Willie died, without realizing fully these things. That blow overwhelmed me. It showed me my weakness as I had never felt it before, and if I can take what you have stated as a *test*, I think I can safely say that I know something of that *change* of which you speak; and I will further add, that it has been my intention for some time, at a suitable opportunity, to make a public religious profession."

Mr. Noah Brooks, in some "reminiscences," already quoted from in these pages, gives the following upon this subject:—

"Just after the last Presidential election he said, 'Being only mortal, after all, I should have been a little mortified if I had been beaten in this canvass; but that sting would have been more than compensated by the thought that the people had notified me that all my official responsibilities were soon to be lifted off my back.' In reply to the remark that he might remember that in all these cares he was daily remembered by those who prayed, not to be heard of men, as no man had ever before been remembered, he caught at the homely phrase, and said, 'Yes, I like that phrase, "not to be heard of men," and guess it is generally true, as you say; at least, I have been told so, and I have been a good deal helped by just that thought.' Then he solemnly and slowly added: 'I should be the most presumptuous blockhead upon this footstool, if I for one day thought that I could discharge the duties which have come upon me since I came into this place, without the aid and enlightenment of One who is stronger and wiser than all others.'"

"At another time he said cheerfully, 'I am very sure that if I do not go away from here a wiser man, I shall go away a better man, for having learned here what a very poor sort of a man I am.' Afterwards, referring to what he called a change of heart, he said he did not remember any precise time when he passed through any special change of purpose, or of heart; but he would say, that his own election to office, and the crisis immediately following, influentially determined him in what he called 'a process of crystallization,' then going on in his mind. Reticent as he was, and shy of discoursing much of his own mental exercises, these few utterances now have a value with those who knew him, which his dying words would scarcely have possessed."

"On Thursday of a certain week, two ladies, from Tennessee, came before the President, asking the release of their husbands, held as prisoners of war at Johnson's Island. They were put off until Friday, when they came again, and were again put off until Saturday. At each of the interviews one of the ladies urged that her husband was a religious man. On Saturday, when the President ordered the release of the prisoner, he said to this lady,—'You say your husband is a religious man; tell him when you meet him, that I say I am not much of a judge of religion, but that in my opinion the religion which sets men to rebel and fight against their government, because, as they think, that government does not sufficiently help *some* men to eat their bread in the sweat of *other* men's faces, is not the sort of religion upon which people can get to heaven.'"

"On an occasion I shall never forget," says the Hon. H. C. Deming, of Connecticut, "the conversation turned upon religious subjects, and Mr. Lincoln made this impressive remark: 'I have never united myself to any church, because I have found difficulty in giving my assent, without mental reservation, to the long, complicated statements of Christian doctrine which characterize their Articles of Belief and Confessions of Faith. When any church will inscribe over its altar, as its sole qualification for membership,' he continued, 'the Saviour's condensed statement of the substance of both Law and Gospel, "Thou shalt love the Lord thy God with all thy heart, and with all thy soul, and with all thy mind, and thy neighbor as thyself," that church will I join with all my heart and all my soul.'"

At a dinner-party in Washington, composed mainly of opponents of the war and the administration, Mr. Lincoln's course and policy was, as usual with this class, the subject of vehement denunciation. This had gone on for some time, when one of the company, who had taken no part in the discussion, asked the privilege of saying a few words.

"Gentlemen," said he, "you may talk as you please about Mr. Lincoln's capacity; I don't believe him to be the ablest statesman in America, by any means, and I voted against him on both occasions of his candidacy. But I happened to see, or, rather, to hear something, the other day, that convinced me that, however deficient he may be in the head, he is all right in the heart. I was up at the White House, having called to see the President on business. I was shown into the office of his private secretary, and told that Mr. Lincoln was busy just then, but would be disengaged in a short time. While waiting, I heard a very earnest prayer being uttered in a loud female voice in the adjoining room. I inquired what it meant, and was told that an old Quaker lady, a friend of the President's, had called that afternoon and taken tea at the White House, and that she was then praying with Mr. Lincoln. After the lapse of a few minutes the prayer ceased, and the President, accompanied by a Quakeress not less than eighty years old, entered the room where I was sitting. I made up my mind then, gentlemen, that Mr. Lincoln was not a bad man; and I don't think it will be easy to efface the impression that the scene I witnessed and the voice I heard made on my mind!"

Nothing has been given to the public since Mr. Lincoln's death, more interesting and valuable than the following, from the pen of Dr. Holland:—*

"At the time of the nominations at Chicago, Mr. Newton Bateman, Superintendent of Public Instruction for the State of Illinois, occupied a room adjoining and opening into the Executive Chamber at Springfield. Frequently this door was open during Mr. Lincoln's receptions, and throughout the seven months or more of his occupation, he saw him nearly every day. Often when Mr. Lincoln was tired, he closed the door against all intruders, and called Mr. Bateman into his room for a quiet talk. On one of these occasions Mr. Lincoln took up a book containing a careful canvass of the city of Springfield in which he lived, showing the candidate for whom each citizen had declared it his intention to vote in the approaching election. Mr. Lincoln's friends had, doubtless at his own request, placed the result of the canvass in his hands. This was towards the close of October, and only a few days before election. Calling Mr. Bateman to a seat by his side, having previously locked all the doors, he said: 'Let us look over this book; I wish particularly to see how the ministers of Springfield are going to vote.' The leaves were turned, one

---

*Holland's *Life of Abraham Lincoln.*

by one, and as the names were examined Mr. Lincoln frequently asked if this one and that were not a minister, or an elder, or a member of such or such church, and sadly expressed his surprise on receiving an affirmative answer. In that manner they went through the book, and then he closed it and sat silently for some minutes, regarding a memorandum in pencil which lay before him. At length he turned to Mr. Bateman, with a face full of sadness, and said: 'Here are twenty-three ministers, of different denominations, and all of them are against me but three; and here are a great many prominent members of the churches, a very large majority are against me. Mr. Bateman, I am not a Christian,—God knows I would be one,—but I have carefully read the Bible, and I do not so understand this book;' and he drew forth a pocket New Testament. 'These men well know,' he continued, 'that I am for freedom in the Territories, freedom everywhere as free as the Constitution and the laws will permit, and that my opponents are for slavery. They *know* this, and yet, with this book in their hands, in the light of which human bondage cannot live a moment, they are going to vote against me; I do not understand it at all.'

"Here Mr. Lincoln paused,—paused for long minutes,—his features surcharged with emotion. Then he rose and walked up and down the reception-room in the effort to retain or regain his self-possession. Stopping at last, he said, with a trembling voice and his cheeks wet with tears: 'I know there is a God, and that He hates injustice and slavery. I see the storm coming, and I know that his hand is in it. If He has a place and work for me—and I think He has—I believe I am ready. I am nothing, but Truth is everything. I know I am right, because I know that liberty is right, for Christ teaches it, and Christ is God. I have told them that a house divided against itself cannot stand; and Christ and Reason say the same; and they will find it so.'

"'Douglas don't care whether slavery is voted up or down, but God cares, and humanity cares, and I care; and with God's help I shall not fail. I may not see the end; but it will come, and I shall be vindicated; and these men will find that they have not read their Bibles right.'

"Much of this was uttered as if he was speaking to himself, and with a sad, earnest solemnity of manner impossible to be described. After a pause, he resumed: 'Doesn't it appear strange that men can ignore the moral aspect of this contest? A revelation could not make it plainer to me that slavery or the Government must be destroyed. The future would be something awful, as I look at it, but for this rock on which I stand,' (alluding to the Testament which he still held in his hand,) 'especially with the knowledge of how these ministers are going to vote. It seems as if God had borne with this thing [slavery] until the very teachers of religion had come to defend it from the Bible, and to claim for it a divine character and sanction; and now the cup of iniquity is full, and the vials of wrath will be poured out.' After this the conversation was continued for along time. Everything he said was of a peculiarly deep, tender, and religious tone, and all was tinged with a touching melancholy. He repeatedly referred to his conviction that the day of wrath was at hand, and that he was to be an actor in the terrible struggle which would issue in the overthrow of slavery, though he might not live to see the end.

"After further reference to a belief in Divine Providence, and the fact of God in history, the conversation turned upon prayer. He freely stated his belief in the duty, privilege, and efficacy of prayer, and intimated, in no unmistakable terms, that he had sought in that way the Divine guidance and favor. The effect of this conversation upon the mind of Mr. Bateman, a Christian gentleman whom Mr. Lincoln profoundly respected, was to convince him that Mr. Lincoln had, in his quiet way, found a path to the Christian standpoint—that he had found God, and rested on the eternal truth of God. As the two men were about to separate, Mr. Bateman remarked: 'I have not supposed that you were accustomed to think so much upon this class of subjects; certainly your friends generally are ignorant of the sentiments you have expressed to me.' He replied quickly: 'I know they are, but I think more on these subjects than upon all others, and I have done so for years; and I am willing you should know it.'"

Schuyler Colfax once said to me that "Mr. Lincoln had two ruling ideas, or principles, which governed his life. The first was hatred of slavery, which he inherited in part from his parents; the other was sympathy with the lowly born and humble, and the desire to lift them up." I know of no better epitaph for his tombstone than this, save that suggested by Theodore Tilton, the editor of the New York "Independent,"—"He bound the nation, and unbound the slave."

LVII.

On the Fourth of July an unprecedented event was witnessed in Washington. By special consent of the President, the White House grounds were granted to the colored people of the city for a grand Sunday-school festival, and never did they present a busier or more jubilant scene. Inside the grounds a platform was erected, upon which accommodations were placed for speakers. Around this were rows of benches, which, during the greater part of the day, were not only well filled but crowded. Meanwhile groups reposed under every tree or walked to and fro along the shaded paths. From the thick-leaved branches of the trees were suspended swings, of which all, both old and young, made abundant use. Every contrivance which could add to the pleasure of the time was brought into energetic requisition, and altogether no celebration of the day presented a greater appearance of enjoyment and success.

By the Act of Emancipation, Mr. Lincoln built for himself the first place in the affections of the African race on this continent. The love and reverence manifested for his name and person on all occasions during the last two years of his life, by this down-trodden people, were always remarkable, and sometimes of a thrilling character. In the language of one of the poor creatures who stood weeping and moaning at the gateway of the avenue in front of the White House, while the beloved remains were lying in state in the East Room, "*they* had him.*"

No public testimonial of regard, it is safe to say, gave Mr. Lincoln more sincere pleasure during his entire public life, than that presented by the colored people of the city of Baltimore, in the summer of 1864, consisting of an elegant copy of the Holy Bible. The volume was of the usual pulpit size, bound in violet-colored velvet. The corners were bands of solid gold, and carved upon a plate also of gold, not less than one fourth of an inch thick. Upon the left-hand cover, was design representing the President in a cotton-field knocking the shackles off the wrists of a slave, who held one hand aloft as if invoking blessings upon the head of his benefactor,—at whose feet was a scroll upon which was written "Emancipation"; upon the other cover was a similar plate bearing the inscription:—

"To ABRAHAM LINCOLN, President of the United States, the friend of Universal Freedom. From the loyal colored people of Baltimore, as a token of respect and gratitude. Baltimore, July 4th, 1864."

The presentation was made by a committee of colored people, consisting of three clergymen and two laymen, who were received by the President in the most cordial manner, after which the Rev. S. W. Chase, on the part of the committee, said:—

"MR. PRESIDENT: The loyal colored people of Baltimore have delegated to us the authority to present this Bible, as a token of their appreciation of your humane part towards the people of our race. While all the nation are offering their tributes of respect, we cannot let the occasion pass by without tendering ours. Since we have been incorporated in the American family we have been true and loyal, and we now stand by, ready to defend the country. We are ready to be armed and trained in military matters, in order to protect and defend the Star-spangled Banner.

"Our hearts will ever feel the most unbounded gratitude towards you. We come forward to present a copy of the Holy Scriptures as a token of respect to you for your active part in the cause of emancipation. This great event will be a matter of history. In future, when our sons shall ask what mean these tokens, they will be told of your mighty acts, and rise up and call you blessed.

"The loyal colored people will remember your Excellency at the throne of Divine Grace. May the King Eternal, an all-wise Providence, protect and keep you, and when you pass from this world, may you be borne to the bosom of your Saviour and God."

The President, in reply, said:—

"It would be a very fitting occasion to make a response at length to the very appropriate address which you have just made. I would do so if I were prepared. I would promise you to make a response in writing, had not experience taught me that business will not allow me to do so. I can only say now, as I have often said before, it has always been a sentiment with me that all mankind should be free.

"So far as I have been able, so far as came within my sphere, I have always acted as I believed was right and just, and done all I could for the good of mankind. I have, in letters and documents sent forth from this office, expressed myself better than I can now. In regard to the great book, I have only to say, it is the best gift which God has ever given man.

"All the good from the Saviour of the World is communicated to us through this book. But for that book we could not know right from wrong. All those things desirable to man are contained in it. I return you my sincere thanks for this very elegant copy of the great book of God which you present."

After some time spent in the examination of the gift, which drew out many expressions of admiration from the President, the party withdrew, Mr. Lincoln taking each of them by the hand as they passed out.

Caroline Johnson, an estimable colored woman of Philadelphia, an active nurse in the hospitals during the war, who had once been a slave, as an expression of reverence and affection for President Lincoln, prepared, with much taste and ingenuity, a superb collection of wax fruits, together with a stem-table, appropriately ornamented, which she desired to present to the President. Through a friend an opportunity was secured, and she went to Washington, with her minister, to attend personally to the setting up of the stand and fruit.

The result is given by a correspondent of the "Anti-Slavery Standard," in her own words:—

"The Commissioner, Mr. Newton, received us kindly, and sent the box to the White House, with directions that it should not be opened until I came. The next day was reception day, but the President sent me word that he would receive me at one o'clock. I went and arranged the table, placing it in the centre of the room. Then I was introduced to the President and his wife. He stood next to me; then Mrs. Lincoln, Mr. Newton, and the minister; the others outside. Mr. Hamilton (the minister) made an appropriate speech, and at the conclusion said: 'Perhaps Mrs. Johnson would like to say a few words?' I looked down to the floor, and felt that I had not a word to say, but after a moment or two, the fire began to burn, (laying her hand on her breast,) and it burned and burned till it went all over me. I think it was the Spirit, and I looked up to him and said: 'Mr. President, I believe God has hewn you out of a rock, for this great and mighty purpose. Many have been led away by bribes of gold, of silver, of presents; but you have stood firm, because God was with you, and if you are faithful to the end, he will be with you.' With his eyes full of tears, he walked round and examined the present, pronounced it beautiful, thanked me kindly, but said: 'You must not give me the praise—it belongs to God.'"

LVIII.

"Sojourner Truth," the slave preacher whom Mrs. Stowe has described as embodying all the elements of an African prophetess or sibyl, when over eighty years old, left her home, at Battlecreek, Michigan, with the unalterable purpose of seeing the Emancipator of her race before her death. Provided for throughout her journey, she reached Washington the last of October, 1864, and subsequently, at her dictation, the following account of her interview with Mr. Lincoln was written out by a friend:—

"It was about eight o'clock, A.M., when I called on the President. Upon entering his reception-room we found about a dozen persons in waiting, among them two colored women. I had quite a pleasant time waiting until he was disengaged, and enjoyed his conversation with others; he showed as much kindness and consideration to the colored persons as to the whites,—if there was any difference, more. One case was that of a colored woman, who was sick and likely to be turned out of her house on account of her inability to pay her rent. The President listened to her with much attention, and spoke to her with kindness and tenderness. He said he had given so much he could give no more, but told her where to go and get the money, and asked Mrs. C——, who accompanied me, to assist her, which she did.

"The President was seated at his desk. Mrs. C. said to him: 'This is Sojourner Truth, who has come all the way from Michigan to see you.' He then arose, gave me his hand, made a bow, and said: 'I am pleased to see you.'

"I said to him: 'Mr. President, when you first took your seat I feared you would be torn to pieces, for I likened you unto Daniel, who was thrown into the lions' den; and if the lions did not tear you into pieces, I knew that it would be God that had saved you; and I said if He spared me I would see you before the four years expired, and He has done so, and now I am here to see you for myself.'

"He then congratulated me on my having been spared. Then I said: 'I appreciate you, for you are the best President who has ever taken the seat.' He replied thus: 'I expect you have reference to my having emancipated the slaves in my proclamation. But,' said he, mentioning the names of several of his predecessors, (and among them emphatically that of Washington,) 'they were all just as good, and would have done just as I have done if the time had come. If the people over the river (pointing across the Potomac) had behaved themselves, I could not have done what I have; but they did not, and I was compelled to do these things.' I then said: 'I thank God that you were the instrument selected by Him and the people to do it.'

"He then showed me the Bible presented to him by the colored people of Baltimore, of which you have heard. I have seen it for myself, and it is beautiful beyond description. After I had looked it over, I said to him: 'This is beautiful indeed; the colored people have given this to the Head of the Government, and that Government once sanctioned laws that would not permit its people to learn enough to enable them to read this Book. And for what? Let them answer who can.'

"I must say, and I am proud to say, that I never was treated by any one with more kindness and cordiality than was shown me by that great and good man, Abraham Lincoln, by the grace of God President of the United States for four years more. He took my little book, and with the same hand that signed the death-warrant of slavery, he wrote as follows:—

'For Aunty Sojourner Truth,
    'Oct. 29, 1864.   A. LINCOLN.'

"As I was taking my leave, he arose and took my hand, and said he would be pleased to have me call again. I felt that I was in the presence of a friend, and I now thank God from the bottom of my heart that I always have advocated his cause, and have done it openly and boldly. I shall feel still more in duty bound to do so in time to come. May God assist me."

Mr. Lincoln's cordial reception of Frederick Douglass, the distinguished anti-slavery orator, also once a slave, was widely made known through that gentleman's own account of it in one his public lectures.

In August or September, 1864, Mr. Douglass again visited Washington. The President heard of his being in the city, and greatly desiring a second conversation upon points on which he considered the opinion and advice of a man of Mr. Douglass's antecedents valuable, he sent his carriage to the boarding-house where he was staying, with a request that Mr. D. would "come up and take a cup of tea" with him. The invitation was accepted; and probably never before, in our history, was the executive carriage employed to convey *such* a guest to the White House. Mr. Douglass subsequently remarked that "Mr. Lincoln was one of the few white men he ever passed an hour with, who failed to remind him in some way, before the interview terminated, that he was a 'negro.'"

A memorial, on a certain occasion, was presented to the President from the children and young people of Concord, Mass., petitioning for the freedom of all slave children. In reply, he wrote the following:—

"Tell those little people I am very glad their young hearts are so full of just and generous sympathy, and that while I have not the power to grant all they ask, I trust they will remember that GOD has; and that as it seems He *wills* to do it.

A. LINCOLN."

LIX.

"On New Year's day, 1865," wrote a correspondent of the New York "Independent," "a memorable incident occurred, of which the like was never before seen at the White House. I had noticed, at sundry times during the summer, the wild fervor and strange enthusiasm which our colored friends always manifest over the name of Abraham Lincoln. His name with them seems to be associated with that of his namesake, the Father of the Faithful. In the great crowds which gather from time to time in front of the White House, in honor of the President, none shout so loudly or so wildly, and swing their hats with such utter abandon, while their eyes are beaming with the intensest joy, as do these simple-minded and grateful people. I have often laughed heartily at these exhibitions. But the scene yesterday excited far other emotions. As I entered the door of the President's House, I noticed groups of colored people gathered here and there, who seemed to be watching earnestly the inpouring throng. For nearly two hours they hung around, until the crowd of white visitors began sensibly to diminish. Then they summoned up courage, and began timidly to approach the door. Some of them were richly and gayly dressed; some were in tattered garments, and other in the most fanciful and grotesque costume. All pressed eagerly forward. When they came into the presence of the President, doubting as to their reception, the feelings of the poor creatures overcame them, and here the scene baffles my powers of description.

"For two long hours Mr. Lincoln had been shaking the hands of the 'sovereigns,' and had become excessively weary, and his grasp languid; but here his nerves rallied at the unwonted sight, and he welcomed this motley crowd with a heartiness that made them wild with exceeding joy. They laughed and wept, and wept and laughed,—exclaiming, through their blinding tears: 'God bless you!' 'God bless Abraham Lincoln!' 'God bress Massa Linkum!' Those who witnessed this scene will not soon forget it. For a long distance down the Avenue, on my way home, I heard fast young men cursing the President for this act; but all the way the refrain rang in my ears,—'God bless Abraham Lincoln!'"

Miss Betsey Canedy, of Fall River, Massachusetts, while engaged in teaching a school among the colored people of Norfolk, Virginia, had in her school-room a plaster bust of the President. One day she called some colored carpenters who were at work on the building, and showed it to them, writing down their remarks, some of which were as follows:—

"He's brought us safe through the Red Sea." "He looks as deep as the sea himself." "He's king of the United States." "He ought to be king of all the world." "We must all pray to the Lord to carry him safe through, for it 'pears like he's got everything hitched to him." "There has been a right smart praying for him, and it mustn't stop now."

A southern correspondent of the New York "Tribune," in Charleston, South Carolina, the week following the assassination, wrote:—

"I never saw such sad faces, or heard such heavy hearts beatings, as here in Charleston the day the dreadful news came! The colored people—the native loyalists—were like children bereaved of an only and loved parent. I saw one old woman going up the street wringing her hands and saying aloud, as she walked looking straight before her, so absorbed in her grief that she noticed no one,—

"'O Lord! O Lord! O Lord! Massa Sam's dead! Massa Sam's dead! O Lord! Massa Sam's dead!'

"'Who's dead, Aunty?' I asked her.

"'Massa Sam!' she said, not looking at me,—renewing her lamentations: 'O Lord! O Lord! Lord! Massa Sam's dead!'

"'Who's Massa Sam?' I asked.

"'Uncle Sam!' she said. 'O Lord! Lord!

"I was not quite sure that she meant the President, and I spoke again:—

"'Who's Massa Sam, Aunty?'

"'Mr. Lincum!' she said, and resumed wringing her hands and moaning in utter hopelessness of sorrow. The poor creature was too ignorant to comprehend any difference between the very unreal Uncle Sam and the actual President; but her heart told her that he whom Heaven had sent in answer to her prayers was lying in a bloody grave, and she and her race were left—*fatherless*."

In 1863, Colonel McKaye, of New York, with Robert Dale Owen and one or two other gentlemen, were associated as a committee to investigate the condition of the freedmen on the coast of North Carolina. Upon their return from Hilton Head they reported to the President; and in the course of the interview Colonel McKaye related the following incident.

He had been speaking of the ideas of power entertained by these people. He said they had an idea of God, as the Almighty, and they had realized in their former condition the power of their masters. Up to the time of the arrival among them of the Union forces, they had no knowledge of any other power. Their masters fled upon the approach of our soldiers, and this gave the slaves a conception of a power greater than that exercised by them. This power they called "Massa Linkum."

Colonel McKaye said that their place of worship was a large building which they called "the praise house;" and the leader of the meeting, a venerable black man, was known as "the praise man." On a certain day, when there was quite a large gathering of the people, considerable confusion was created by different persons attempting to tell who and what "Massa Linkum" was. In the midst of the excitement the white-headed leader commanded silence. "Brederin," said he, "you don't know nosen' what you'se talkin' 'bout. Now, you just listen to me. Massa Linkum, he everywhar. He know eberyting." Then, solemnly looking up, he added,—"*He walk de earf like de Lord!*"

Colonel McKaye told me that Mr. Lincoln seemed much affected by this account. He did not smile, as another man might have done, but got up from his chair, and walked in silence two or three times across the floor. As he resumed his seat, he said, very impressively: "It is a momentous thing to be the instrument, under Providence, of the liberation of a race."

LX.

The famous "peace" conference, on board the *River Queen*, in Hampton Roads, between President Lincoln and Secretary Seward, and the Rebel commissioners Stephens, Hunter, and Campbell, took place the 3d of February, 1865. A few days afterward* I asked the President if it was true, as reported by the

---

*My "six months" proper, at the White House, terminated, as will be seen, the last week in July, 1864. February and a part of March following I passed in Washington, and was privileged with a renewal of my previous intercourse with Mr. Lincoln.

New York "Herald," that he told a "little story" on that occasion?—"Why," said he, "has it leaked out? I was in hopes nothing would be said about *that*, lest some oversensitive people should imagine there was a degree of levity in the intercourse between us." He then went on to relate the circumstances which called it out. "You see," said he, "we had reached and were discussing the *slavery* question. Mr. Hunter said, substantially, that the slaves, always accustomed to an overseer, and to work upon compulsion, suddenly freed, as they would be if the South should consent to peace on the basis of the 'Emancipation Proclamation,' would precipitate not only themselves but the entire Southern society into irremediable ruin. No work would be done, nothing would be cultivated, and both blacks and whites would *starve!*" Said the President, "I waited for Seward to answer that argument, but as he was silent, I at length said: 'Mr. Hunter, *you* ought to know a great deal better about this matter than *I*, for you have always lived under the slave system. I can only say, in reply to your statement of the case, that it reminds me of a man out in Illinois, by the name of Case, who undertook, a few years ago, to raise a very large herd of hogs. It was a great trouble to *feed* them, and how to get around this was a puzzle to him. At length he hit on the plan of planting an immense field of potatoes, and, when they were sufficiently grown, he turned the whole herd into the field, and let them have full swing, thus saving not only the labor of feeding the hogs, but also that of digging the potatoes. Charmed with his sagacity, he stood one day leaning against the fence, counting his hogs, when a neighbor came along. 'Well, well,' said he, 'Mr. Case, this is all very fine. Your hogs are doing very well just now, but you know out here in Illinois the frost comes early, and the ground freezes a foot deep. Then what are they going to do?' This was a view of the matter Mr. Case had not taken into account. Butchering-time for hogs was 'way on in December or January. He scratched his head, and at length stammered, 'Well, it may come pretty hard on their *snouts*, but I don't see but that it will be "root, hog, or die!"'

"Shortly afterward," he continued, "a reference was casually made to Colonel Hardin, who was killed in the Mexican War,—who at one time was a representative in Congress from Illinois; and this drew out a story from Stephens. 'On a certain occasion,' he said, 'when the House was in session, a dispute arose between Hardin and others of the Illinois delegation as to the proper pronunciation of the name of their State. Some insisted it was "*Illinoy*," others as stoutly that it was "*Illinois*." Hardin at length appealed to the venerable John Quincy Adams. "If one were to judge from the character of the representatives in this Congress from that State," said the old man, with a malicious smile, "I should decide unhesitatingly that the proper pronunciation was '*All noise!*'"""

In the Augusta (Ga.) "Chronicle," of the 17th of June, 1865, there appeared a report of this conference, purporting to have been written out from the lips of Mr. Stephens, so characteristic of Mr. Lincoln, that I subjoin the following extracts:—

"There three Southern gentlemen met Mr. Lincoln and Mr. Seward, and after some preliminary remarks, the subject of peace was opened. Mr. Stephens, well aware that one who asks much may get more than he who confesses to humble wishes at the outset, urged the claims of his section with that skill and address for which the Northern papers have given him credit. Mr. Lincoln, holding the vantage-ground of conscious power, was, however, perfectly frank, and submitted his views almost in the form of an argument.

. . . "Davis had on this occasion, as on that of Mr. Stephens's visit to Washington, made it a condition that no conference should be had unless his rank as commander or President should first be recognized. Mr. Lincoln declared that the only ground on which he could rest the justice of the war— either with his own people or with foreign powers—was that it was not a war for conquest, for that the States had never been separated from the Union. Consequently, he could not recognize another government inside of the one of which he alone was President, nor admit the separate independence of States that were yet a part of the Union. 'That,' said he, 'would be doing what you have so long asked Europe to do in vain, and be resigning the only thing the armies of the Union are fighting for.'

"Mr. Hunter made a long reply to this, insisting that the recognition of Davis's power to make a treaty was the first and indispensable step to peace, and referred to the correspondence between King Charles I and his Parliament, as a trustworthy precedent of a constitutional ruler treating with rebels.

"Mr. Lincoln's face then wore that indescribable expression which generally preceded his hardest hits, and he remarked: 'Upon questions of history I must refer you to Mr. Seward, for he is posted in such things, and I don't pretend to be bright. My only distinct recollection of the matter is, that Charles lost his head.' That settled Mr. Hunter for a while."

* * * * * * * *

"During the interview it appears that Hunter declared that he had never entertained any fears for his person of life from so mild a government as that of the United States. To which Mr. Lincoln retorted that he, also, had felt easy as to the Rebels, but not always so easy about the lamp-posts around Washington City,—a hint that he had already done more favors for the Rebels than was exactly popular with the radical men of his own party.

"Mr. Lincoln's manner had now grown more positive. He suggested that it would be better for the Rebel States to return at once than to risk the chances of continuing the war, and the increasing bitterness of feeling in Congress. The time might come, he said, when they would not be considered as an erring people invited back to citizenship, but would be looked upon as enemies to be exterminated or ruined.

"During the conference, the amendment to the Federal Constitution, which has just been adopted by Congress, was read, providing that neither slavery nor involuntary servitude, except for crime, should exist with the United States, or any place within its jurisdiction, and Congress should have power to enforce the amendment by appropriate legislation." The report says, "Mr. Seward then remarked: Mr. President, it is as well to inform these gentlemen that yesterday Congress acted upon the amendment of the Constitution abolishing slavery."

"Mr. Lincoln stated this to be true, and suggested that there was a question as to the right of the insurgent States to return at once and claim a right to vote upon the amendment, to which the concurrence of two thirds of the States was required. He stated that it would be desirable to have the institution of slavery abolished by the consent of the people as soon as possible,—he hoped with six years. He also stated that four hundred millions of dollars might be offered as compensation to the owners, and remarked, 'You would be surprised were I to give you the names of those who favor that.'"

*   *   *   *   *   *   *   *

"Mr. Stephens came home with a new cause of sorrow, and those who said he talked of coming home to make war speeches and denounce the terms offered, simply lied. Before Mr. Lincoln's death, he thought he was doing a favor to him not to include that offer of four hundred millions in gold for the Southern slaves in the published report, for it would be used to the injury of Mr. Lincoln by those of his enemies who talk about taxation and the debt.

"Mr. Stephens has frequently expressed no apprehensions should the fortunes of war throw him into the hands of Mr. Lincoln, and said he would not get out of the way of a raid were it not for appearances, on account of the office he held. He spoke of Mr. Lincoln as an old friend who had generally voted with him in Congress, and who had a good heart and fine mind, and was undoubtedly honest."

LXI.

Visitors to the Executive Chamber, during the administration of Mr. Lincoln, will remember the lithographic map, showing the slave population of the Southern States in graduated

light and shade, which usually leaned against a leg of his desk
or table, and bore the marks of much service. The States and
counties most abounding in slaves were indicated on this map
by degrees of blackness, so that by a glance the proportion of
whites and blacks in the different States at the commencement
of the Rebellion could be easily comprehended.

Wishing to introduce this map into my picture, I carried it
off one day, without the President's knowledge, and as the
copying of it was a tedious affair, it remained in the studio for
some time. This chanced to be during the week of Kilpatrick's
great cavalry raid in Virginia. One afternoon the President
came in alone, as was his wont,—the observation of the daily
progress of the picture appearing to afford him a species of
recreation. Presently his eye fell upon the map, leaning against
a chair, as I had left it after making the study. "Ah!" said he,
"*you* have appropriated my map, have you? I have been looking
all around for it." And with that he put on his spectacles, and,
taking it up, walked to the window; and sitting down upon a
trunk began to pore over it very earnestly. He pointed out
Kilpatrick's position, when last heard from, and said:—

"It is just as I thought it was. He is close upon——County,
where the slaves are thickest. Now we ought to get a 'heap' of
them, when he returns."

This conversation occurred, I recollect, just after his solitary lunch,—the family being away at the time. It was often a

matter of surprise to me how the President sustained life; for it seemed, some weeks, as though he neither ate nor slept. His habits continued as simple as when he was a practising lawyer in Springfield, but they came to be very irregular. During the months of my intercourse with him he rarely entertained company at dinner. Almost daily, at this hour, I met a servant carrying a simple meal upon a tray up-stairs, where it was received, perhaps two hours later, in the most unceremonious manner. I knew this irregularity of life was his own fault; but the wonder as to how his system endured the strain brought to bear upon it was not lessened by this knowledge.

All familiar with him will remember the weary air which became habitual during his last years. This was more of the mind than the body, and no rest and recreation which he allowed himself could relieve it. As he sometimes expressed it, the remedy "seemed never to reach the *tired* spot."

Mr. Lincoln's height was six feet three and three-quarter inches "in his stocking-feet." He stood up, one day, at the right of my large canvas, while I marked his exact height upon it.

His frame was gaunt but sinewy, and inclined to stoop when he walked. His head was of full medium size, with a broad brow, surmounted by rough, unmanageable hair, which, he once said, had "a way of getting up as far as possible in the world." Lines of care ploughed his face,—the hollows in his cheeks and under his eyes being very marked. The mouth was his plainest feature, varying widely from classical models,—nevertheless expressive of much firmness and gentleness of character.

His complexion was inclined to sallowness, though I judged this to be the result in part, of his anxious life in Washington. His eyes were blueish-gray in color,—always in deep shadow, however, from the upper lids, which were unusually heavy, (reminding me, in this respect, of Stuart's portrait of Washington,)—and the expression was remarkably pensive and tender, often inexpressibly sad, as if the reservoir of tears lay very near the surface,—a fact proved not only by the response which accounts of suffering and sorrow invariably drew forth, but by circumstances which would ordinarily affect few men in his position.

The Hon. Mr. Frank, of New York, told me that just after the nomination of Mr. Chase as Chief Justice, a deeply interesting conversation upon this subject took place one evening between himself and the President, in Mrs. Lincoln's private sitting-room. Mr. Lincoln reviewed Mr. Chase's political course and aspirations at some length, alluding to what he had felt to be an estrangement from him personally, and to various sarcastic and bitter expressions reported to him as having been indulged in by the ex-Secretary, both before and after his resignation. The Congressman replied that such reports were always exaggerated, and spoke very warmly of Mr. Chase's great services in the hour of the country's extremity, his patriotism, and integrity to principle. The tears instantly sprang into Mr. Lincoln's eyes. "Yes," said he, "that is true. We have stood together in the time of trial, and I should despise myself if I allowed personal differences to affect my judgment of his fitness for the office of Chief Justice."

LXII.

The President's friend, the Hon. H. C. Deming of Connecticut, once ventured to ask him "if he had ever despaired of the country?" "When the Peninsula campaign terminated suddenly at Harrison's Landing," rejoined Mr. Lincoln, "I was as nearly inconsolable as I could be and live." In the same connection Colonel Deming inquired if there had ever been a period in which he thought that better management upon the part of the commanding general might have terminated the war? "Yes," answered the President, "there were three: at 'Malvern Hill,' when McClellan failed to command an immediate advance upon Richmond; at 'Chancellorville,' when Hooker failed to reënforce Sedgwick, after hearing his cannon upon the extreme right; and at 'Gettysburg,' when Meade failed to attack Lee in his retreat at the bend of the Potomac." After this commentary, the Congressman waited for an outburst of denunciation—for a criticism, at least—upon the delinquent officers; but he waited in vain. So far from a word of censure escaping

Mr. Lincoln's lips, he soon added, that his first remark might not appear uncharitable: "I do not know that I could have given any different orders had I been with them myself. I have not fully made up my mind how I should behave when minie-balls were whistling, and those great oblong shells shrieking in my ear. I might run away."

The interview at which this conversation took place, occurred just after General Fremont had declined to run against him for the presidency. The magnificent Bible which the negroes of Baltimore had just presented to him lay upon the table, and while examining it, Colonel Deming recited the somewhat remarkable passage from the Chronicles: "Eastward were six Levites, northward four a day, southward four a day, and toward Assuppim, two and two. At Parbar westward, four at the causeway, and two at Parbar." The President immediately challenged his friend to find any such passage in *his* Bible. After it was pointed out to him, and he was satisfied of its genuineness, he asked the Congressman if he remembered the text which his friends had recently applied to Fremont, and instantly turned to a verse in the first of Samuel, put on his spectacles, and read in his slow, peculiar, and waggish tone: "And every one that was in distress, and every one that was in debt, and every one that was discontented, gathered themselves unto him, and he became a captain over them, and there were with him about four hundred men."

LXIII.

The letter of General Fremont withdrawing from the presidential canvass of 1864, after having accepted the nomination of the Cleveland Convention, was an unfortunate one for his political reputation, whatever may have been thought of the military career of that once popular leader. Without attempting any discussion of the merits of the controversy between him and the Government, I think it cannot be denied that Mr. Lincoln ever bore toward General Fremont the sincerest good will, though for reasons perhaps not yet fairly estimated, as a commander he had failed to realize the public expectation.

Some months subsequent to Fremont's removal from the Western Department, one of his personal friends, Mr. Henry C. Bowen, of Brooklyn, happened to be in Washington. Passing the Executive Chamber, on his way to the private secretary's office one day, he observed the door ajar, and the President standing near it, in the act of taking down a book from the bookcase. Catching a glimpse of him, Mr. Lincoln said, "Come in; you are the very man I want to see." Mr. Bowen entered the office, and the President, laying aside other business, said: "I have been thinking a great deal lately about Fremont; and I want to ask you, as an old friend of his, what is thought about his continuing inactive?" "Mr. President," returned Mr. Bowen, "I will say to you frankly, that a large class of people feel that

General Fremont has been badly treated, and nothing would give more satisfaction, both to him and to his friends, than his re-appointment to a command commensurate, in some degree, with his rank and ability." "Do you think he would accept an inferior position to that he occupied in Missouri?" asked the President. "I have that confidence in General Fremont's patriotism, that I venture to promise for him in advance," was the earnest reply. "Well," rejoined Mr. Lincoln, thoughtfully, "I have had it on my mind for some time that Fremont should be given a chance to redeem himself. The great hue and cry about him has been concerning his expenditure of the public money. I have looked into the matter a little, and I can't see as he has done any worse or any more, in that line, than our *Eastern* commanders." At any rate, he shall have another trial!" The result, close upon this interview, was the appointment of Fremont to the "Mountain Department of Western Virginia."

While Mr. Bowen was in Washington, he drove out, by invitation one evening, with one or two friends, to the Soldier's Home, where the President spent the nights of midsummer. More at leisure there than at the "shop," as he was in the habit of calling his official chamber at the White House, Mr. Lincoln sat down with the party for a leisurely conversation. "I know," he said to Mr. Bowen, "that you are a great admirer of Mr. Chase and Mr. Seward. Now, I will tell you a circumstance that may please you. Before sunset of election-day, in 1860, I was pretty sure, from the despatches I received, that I was elected. The very first thing that I settled in my mind, after reaching this conclusion, was that these two great leaders of the party should occupy the two first places in my cabinet."

LXIV.

"The Soldier's Home," writes a California lady,* who visited Mr. Lincoln there, "is a few miles out of Washington on the Maryland side. It is situated on a beautifully wooded hill, which you ascend by a winding path, shaded on both sides by wide-spread branches, forming a green arcade above you. When you reach the top you stand between two mansions, large, handsome, and substantial, but with nothing about them indicative of the character of either. That on your left is the Presidential country-house; that directly before you, the 'Rest' for soldiers who are too old for further service. . . . The 'Home' only admitted soldiers of the regular army; but in the graveyard near at hand there are numberless graves—some without a spear of grass to hide their newness—that hold the bodies of volunteers.

"While we stood in the soft evening air, watching the faint trembling of the long tendrils of waving willow, and feeling the dewy coolness that was flung out by the old oaks above us, Mr. Lincoln joined us, and stood silent, too, taking in the scene.

San Francisco Bulletin.

"'How sleep the brave, who sink to rest
    By all their country's wishes blest,'—

he said, softly.

"There was something so touching in the picture opened before us,—the nameless graves, the solemn quiet, the tender twilight air, but more particularly our own feminine disposition to be easily melted, I suppose,—that it made us cry as if we stood beside the tomb of our own dead, and gave point to the lines which he afterwards quoted:—

"'And women o'er the graves shall weep,
    Where nameless heroes calmly sleep.'"

*   *   *   *   *   *   *   *

"Around the 'Home' grows every variety of tree, particularly of the evergreen class. Their branches brushed into the carriage as we passed along, and left with us that pleasant, woody smell belonging to leaves. One of the ladies, catching a bit of green from one of these intruding branches, said it was cedar, and another thought it spruce.

"'Let me discourse on a theme I understand,' said the President. 'I know all about trees in right of being a backwoodsman. I'll show you the difference between spruce, pine, and cedar, and this shred of green, which is neither one nor the other, but a kind of illegitimate cypress.' He then proceeded to gather specimens of each, and explain the distinctive formation of foliage belonging to every species. 'Trees,' he said, 'are as deceptive in their likeness to one another as are certain classes of men, amongst whom none but a physiognomist's eye can detect dissimilar moral features until events have developed them. Do you know it would be a good thing if in all the schools proposed and carried out by the improvement of modern thinkers, we could have a school of events?'

"'A school of events?' repeated the lady he addressed.

"'Yes,' he continued, 'since it is only by that active development that character and ability can be tested. Understand me, I now mean men, not trees; *they* can be tried, and an analysis of their strength obtained less expensive to life and human interests than man's. What I say now is a mere whimsey, you know; but when I speak of a school of events, I mean one in which, before entering real life, students might pass through the mimic vicissitudes and situations that are necessary to bring out their powers and mark the calibre to which they are assigned. Thus, one could select from the graduates an invincible soldier, equal to any position, with no such word as fail; a martyr to Right, ready to give up life in the cause; a politician too cunning to be outwitted; and so on. These things have all to be tried, and their sometime failure creates confusion as well as disappointment.

There is no more dangerous or expensive analysis than that which consists of trying a man.'

"'Do you think all men are tried?' was asked.

"'Scarcely,' said Mr. Lincoln, 'or so many would not fit their place so badly. Your friend, Mr. Beecher, being an eloquent man, explains this well in his quaint illustration of people out of their sphere,—the clerical faces he has met with in gay, rollicking life, and the natural wits and good brains that have by a freak dropped into ascetic robes.'

"'Some men seem able to do what they wish in any position, being equal to them all,' said some one.

"'Versatility,' replied the President, 'is an injurious possession, since it never can be greatness. It misleads you in your calculations from its very agreeability, and it inevitably disappoints you in any great trust from its want of depth. A versatile man; to be safe from execration, should never soar; mediocrity is sure of detection.'

"On our return to the city we had reached that street—I forget its name—crossing which you find yourself out of Maryland and in the District of Columbia. Wondering at this visible boundary that made certain laws and regulations apply to one side of a street that did not reach the other, I lost the conversation, till I found it consisted of a discursive review of General McClellan's character, in which I was directly appealed to to know if we had not at one time considered him the second Napoleon in California.

"I hastened to say that I had found, in traveling in the New England States, more fervent admirers of the Unready than I had ever known to expend speculative enthusiasm upon him among us.

"'So pleasant and scholarly a gentleman can never fail to secure personal friends,' said the President. 'In fact,' he continued, kindly,

"'Even his failings lean to virtue's side."

A keen sense of genius in another, and a reverence for it that forced expression, was out of place at Seven Oaks, as beautiful things sometimes will be. He was lost in admiration of General Lee, and filled with that feeling, forebore to conquer him. The quality that would prove noble generosity in a historian, does not fit the soldier. Another instance of the necessity for my suggestion being carried into effect,' he added, smiling.

"When in New York a few months afterwards, I heard the regular dinner-table conversation turn on the 'Nero who cracked jokes while Rome was burning,' and the hundred and one wicked things the McClellanites said of Mr. Lincoln, I recalled the gentle verdict I had heard, and acknowledged how bitterly a noble Christian gentleman may be belied. It was after McClellan's speech at West Point, and his admirers were wild with enthusiasm over the learning and classic taste it displayed. The word 'scholarly' rang from mouth to mouth in characterizing it,—the very word Mr. Lincoln had used months before in finding a merciful excuse for his inefficiency.

"There is one little incident connected with this visit to the Soldier's Home that remains with me as connected with my home here. I had always noticed that the bare mention of our California cemetery filled the minds of those who heard it with a solemn sense of awe and sorrow,—'Lone Mountain!' It seemed to rise before them out of the quiet sea, a vast mausoleum from the hand of God, wherein to lay the dead. I was not astonished, therefore, when Mr. Lincoln alluded to it in this way, and gave, in a few deep-toned words, a eulogy on one of its most honored dead, Colonel Baker. Having witnessed the impressive spectacle of that glorious soldier's funeral, I gave him the meagre outline one can convey in words, of something which, having been once seen, must remain a living picture in the memory forever. I tried to picture the solemn hush that lay like a pall on the spirit of the people while the grand procession wound its mournful length through the streets of the city out on that tearstained road to the gate of the cemetery, where the body passed beneath the prophetic words of California's most eloquent soul, 'Hither in future ages they shall bring,' etc. When I spoke of 'Starr King,' I saw how strong a chord I had touched in the great appreciative heart I addressed; and giving a weak dilution of that wondrous draught of soul-lit eloquence, that funeral hymn uttered by the priest of God over the sacred ashes of the advocate and soldier of liberty, whose thrilling threnody seems yet to linger in the sighing wind that waves the grass upon the soil made sacred by the treasure it received that day, I felt strangely impressed as to the power and grandeur of that mind, whose thoughts, at second-hand and haltingly given from memory, could move and touch the soul of such a man as Abraham Lincoln as I saw it touched when he listened. It is the electric chain with which all genius and grandeur of soul whatsoever is bound,—the freemasonry by which spirit hails spirit, though unseen. Now they all three meet where it is not seeing through a glass darkly, but in the light of a perfect day."

LXV.

On the morning of Mr. Lincoln's arrival in Washington, just before his inauguration, it will be remembered that the Peace Convention was in session. Among those who were earliest to call upon him was a gentleman from Pennsylvania, who had been in Congress with him, and who was a member of the Peace Convention. He at once commenced plying the President elect with urgent reasons for *compromising* matters in dispute, saying, "It must be done sooner or later, and that this seemed the propitious moment." Listening attentively to all that was said, Mr. Lincoln finally replied: "Perhaps your reasons for compromising the alleged difficulties are correct, and that now is the favorable time to do it; still, if I remember correctly, *that* is not what *I* was elected for!"

The same day, at Willard's Hotel, a gentleman from Connecticut was introduced, who said he wanted nothing but to take the incoming President by the hand. Mr. Lincoln surveyed him from head to foot, and giving him a cordial grasp, replied: "You are a *rare* man."

During the brief period that the Rev. Henry Ward Beecher was editor-in-chief of the "Independent," in the second year of the war, he felt called upon to pass some severe strictures upon the course of the administration. For several weeks the successive leaders of the editorial page were like bugle-blasts, waking the echoes throughout the country. Somebody cut these editorials out of the different numbers of the paper, and mailed them all to the President under one envelop. One rainy Sunday he took them from his drawer, and read them through to the very last word. One or two of the articles were in Mr. Beecher's strongest style, and criticized the President in no measured terms. As Mr. Lincoln finished reading them, his face flushed up with indignation. Dashing the package to the floor, he exclaimed, "Is thy servant a *dog*, that he should do this thing?"

The excitement, however, soon passed off, leaving no trace behind of ill-will toward Mr. Beecher; and the impression made upon his mind by the criticism was lasting and excellent in its effects.

Mr. Lincoln's popularity with the soldiers and the people is well illustrated in the following incidents.

Just after the presidential nominations had been made in 1864, a discussion arose in a certain regiment in the Army of the Potomac as to the merits of the two candidates. Various opinions had been warmly expressed, when at length a German spoke. "I goes," said he, "for Fader Abraham. Fader Abraham, he likes the soldier-boy. Ven he serves tree years he gives him four hundred tollar, and reënlists him von veteran. Now Fader Abraham, he serve four years. We reënlist him four years more, and make *von veteran of him.*"

The night following the election, a clergyman of Middletown, Conn., at a torchlight display, exhibited a transparency over his door, with a quotation from Genesis xxii. 15,—"The angel of the Lord called unto Abraham out of heaven a second time."

A few days before the reinauguration of Mr. Lincoln, my picture was placed temporarily on exhibition in the Rotunda of the Capitol. As the workmen were raising it to its place, over the northern door leading to the Senate Chamber, a group gathered in front of it, among whom was policeman R——, of the Capitol squad. As the painting reached its position, a wandering sunbeam crept in from the top of the great dome and settled full upon the head of Mr. Lincoln, leaving all the rest of the picture in shadow. The effect was singular and wonderful. "Look!" exclaimed the enthusiastic R——, pointing to the canvas; "that is as it should be. God bless him; may the sun shine upon his head forever."

LXVI.

The 22d of February, 1865, Lieutenant Cushing of the Navy reached Washington, from the fleet at Wilmington, with the news of the capture of Fort Anderson. This gallant officer, only twenty or twenty-one years of age, had greatly distinguished himself by planning and successfully accomplishing the destruction of the rebel ram *Savannah*, also in the construction of the "bogus" monitor which played so effectual a part in the capture of Fort Anderson. He was introduced to the President by the Secretary of the Navy, and was received in the most cordial manner. Sitting down for an hour's talk, Mr. Lincoln, who was in high spirits over the late military successes, sparkled with humor. Temporarily upon the wall of the room was a portrait of himself recently painted for Secretary Welles by a

Connecticut artist friend. Turning to the picture, Mr. Welles remarked that he thought it a successful likeness. "Yes," returned the President, hesitatingly; and then came a story of a western friend whose wife pronounced her husband's portrait, painted secretly for a birth day present, "horridly like;" "and that," said he, "seems to me a just criticism of this!" The liability to "mistakes," so many instances of which had occurred during the war, both on land and sea, was illustrated by reference to a charitably disposed woman, with a very indifferent face, who, while visiting the rooms of the Young Men's Christian Association, or a similar institution, caught sight of her own reflection in a concealed looking-glass, upon which she retired in great confusion, saying she would have nothing more to do with an institution which one could not visit without meeting disreputable characters.

Lieutenant Cushing related a circumstance showing the estimation in which General Sherman was held by the rebel privates. A deserter of this class had lately fallen into his hands. "Our boys," said he, speaking of the Rebels, "say General Sherman never makes but one speech. When ready for a movement, he says: 'Now boys, let's get ready to go;' and they get ready," said the deserter, "on both sides."

"There is a good deal of mother-wit in some of those fellows," rejoined Mr. Lincoln, much amused. "That puts me in mind of a conversation between two opposing pickets, just after

Hooker fell back across the Rappahannock, after the battle of Chancellorville. 'Where's Old Joe?' called out a 'butternut' one frosty morning. 'Gone to Stonewall Jackson's funeral,' was the ready reply. 'What is the reason you "Johnnies" never have any decent clothes?' hallooed the 'Union' boy back. 'We-uns don't put on our best to kill hogs in,' was the retort."

I was sitting in the President's office with Mr. G. B. Lincoln, of Brooklyn, and the Hon. John A. Bingham, of Ohio,—who were there by appointment of the President,—the Sunday evening before the reinauguration, when Mr. Lincoln came in through the side passage which had lately been constructed, holding in his hand a roll of manuscripts.

"Lots of wisdom in that document, I suspect," said he; "it is what will be called my 'second inaugural,' containing about six hundred words. I will put it away here in this drawer until I want it."

Seating himself by the open grate, he commenced conversation in a familiar and cheerful mood, referring to his early life in Illinois. Nothing, he said, had ever gratified him so much as his first election to the legislature of that State, just after his return from the Black-Hawk war. In the election district a large majority were Democrats, and he was known as a "talking Whig." Nevertheless, he said, in a vote of two hundred, he received all but three.

LXVII.

"The world," writes one who knew Mr. Lincoln well, "will never hear the last of the 'little stories' with which the President garnished or illustrated his conversation and his early stump-speeches. He once, said, however, that as near as he could reckon, about one sixth only of those credited to him were old acquaintances,—all the rest were the productions of other and better story-tellers than himself. 'I remember a good story when I hear it,' he continued; 'but I never invented anything original; I am only a retail-dealer.'"*

"Mr. Lincoln's jocoseness," wrote another, "though sometimes grim and sarcastic, was *never* abusive, and seldom wounded. Often nicely adapted to the place and the occasion, it was used, as the case might be, either as a shield or a weapon,"†

Humor and shrewdness, together with a certain nameless individuality, were combined in his stories in a degree that will secure for many of them enduring interest. These characteristics, marked and prominent as they were, are directly traceable to the powerful effect produced upon the plastic mind of the pioneer boy, by the early study of Æsop's Fables, and the "Pilgrim's Progress." His lightest as well as his most powerful thought almost invariably took on the form of a figure in speech, which

---

*Noah Brooks, *Harper's Monthly*, July, 1865.
†*Boston Watchman and Reflector.*

drove the point *home*, and *clinched* it, as few abstract reasoners are able to do.

The character of this volume, necessarily rambling and fragmentary, seems to present a legitimate field for the incorporation and preservation of some of the best of Mr. Lincoln's "little stories" and quaint sayings, other than those which came within my own personal observation. Beside these, there has accumulated in my possession a variety of incidents, many of which have never been published, throwing light not only upon the character of the man, but upon many events and circumstances connected with the war and the administration.

Believing everything of this to have more than a temporary interest and value, I devote the following section to their embodiment.

LXVIII.

Mr. Lincoln made his first political speech in 1832, at the age of twenty-three, when he was a candidate for the Illinois Legislature. His opponent had wearied the audience by a long speech, leaving him but a short time in which to present his views. He condensed all he had to say into a few words, as follows:—

"Gentlemen, Fellow-citizens: I presume you know who I am. I am humble Abraham Lincoln. I have been solicited by many friends to become a candidate for the legislature. My politics can be briefly stated. I am in favor of a national bank. I am in favor of the internal improvement system, and a high protective tariff. These are my sentiments and political principles. If elected, I shall be thankful. If not, it will be all the same."

The contrast between Mr. Lincoln and Senator Douglas is well brought out in the following extract from a speech by Hon. I. N. Arnold of Illinois, in 1863. Speaking of their great contest for the senatorship, Mr. Arnold said:—

"Douglas went through this campaign like a conquering hero. He had his special train of cars, his band of music, his body-guard of devoted friends, a cannon carried on the train, the firing from which announced his approach to the place of meeting. Such a canvass involved, necessarily, very large expenditures; and it has been said that Douglas did not expend less than $50,000 in this canvass. Some idea of the plain, simple, frugal habits of Mr. Lincoln may be gathered, when I tell you that at its close, having occupied several months, Mr. Lincoln said, with the idea, apparently, that he had been somewhat extravagant: 'I do not believe I have spent a cent less than five hundred dollars in this canvass.'"

Soon after Mr. Lincoln entered upon the practice of his profession at Springfield, he was engaged in a criminal case in which it was thought there was little chance of success. Throwing all his powers into it, he came off victorious, and promptly received for his services five hundred dollars. A legal friend calling upon him the next morning found him sitting before a table, upon which his money was spread out, counting it over and over. "Look here, Judge," said he; "see what a heap of money I've got from the——case. Did you ever see anything like it? Why, I never had so much money in my life before, put it all together!" Then crossing his arms upon the table, his manner sobering down, he added. "I have got just five hundred dollars: if it was only seven hundred and fifty, I would go directly and purchase a quarter section of land, and settle it upon my old step-mother." His friend said that if the deficiency was all he needed, he would loan him the amount, taking his note, to which Mr. Lincoln instantly acceded.

His friend then said: "Lincoln, I would not do just what you have indicated. Your step-mother is getting old, and will not probably live many years. I would settle the property upon her for her use during her lifetime, to revert to you upon her death."

With much feeling, Mr. Lincoln replied: "I shall do no such thing. It is a poor return, at the best, for all the good woman's devotion and fidelity to me, and there is not going to be any half-way business about it;" and so saying, he gathered up his money, and proceeded forthwith to carry his long-cherished purpose into execution.

Among the numerous delegations which thronged Washington in the early part of the war was one from New York, which urged very strenuously the sending of a fleet to the southern cities,—Charleston, Mobile, and Savannah,—with the object of drawing off the rebel army from Washington. Mr. Lincoln said the project reminded him of the case of a girl in New Salem, who was greatly troubled with a "singing" in her head. Various remedies were suggested by the neighbors, but nothing tried afforded any relief. At last a man came along,—"a common-sense sort of a man," said he, inclining his head towards the gentleman complimentarily,—"who asked to prescribe for the difficulty. After due inquiry and examination, he said the cure was very simple. 'What is it?' was the anxious question. 'Make a plaster of *psalm-tunes*, and apply to her feet, and draw the "singing" *down*,' was the rejoinder."

On another occasion, an antislavery delegation, also from New York, were pressing the adoption of the emancipation policy. During the interview the "chairman," Rev. Dr. C——, made a characteristic and powerful appeal, largely made up of quotations from the Old Testament Scriptures. Mr. Lincoln received the "bombardment" in silence. As the speaker concluded, he continued for a moment in thought, and then, drawing a long breath, responded: "Well gentlemen, it is not often one is favored with a delegation *direct* from the Almighty!"

One of Mr. Lincoln's Springfield neighbors, a clergyman, visiting Washington early in the administration, asked the President what was to be his policy on the slavery question. "Well," said he, "I will answer by telling you a story. You know Father B., the old Methodist preacher? and you know Fox River and his freshets? Well, once in the presence of Father B., a young Methodist was worrying about Fox River, and expressing fears that he should be prevented from fulfilling some of his appointments by a freshet in the river. Father B. checked him in his gravest manner. Said he: 'Young man, I have always made it a rule in my life not to cross Fox River till I get to it!' And," added Mr. Lincoln, "I am not going to worry myself over the slavery question till I get to it."

General Garfield, of Ohio, received from the President an account of the capture of Norfolk, similar to that recorded on a previous page, with the following preface:—

"By the way, Garfield," said Mr. Lincoln, "you never heard, did you, that Chase, Stanton, and I, had a campaign of our own? We went down to Fortress Monroe in Chase's revenue cutter, and consulted with Admiral Goldsborough as to the feasibility of taking Norfolk by landing on the north shore and making a march of eight miles. The Admiral said, very positively, there was no landing on that shore, and we should have to double the cape and approach the place from the south side, which would be a long and difficult journey. I thereupon asked him if he had ever tried to find a landing, and he replied that he had not. 'Now,' said I, 'Admiral, that reminds me of a chap out West who had studied law, but had never tried a case. Being sued, and not having confidence in his ability to manage his own case, he employed a fellow-lawyer to manage it for him. He had only a confused idea of the meaning of law terms, but was anxious to make a display of learning, and on the trial constantly made suggestions to his lawyer, who paid no attention to him. At last, fearing that his lawyer was not handling the opposing counsel very well, he lost all patience, and springing to his feet cried out, "Why don't you go at him with a *capias*, or a *surre-butter*, or something, and not stand there like a confounded old *nudum-pudum?*"'"

An officer of the Government called one day at the White House, and introduced a clerical friend. "Mr. President," said he, "allow me to present to you my friend, the Rev. Mr. F., of——. Mr. F. has expressed a desire to see you and have some conversation with you, and I am happy to be the means of introducing him." The President shook hands with Mr. F., and desiring him to be seated took a seat himself. Then, his countenance having assumed an air of patient waiting, he said: "I am now ready to hear what you have to say." "Oh, bless you, sir," said Mr. F., "I have nothing special to say; I merely called to pay my respects to you, and, as one of the million, to assure you of my hearty sympathy and support."

"My dear sir," said the President, rising promptly, his face showing instant relief, and with both hands grasping that of his visitor, "I am very glad to see you, indeed. *I thought you had come to preach me!*"

On the way to the cemetery dedication at Gettysburg, Mr. Lincoln said to his friend, McVeagh, of Pennsylvania, speaking of Governor Gamble and the administration troubles in Missouri:—"I do not understand the spirit of those men who, in such a time as this, because they cannot have a whole loaf will take no bread. For my part, I am willing to receive any man, or class of men, who will help us even *little*."

On the same occasion, when the Presidential party reached Hanover Junction they found a large concourse of people assembled to greet them. Mr. Lincoln and Secretary Seward, an hour previous, had gone into the sleeping-car attached to the train, for some rest. In response to the clamor of the crowd, a friend intruded upon them, saying to the President that he was "expected to make a speech."

"No!" he rejoined, very emphatically; "I had enough of that sort of thing all the way from Springfield to Washington. "Seward," said he, turning over in his berth, "you go out and repeat some of your '*poetry*' to the people!"

Upon the betrothal of the Prince of Wales to the Princess Alexandra, Queen Victoria sent a letter to each of the European sovereigns, and also to President Lincoln, announcing the fact.

Lord Lyons, her ambassador at Washington,—a "bachelor," by the way,—requested an audience of Mr. Lincoln, that he might present this important document in person. At the time appointed he was received at the White House, in company with Mr. Seward.

"May it please your Excellency," said Lord Lyons, "I hold in my hand an autograph letter from my royal mistress, Queen Victoria, which I have been commanded to present to your Excellency. In it she informs your Excellency that her son, his Royal Highness the Prince of Wales, is about to contract a matrimonial alliance with her Royal Highness the Princess Alexandra of Denmark."

After continuing in this strain for a few minutes, Lord Lyons tendered the letter to the President and awaited his reply. It was short, simple, and expressive, and consisted simply of the words:—

"Lord Lyons, go thou and do likewise."

It is doubtful if an English ambassador was ever addressed in this manner before, and it would be interesting to learn what success he met with in putting the reply in diplomatic language when he reported it to her Majesty.

The antagonism between the northern and southern sections of the Democratic party, which culminated in the nomination of two separate tickets in 1860, was a subject to draw out one of Mr. Lincoln's hardest hits.

"I once knew," said he, "a sound churchman by the name of Brown, who was a member of a very sober and pious committee having in charge the erection of a bridge over a dangerous and rapid river. Several architects failed, and at last Brown said he had a friend named Jones, who had built several bridges and undoubtedly could build that one. So Mr. Jones was called in. 'Can you build this bridge?' inquired the committee. 'Yes,' replied Jones, 'or any other. I could build a bridge to the infernal regions, if necessary!' The committee were shocked, and Brown felt called upon to defend his friend. 'I know Jones so well,' said he, 'and he is so honest a man and so good an architect, that if he states soberly and positively that he can build a bridge to—to——, why, I believe it; but I feel bound to say that I have my doubts about the abutment on the infernal side.' So," said Mr. Lincoln, "when politicians told me that the northern and southern wings of the Democracy could be harmonized, why, I believed them, of course; but I always had my doubts about the 'abutment' on the *other* side."*

About the time Mr. Lincoln began to be known as a successful lawyer, he was waited upon by a lady, who held a real-estate claim which she desired to have him prosecute,— putting into his hands, with the necessary papers, a check for two hundred and fifty dollars, as a retaining fee. Mr. Lincoln

---

*Abbott's *History of Civil War*.

said he would look the case over, and asked her to call again the next day. Upon presenting herself, Mr. Lincoln told her that he had gone through the papers very carefully, and he must tell her frankly that there was not a "peg" to hang her claim upon, and he could not conscientiously advise her to bring an action. The lady was satisfied, and, thanking him, rose to go. "Wait," said Mr. Lincoln, fumbling in his vest pocket; "here is the check you left with me." "But, Mr. Lincoln," returned the lady, "I think you have earned *that*." "No, no," he responded, handing it back to her; "that would not be right. I can't take *pay* for doing my duty."

Mr. Lincoln liked to feel himself the attorney of the people, not their ruler. Speaking once of the probability of his renomination, he said: "If the people think I have managed their 'case' for them well enough to trust me to carry it up to the next term, I am sure I shall be glad to take it."

"Judge Baldwin of California, being in Washington, called one day on General Halleck, and, presuming upon a familiar acquaintance in California a few years before, solicited a pass outside of our lines to see a brother in Virginia, not thinking that he would meet with a refusal, as both his brother and himself were good Union men. "We have been deceived too often." said General Halleck, "and I regret I can't grant it." Judge B. then went to Stanton, and was very briefly disposed of, with the same result. Finally, he obtained an interview with

Mr. Lincoln, and stated his case. "Have you applied to General Halleck?" inquired the President. "Yes, and met with a flat refusal," said Judge B. "Then you must see Stanton," continued the President. "I have, and with the same result," was the reply. "Well, then," said Mr. Lincoln, with a smile, "I can do nothing; for you must know *that I have very little influence with this Administration.*"

Mr. Colfax told me of a gentleman's going to the President, one day, with a bitter denunciation of Secretary Stanton and his management of the War Department. "Go home, my friend," interrupted Mr. Lincoln, "and read attentively the tenth verse of the thirtieth chapter of Proverbs!"*

A lieutenant, whom debts compelled to leave his fatherland and service, succeeded in being admitted to President Lincoln, and, by reason of his commendable and winning deportment and intelligent appearance, was promised a lieutenant's commission in a cavalry regiment. He was so enraptured with his success, that he deemed it a duty to inform the President that he belonged to one of the oldest noble houses in Germany, "Oh, never mind that," said Mr. Lincoln; "you will not find that to be an obstacle to your advancement."

---

*"Accuse not a servant to his master, lest he curse thee, and thou be found guilty."

Just previous to the fall of Vicksburg, a self-constituted committee, solicitous for the *morale* of our armies, took it upon themselves to visit the President and urge the removal of General Grant. In some surprise Mr. Lincoln inquired, "For what reason?" "Why," replied the spokesman, "he drinks too much whiskey." "Ah!" rejoined Mr. Lincoln, dropping his lower lip. "By the way, gentlemen, can either of you tell me where General Grant procures his whiskey? because, if I can find out, I will send every general in the field a barrel of it!"

When the telegram from Cumberland Gap reached Mr. Lincoln that "firing was heard in the direction of Knoxville," he remarked that he was "glad of it." Some person present, who had the perils of Burnside's position uppermost in his mind, could not see *why* Mr. Lincoln should be *glad* of it, and so expressed himself. "Why, you see," responded the President, "it reminds me of Mistress Sallie Ward, a neighbor of mine, who had a very large family. Occasionally one of her numerous progeny would be heard crying in some out-of-the-way place, upon which Mrs. Ward would exclaim, 'There's one of my children that isn't dead yet.'"

A gentleman once complimented the President on having no vices, neither drinking nor smoking. "That is a doubtful compliment," answered the President; "I recollect once being outside a stagecoach, in Illinois, and a man sitting by me offered me a cigar. I told him I had no vices. He said nothing, but smoked for some time, and then growled out: 'It's my experience that folks who have no vices have generally very few virtues.'"

Mr. Lincoln's aversion to calls for a speech that must be merely "off-hand," was decided; yet, unwilling altogether to disappoint the crowds, who perhaps too often made such demands of him, he seldom excused himself altogether from speaking. One evening a friend was conversing with him in his room, when his quick ear caught the sound of approaching music, and his countenance suddenly changed, as he inquired its meaning, though readily divining it. A serenade was presently announced by an usher, and Mr. Lincoln, as he arose to go forward to the front window, lingered a moment, and said:—

"These 'serenade' speeches bother me a good deal, they are so hard to make. I feel very much like the steam doctor, who said he could get along very well in his practice with almost every case, but he was always a little puzzled when it came to mending a broken leg."

It has been repeatedly said that Mr. Lincoln lacked imagination and poetic sensibility. Surely, the soul which could conceive the last inaugural, or indite the closing sentence of the first, was not wanting in these elements:—

"The mystic chords of memory, stretching from every battle-field and patriot grave to every living heart and hearthstone all over this broad land, will yet swell the chorus of the Union, when again touched, as surely they will be, by the better angels of our nature."

Neither was the mind deficient in enthusiasm, which could prophesy:—

"There are already those among us, who, if the Union be preserved, will live to see it contain two hundred and fifty millions. The struggle *of* to-day is not altogether *for* to-day; it is for a vast future also."

"The President," said a leading member of the Cabinet, on one occasion, "is his own War-Minister. He directs personally the movements of the armies, and is fond of strategy; but pays much less attention to official details than is generally supposed."

Mr. Lincoln's wit was never malicious nor rudely personal. Once when Mr. Douglas had attempted to parry an argument by impeaching the veracity of a senator whom Mr. Lincoln had quoted, he answered that the question was not one of veracity, but simply one of argument. "By a course of reasoning, Euclid proves that all the angles in a triangle are equal to two right angles. Now, if you undertake to disprove that proposition, would you prove it to be false by calling Euclid a liar?"[*]

A couple of well-known New York gentlemen called upon the President one day to solicit a pardon for a man who, while

---

[*]Speech at Charleston, September 18th, 1858.

acting as mate of a sailing vessel, had struck one of his men a blow which resulted in his death. Convicted and sentenced for manslaughter, a powerful appeal was made in his behalf, as he had previously borne an excellent character. Giving the facts a hearing, Mr. Lincoln responded:—

"Well, gentlemen, leave your papers, and I will have the Attorney-General, Judge Bates, look them over, and we will see what can be done. Being both of us '*pigeon-hearted*' fellows, the chances are that, if there is any ground whatever for interference, the scoundrel will get off."

Attorney-General Bates was once remonstrating with the President against the appointment to a judicial position of considerable importance of a western man, who, though once on the "bench," was of indifferent reputation as a lawyer.

"Well now, Judge," returned Mr. Lincoln, "I think you are rather too hard on——. Besides that, I must tell you, he did me a good turn long ago. When I took to the law, I was going to court one morning, with some ten or twelve miles of bad road before me, when——overtook me in his wagon. 'Hallo, Lincoln!' said he; 'going to the court-house? come in and I will give you a seat.' Well, I got in, and——went on reading his papers. Presently the wagon struck a stump on one side of the road; then it hopped off to the other. I looked out and saw the driver was jerking from side to side in his seat: so said I, 'Judge, I think your coachman has been taking a drop too much this morning.'

'Well, I declare, Lincoln,' said he, 'I should not much wonder if you are right, for he has nearly upset me half-a-dozen times since starting.' So, putting his head out of the window, he shouted, 'Why, you infernal scoundrel, you are drunk!' Upon which, pulling up his horses and turning round with great gravity, the coachman said: 'Bedad! but that's the first rightful decision your honor has given for the last twelve months.'"

Some gentlemen fresh from a western tour, during a call at the White House, referred in the course of conversation to a body of water in Nebraska which bore an Indian name signifying "weeping water." Mr. Lincoln instantly responded: "As 'laughing water,' according to Longfellow, is 'Minnehaha,' this evidently should be 'Minneboohoo.'"

A farmer from one of the border counties went to the President on a certain occasion with the complaint that the Union soldiers in passing his farm had helped themselves not only to hay but to his horse; and he hoped the proper officer would be required to consider his claim immediately.

"Why, my good sir," replied Mr. Lincoln, "If I should attempt to consider every such individual case, I should find work enough for twenty Presidents! In my early days, I knew one Jack Chase, who was a lumberman on the Illinois, and, when steady and sober, the best raftsman on the river. It was quite a trick twenty-five years ago to take the logs over the rapids, but he was skilful with a raft, and always kept her straight in the channel. Finally a steamer was put on, and Jack—he's dead now, poor fellow!—was made captain of her. He always used to take the wheel going through the rapids. One day, when the boat was plunging and wallowing along the boiling current, and Jack's utmost vigilance was being exercised to keep her in the narrow channel, a boy pulled his coat-tail and hailed him with: 'Say, Mister Captain! I wish you would just stop your boat a minute—I've lost my apple overboard!'"

At a time of financial difficulty, a committee of New York bankers waited upon the Secretary of the Treasury and volunteered a loan to the government, which was gratefully accepted. Mr. Chase subsequently accompanied the gentlemen to the White House and introduced them to the President, saying they had called to have a talk with him about money. "Money," replied Mr. Lincoln; "I don't know anything about '*money*.' I never had enough of my own to fret me, and I have no opinion about it any way."

"It is considered rather necessary to the carrying on of a war, however," returned the Secretary.

"Well, I don't know about that,' rejoined Mr. Lincoln, turning crosswise in his chair, swinging both legs backward and forward. "We don't read that 'Hannibal' had any '*money*' to prosecute his wars with."

The President was one day speaking of a visit he had just received from another delegation of bankers, from New York and Boston, who had been urging the removal of General Cameron from the Cabinet.

"They talked very glibly," said he, "especially a man named G——from Boston; and I finally told them as much—adding, nevertheless, that I was not convinced. 'Now,' said I, 'gentlemen, if you want General Cameron removed, you have only to bring me *one proved* case of dishonesty, and I promise you his "head"; but I assure you I am not going to act on what seems to me the most unfounded gossip.'"

The Hon. Mr. Hubbard of Connecticut once called upon the President in reference to a newly invented gun, concerning which a committee had been appointed to make a report.

The "report" was sent for, and when it came in was found to be of the most voluminous description. Mr. Lincoln glanced at it, and said: "I should want a new lease of life to read this through!" Throwing it down upon the table, he added: "Why can't a committee of this kind occasionally exhibit a grain of common sense? If I send a man to buy a horse for me, I expect him to tell me his '*points*'—not how many *hairs* there are in his tail."

Late one evening, the President brought in to see my picture his friend and biographer, the Hon. J. H. Barrett, and a Mr. M——, of Cincinnati. An allusion to a question of law in the course of conversation suggesting the subject, Mr. Lincoln said: "The strongest example of 'rigid government' and 'close construction' I ever knew, was that of Judge——. It was once said of him that he would *hang* a man for blowing his nose in the street, but that he would *quash* the indictment if it failed to specify which *hand* he blew it with!"

A new levy of troops required, on a certain occasion, the appointment of a large additional number of brigadier and major-generals. Among the immense number of applications, Mr. Lincoln came upon one wherein the claims of a certain worthy (not in the service at all) for a generalship were glowingly set forth. But the applicant didn't specify whether he wanted to be brigadier or major-general. The President observed this difficulty, and solved it by a lucid indorsement. The clerk, on receiving the paper again, found written across its back: "Major-General, I reckon. A. Lincoln."

A juvenile "Brigadier" from New York, with a small detachment of cavalry, having imprudently gone within the Rebel lines near Fairfax Court House, was captured by "guerillas." Upon the fact being reported to Mr. Lincoln, he said that he was very sorry to lose the horses!

"What do you mean?" inquired his informant.

"Why," rejoined the President, "I can make a better 'brigadier' any day; but those horses cost the government a hundred and twenty-five dollars a head!"

Mr. Lincoln sometimes had a very effective way of dealing with men who troubled him with questions. A visitor once asked him how many men the Rebels had in the field. The President replied, very seriously, "Twelve hundred thousand, according to the best authority." The interrogator blanched in the face, and ejaculated, "Good Heavens!" "Yes sir, twelve hundred thousand—no doubt of it. You see, all of our generals, when they get whipped, say the enemy outnumbers them from three or five to one, and I must believe them. We have four hundred thousand men in the field, and three times four make twelve. Don't you see it!"

Some gentlemen were discussing in Mr. Lincoln's presence on a certain occasion General McClellan's military capacity. "It is doubtless true that he is a good 'engineer,' said the President; but he seems to have a special talent for developing a 'stationary' engine."

When Mr. Lincoln handed to his friend Gilbert his appointment as assessor in the Wall Street district, New York, he said: "Gilbert, from what I can learn, I judge that you are going upon good 'missionary' ground. Preach God and Liberty to the 'bulls' and 'bears,' and get all the money you can for the government!"

A gentleman calling at the White House one evening carried a cane, which, in the course of conversation, attracted the President's attention. Taking it in his hand, he said: "I always used a cane when I was a boy. It was a freak of mine. My favorite one was a knotted beech stick, and I carved the head myself. There's a mighty amount of character in sticks. Don't you think so? You have seen these fishing-poles that fit into a cane? Well that was an old idea of mine. Dogwood clubs were favorite ones with the boys. I suppose they use them yet. Hickory is too heavy, unless you get it from a young sapling. Have you ever noticed how a stick in one's hand will change his appearance? Old women and witches wouldn't look so without sticks. Meg Merrilies understands that."

One of Mr. Lincoln's "illustrations" in my hearing, on one occasion, was of a man who, in driving the hoops of a hogshead to "head" it up, was much annoyed by the constant falling in of the top. At length the bright idea struck him of putting his little boy inside to "hold it up." This he did; it never occurring to him till the job was done, how he was to get his child out. "This," said he, "is a fair sample of the way some people always do business."

In a time of despondency, some visitors were telling the President of the "breakers" so often seen ahead—"this time surely coming." "That," said he, "suggests the story of the school-boy, who never could pronounce the names 'Shadrach,' 'Meshach,' and 'Abednego.' He had been repeatedly whipped for it without effect. Sometime afterwards he saw the names in the regular lesson for the day. Putting his finger upon the place, he turned to his next neighbor, an older boy, and whispered, 'Here come those "tormented Hebrews" again.'"

Referring to the divisions upon the Missouri Compromise, Mr. Lincoln once said: "It used to amuse me to hear the slaveholders talk about wanting more territory, because they had not *room* enough for their slaves; and yet they complained of not having the slave-trade, because they wanted more slaves for their room."

Speaking on a certain occasion, of a prominent man who had the year before been violent in his manifestations of hostility to the Administration, but was then ostensibly favoring the same policy previously denounced, Mr. Lincoln expressed his entire readiness to treat the past as if it had not been, saying, "I choose always to make my 'statute of limitations' a short one."

At the White House one day some gentlemen were present from the West, excited and troubled about the commissions or omissions of the Administration. The President heard them patiently, and then replied: "Gentlemen, suppose all the property you were worth was in gold, and you had put it in the hands of Blondin to carry across the Niagara River on a rope, would you shake the cable, or keep shouting out to him, 'Blondin, stand up a little straighter—Blondin, stoop a little more—go a little faster—lean a little more to the north—lean a little more to the south.' No, you would hold your breath as well as your tongue, and keep your hands off until he was safe over. The Government are carrying an immense weight. Untold treasures are in their hands. They are doing the very best they can. Don't badger them. Keep silence, and we'll get you safe across."

The President was once speaking of an attack made on him by the Committee on the Conduct of the War, for a certain alleged blunder, or some thing worse, in the Southwest—the matter involved being one which had fallen directly under the observation of the officer to whom he was talking, who possessed official evidence completely upsetting all the conclusions of the Committee.

"Might it not be well for me," queried the officer, "to set this matter right in a letter to some paper, stating the facts as they actually transpired?"

"Oh, no," replied the President, "at least, not now. If I were to try to read, much less answer, all the attacks made on me, this shop might as well be closed for any other business. I do the very best I know how—the very best I can; and I mean to keep doing so until the end. If the end brings me out all right, what is said against me won't amount to anything. If the end brings me out of wrong, ten angels swearing I was right would make no difference."

"I shall ever cherish among the brightest memories of my life," says the Rev. J. P. Thompson, of New York, "the recollection of an hour in Mr. Lincoln's working-room in September, '64, which was one broad sheet of sunshine. . . . I spoke of the rapid rise of Union feeling since the promulgation of the

Chicago Platform, and the victory at Atlanta; and the question was started, which had contributed the most to the reviving of Union sentiment—the victory or the platform. 'I guess,' said the President, 'it was the victory; at any rate, I'd rather have that repeated,'"

Being informed of the death of John Morgan, he said: "Well, I wouldn't crow over anybody's death; but I can take this as *resignedly* as any dispensation of Providence."

The celebrated case of Franklin W. Smith and brother, was one of those which most largely helped to bring military tribunals into public contempt. Those two gentlemen were arrested and kept in confinement, their papers seized, their business destroyed, their reputation damaged, and a naval court-martial, "organized to convict," pursued them unrelentingly till a wiser and juster hand arrested the malice of their persecutors. It is known that President Lincoln, after full investigation of the case, annulled the whole proceedings, but it is remarkable that the actual record of his decision could never be obtained from the Navy Department. An exact copy being withheld, the following was presented to the Boston Board of Trade as being very nearly the words of the late President:—

"*Whereas*, Franklin W. Smith had transactions with the Navy Department to the amount of one million and a quarter of a million of dollars; and *whereas*, he had the chance to steal a quarter of a million, and was only charged with stealing twenty-two hundred dollars—and the question now is about his stealing a hundred—I don't believe he stole anything at all. Therefore, the record and findings are disapproved—declared null and void, and the defendants are fully discharged."

"It would be difficult," says the New York "Tribune," "to sum up the rights and wrongs of the business more briefly than that, or to find a paragraph more characteristically and unmistakably Mr. Lincoln's."

A gentleman was pressing very strenuously the promotion of an officer to a "Brigadiership." "But we have already more generals than we know what to do with," replied the President. "But," persisted the visitor, "my friend is very strongly recommended." "Now, look here," said Mr. Lincoln, throwing one leg over the arm of his chair, "you are a farmer, I believe; if not, you will understand me. Suppose you had a large cattleyard full of sorts of cattle,—cows, oxen, bulls,—and you kept killing and selling and disposing of your cows and oxen, in one way and another,—taking good care of your bulls. By-and-by you would find that you had nothing but a yard full of old bulls, good for nothing under heaven. Now, it will be just so with the army, if I don't stop making brigadier-generals."

Captain Mix, the commander, at one period, of the President's body-guard, told me that on their way to town one sultry morning, from the "Soldiers' Home," they came upon a regiment marching into the city. A "straggler," very heavily loaded with camp equipage, was accosted by the President with the question: "My lad, what is that?" referring to the designation of his regiment. "It's a regiment," said the soldier, curtly, plodding on, his gaze bent steadily upon the ground. "Yes, I see that," rejoined the President, "but I want to know *what* regiment." "——Pennsylvania," replied the man in the same tone, looking neither to the right nor the left. As the carriage passed on, Mr. Lincoln turned to Captain Mix and said, with a merry laugh, "It is very evident that chap smells no blood of '*royalty*' in this establishment."

Captain Mix was frequently invited to breakfast with the family at the "Home" residence. "Many times," said he, "have I listened to our most eloquent preachers, but *never* with the same feeling of awe and reverence, as when our Christian President, his arm around his son, with his deep, earnest tone, each morning read a chapter from the Bible."

Some one was discussing, in the presence of Mr. Lincoln, the character of a time-serving Washington clergyman. Said Mr. Lincoln to his visitor:—

"I think you are rather hard upon Mr.——. He reminds me of a man in Illinois, who was tried for passing a counterfeit bill. It was in evidence that before passing it he had taken it to the cashier of a bank and asked his opinion of the bill, and he received a very prompt reply that it was a counterfeit. His lawyer, who had heard of the evidence to be brought against his client, asked him, just before going into court, 'Did you take the bill to the cashier of the bank and ask him if it was good?' 'I did,' was the reply. 'Well, what was the reply of the cashier?' The rascal was in a corner, but he got out of it in this fashion: 'He said it was a pretty tolerable, respectable sort of a bill.'"

Mr. Lincoln thought the clergyman was "pretty tolerable, respectable sort of a clergyman."

A visitor, congratulating Mr. Lincoln on the prospects of his reëlection, was answered with an anecdote of an Illinois farmer who undertook to blast his own rocks. His first effort at producing an explosion proved a failure. He explained the cause by exclaiming, "Pshaw, this powder has been shot before!"

An amusing, yet touching instance of the President's preoccupation of mind, occurred at one of his levees, when he was shaking hands with a host of visitors passing him in a continuous stream. An intimate acquaintance received the usual conventional hand-shake and salutation, but perceiving that he was not recognized, kept his ground instead of moving on, and spoke again; when the President, roused to a dim consciousness that something unusual had happened, perceived who stood before him, and seizing his friend's hand, shook it again heartily, saying, "How do you do? How do you do? Excuse me for not noticing you, I was thinking of a man down South." He afterward privately acknowledged that the "man down South" was Sherman, then on his march to the sea.

Mr. Lincoln may not have expected death from the hand of an assassin, but he had an impression, amounting to a "presentiment," that his life would end with the war. This was expressed not only to Mr. Lovejoy, as stated on a previous page, but to Mr. Stowe and others.

"He told me, in July, 1864," says a correspondent of the Boston "Journal," "that he was certain he should not outlast the rebellion.

"It was a time of dissension among the Republican leaders. Many of his best friends had deserted him, and were talking of an opposition convention to nominate another candidate; and universal gloom was among the people.

"The North was tired of the war, and supposed an honorable peace attainable. Mr. Lincoln knew it was not,—that any peace at that time would be only disunion. Speaking of it, he said: 'I have faith in the people. They will not consent to disunion. The danger is, in their being misled. Let them know the truth, and the country is safe.' He looked haggard and careworn; and further on in the interview I remarked on his appearance, 'You are wearing yourself out with work.' 'I can't work less,' he answered; 'but it isn't that,—work never troubled me. Things look badly, and I can't avoid anxiety. Personally, I care nothing about a reëlection; but if our divisions defeat us, I fear for the country.' When I suggested that right must eventually triumph, that I had never despaired of the result, he said:—

"'Neither have I, but I may never live to see it. I feel a presentiment that I shall not outlast the Rebellion. When it is over, my work will be done.'"

"The Freedmen," once said the President to the Secretary of War, "are the 'wards' of the nation."

"Yes," replied Stanton, "wards in chancery."

A few days before the President's death, Secretary Stanton tendered his resignation of the War Department. He accompanied the act with a heartfelt tribute to Mr. Lincoln's constant friendship and faithful devotion to the country; saying, also, that he as Secretary had accepted the position to hold it only until the war should end, and that now he felt his work was done, and his duty was to resign.

Mr. Lincoln was greatly moved by the Secretary's words, and tearing in pieces the paper containing the resignation, and throwing his arms about the Secretary, he said: "Stanton, you have been a good friend and a faithful public servant, and it is not for you to say when you will no longer be needed here." Several friends of both parties were present on the occasion, and there was not a dry eye that witnessed the scene.

"On the night of the 3rd of March, the Secretary of War, with others of the Cabinet, were in the company of the President, at the Capitol, awaiting the passage of the final bills of Congress. In the intervals of reading and signing these documents, the military situation was considered,—the lively conversation tinged by the confident and glowing account of General Grant, of his mastery of the position, and of his belief that a few days more would see Richmond in our possession, and the army of Lee either dispersed utterly or captured bodily,— when the telegram from Grant was received, saying that Lee had asked an interview with reference to peace. Mr. Lincoln was elated, and the kindness of his heart was manifest in intimations of favorable terms to be granted to the conquered Rebels.

"Stanton listened in silence, restraining his emotion, but at length the tide burst forth. 'Mr. President,' said he, 'to-morrow is inauguration day. If you are not to be the President of an obedient and united people, you had better not be inaugurated. Your work is already done, if any other authority than yours is for one moment to be recognized, or any terms made that do not signify you are the supreme head of the nation. If generals in the field are to negotiate peace, or any other chief magistrate is to be acknowledged on this continent, then you are not needed, and you had better not take the oath of office.'

"'Stanton, you are right!' said the President, his whole tone changing. 'Let me have a pen.'

"Mr. Lincoln sat down at the table, and wrote as follows:—

"'The President directs me to say to you that he wishes you to have no conference with General Lee, unless it be for the capitulation of Lee's army, or in some minor or purely military manner. He instructs me to say that you are not to decide, discuss, or confer upon any political question. Such questions the President holds in his own hands, and will submit them to no military conferences of conventions. In the mean time you are to press to the utmost your military advantages.'

"The President read over what he had written, and then said:—

"'Now Stanton, date and sign this paper, and send it to Grant. We'll see about this peace business.'

"The duty was discharged only too gladly by the energetic and far-sighted Secretary; with what effect and renown the country knows full well."*

Governor Yates, of Illinois, in a speech at Springfield, quoted one of Mr. Lincoln's early friends—W. T. Greene—as having said that the first time he ever saw Mr. Lincoln, he was in the Sangamon River with his trousers rolled up five feet, more or less, trying to pilot a flat-boat over a mill-dam. The boat was so full of water that it was hard to manage. Lincoln got the prow over, and then, instead of waiting to bail the water out, bored a hole through the projecting part and let it run out; affording a forcible illustration of the ready ingenuity of the future President in the quick invention of moral expedients.

Boston Commonwealth.

"Some two years ago," said Colonel Forney, in a speech at Weldon, Pennsylvania, before the "Soldiers' Aid Society," in 1865, "a deputation of colored people came from Louisiana, for the purpose of laying before the President a petition asking certain rights, not including the right of universal suffrage. The interview took place in the presence of a number of distinguished gentlemen. After reading their memorial, he turned to them and said: 'I regret, gentlemen, that you are not able to secure all your rights, and that circumstances will not permit the government to confer them upon you. I wish you would amend your petition, so as to include several suggestions which I think will give more effect to your prayer, and after having done so please hand it to me.' The leading colored man said: 'If you will permit me, I will do so here.' 'Are you, then, the author of this eloquent production?' asked Mr. Lincoln. 'Whether eloquent or not,' was the reply, 'it is my work;' and the Louisiana negro sat down at the President's side and rapidly and intelligently carried out the suggestions that had been made to him. The Southern gentlemen who were present at this scene did not hesitate to admit that their prejudices had just received another shock.

"To show the magnanimity of Mr. Lincoln, I may mention that on one occasion, when an editorial article appeared in my newspaper, the Washington 'Chronicle,' speaking well of the bravery and the mistaken sincerity of Stonewall Jackson, the news of whose death had been just received, the President wrote me a letter thanking me warmly for speaking kindly of a fallen foe. These were his words:—

"'I honor you for your generosity to one who, though contending against us in a guilty cause, was nevertheless a gallant man. Let us forget his sins over his fresh-made grave.'

"Again, I happened to be in the Executive Chamber when a number of Kentuckians insisted that troops should not be sent through that State for the purpose of putting down the rebel spirit in Tennessee. The President was hesitating what to do, and they were pressing immediate action.

"'I am,' he said, 'a good deal like the farmer who, returning to his home one winter night, found his two sweet little boys asleep with a hideous serpent crawling over their bodies. He could not strike the serpent without wounding or killing the children, so he calmly waited until it had moved away. Now I do not want to act in a hurry about this matter; I don't want to hurt anybody in Kentucky; but I will get the serpent out of Tennessee.'

"And he did march through Kentucky, to the aid of Andrew Johnson's mountaineers."

"The roll containing the Emancipation Proclamation was taken to Mr. Lincoln at noon on the first day of January, 1863, by Secretary Seward and his son Frederick. As it lay unrolled before him, Mr. Lincoln took a pen, dipped it in ink, moved his hand to the place for the signature, held it a moment, and then removed his hand and dropped the pen. After a little hesitation he again took up the pen and went through the same movement as before. Mr. Lincoln then turned to Mr. Seward, and said:—

"'I have been shaking hands since nine o'clock this morning, and my right arm is almost paralyzed. If my name ever goes into history it will be for this act, and my whole soul is in it. If my hand trembles when I sign the Proclamation, all who examine the document hereafter will say, "He hesitated."'

"He then turned to the table, took up the pen again, and slowly, firmly wrote that 'Abraham Lincoln' with which the whole world is now familiar. He looked up, smiled, and said: 'That will do.'"*

What Mr. Lincoln's policy on the subject of "reconstruction" would have been, had he lived, is clearly foreshadowed in the following extract from a letter to General Wadsworth, who was killed in one of the battles of the Wilderness. Few sentences from Mr. Lincoln's lips or pen are more worthy [of] the profound consideration and remembrance of his countrymen.

"You desire to know, in the event of our complete success in the field, the same being followed by a loyal and cheerful submission on the part of the South, if universal amnesty should not be accompanied with universal suffrage.

Rochester (New York) *Express.*

"Now, since you know my private inclinations as to what terms should be granted to the South in the contingency mentioned, I will here add, that if our success should thus be realized, followed by such desired results, I cannot see, if universal amnesty is granted, how, under the circumstances, I can avoid exacting in return universal suffrage, or at least suffrage on the basis of intelligence and military service.

"How to better the condition of the colored race has long been a study which has attracted my serious and careful attention; hence I think I am clear and decided as to what course I shall pursue in the premises, regarding it a religious duty, as the nation's guardian of these people who have so heroically vindicated their manhood on the battle-field, where, in assisting to save the life of the Republic, they have demonstrated in blood their right to the ballot, which is but the humane protection of the flag they have so fearlessly defended."

When Mr. Lincoln was in Congress, General Cass was nominated by the Democratic party for President. In a speech on the floor of the House shortly afterward, Mr. Lincoln subjected the political course of the candidate to scathing criticism. Quoting extracts from the speeches of General Cass, to show his vacillation in reference to the Wilmot Proviso, he added: "These extracts show that in 1846 General Cass was for the Proviso at once; that in March, 1847, he was still for it, but not just then; and that in December, he was against it altogether.

This is a true index of the whole man. When the question was raised in 1846, he was in a blustering hurry to take ground for it, . . . but soon he began to see glimpses of the great Democratic ox-gad waving in his face, and to hear indistinctly a voice saying: 'Back! back, sir! back a little!' He shakes his head, and bats his eyes, and blunders back to his position of March, 1847; but still the 'gad' waves, and the voice grows more distinct and sharper still: 'Back, sir! back, I say! further back!' and back he goes to the position of December, 1847, at which the 'gad' is still, and the voice soothingly says: 'So! stand still at that!'"

A party of gentlemen, among whom was a doctor of divinity of much dignity of manner, calling at the White House one day, was informed by the porter that the President was at dinner, but that he would present their cards. The doctor demurred to this, saying that he would call again. "Edward" assured them that he thought it would make no difference, and went in with the cards. In a few minutes the President walked into the room, with a kindly salutation, and a request that the friends would take seats. The doctor expressed his regret that their visit was so ill-timed, and that his Excellency was disturbed while at dinner. "Oh! no consequence at all," said Mr. Lincoln, good-naturedly. "Mrs. Lincoln is absent at present, and when she is away, I generally '*browse*' around."

"Upon entering the President's office one afternoon," says a Washington correspondent, "I found Mr. Lincoln busily counting greenbacks. 'This sir,' said he, 'is something out of my usual line; but a President of the United States has a multiplicity of duties not specified in the Constitution or acts of Congress. This is one of them. This money belongs to a poor negro who is a porter in the Treasury Department, at present very bad with the small-pox. He is now in hospital, and could not draw his pay because he could not sign his name. I have been at considerable trouble to overcome the difficulty and get it for him, and have at length succeeded in cutting red tape, as you newspaper men say. I am now dividing the money and putting by a portion labelled, in an envelope, with my own hands, according to his wish;' and he proceeded to indorse the package very carefully." No one witnessing the transaction could fail to appreciate the goodness of heart which prompted the President of the United States to turn aside for a time from his weighty cares to succor one of the humblest of his fellow-creatures in sickness and sorrow.

When General Phelps took possession of Ship Island, near New Orleans, early in the war, it will be remembered that he issued a proclamation, somewhat bombastic in tone, freeing the slaves. To the surprise of many people, on both sides, the President took no official notice of this movement. Some time had elapsed, when one day a friend took him to task for his seeming indifference on so important a matter.

"Well," said Mr. Lincoln, "I feel about that a good deal as a man whom I will call 'Jones,' whom I once knew, did about his wife. He was one of your meek men, and had the reputation of being badly henpecked. At last, one day his wife was seen switching him out of the house. A day or two afterward a friend met him in the street, and said: 'Jones, I have always stood up for you, as you know; but I am not going to do it any longer. Any man who will stand quietly and take a switching from his wife, deserves to be horsewhipped.' 'Jones' looked up with a wink, patting his friend on the back. 'Now *don't*,' said he: 'why, it didn't *hurt* me any; and you've no idea what a *power* of *good* it did Sarah Ann?'"

The Rev. Dr. Bellows, of New York, as President of the Sanitary Commission, backed by powerful influences, had pressed with great strenuousness upon the President the appointment of Dr. Hammond as Surgeon-General. For some unexplained reason, there was an unaccountable delay in making the appointment. One stormy evening—the rain falling in torrents—Dr. Bellows, thinking few visitors likely to trouble the President in such a storm, determined to make a final appeal, and stepping into a carriage, he was driven to the White House. Upon entering the Executive Chamber, he found Mr. Lincoln alone, seated at the long table, busily engaged in signing a heap of congressional documents, which lay before him. He barely nodded to Dr. Bellows as he entered, having learned what to expect, and kept straight on with his work. Standing opposite to him, Dr. B. employed his most powerful arguments, for ten or fifteen minutes, to accomplish the end sought, the President keeping steadily on signing the documents before him. Pausing, at length, to take breath, the clergyman was greeted in the most unconcerned manner, the pen still at work, with,— "Shouldn't wonder if Hammond was at this moment 'Surgeon-General,' and had been for some time."

"You don't mean to say, Mr. President," asked Dr. B. in surprise, "that the appointment has been made?"

"I may say to you," returned Mr. Lincoln, for the first time looking up, "that it *has*; only you needn't *tell* of it just yet."

In August, 1864, the prospects of the Union party, in reference to the Presidential election, became very gloomy. A friend, the private secretary of one of the cabinet ministers, who spent a few days in New York at this juncture, returned to Washington with so discouraging an account of the political situation, that after hearing it, the Secretary told him to go over to the White House and repeat it to the President. My friend said that he found Mr. Lincoln alone, looking more than usually careworn and sad. Upon hearing the statement, he walked two or three times across the floor in silence. Returning, he said with grim earnestness of tone and manner: "Well, I cannot run the political machine; I have enough on my hands without *that*.

It is the *people's* business,—the election is in their hands. If they turn their backs to the fire, and get *scorched* in the rear, they'll find they have got to '*sit*' on the 'blister'!"

Mr. Lincoln came to have an almost morbid dread of office-seekers, from whose importunity the executive of a republican government can necessarily never be free. Harassed with applications of every description, he once said that it sometimes seemed as if every visitor "darted at him, and with thumb and finger carried off a portion of his vitality."

As the day of his reinauguration approached, he said to Senator Clark, of New Hampshire, "Can't you and others start a public sentiment in favor of making no changes in offices except for good and sufficient cause? It seems as though the bare thought of going through again what I did the first year here, would *crush* me." To another he said, "I have made up my mind to make very few changes in the offices in my gift for my second term. I think now that I will not remove a single man, except for delinquency. To remove a man is very easy, but when I go to fill his place, there are *twenty* applicants, and of these I must make *nineteen* enemies." "Under these circumstances," says one of his friends, "Mr. Lincoln's natural charity for all was often turned into an unwonted suspicion of the motives of men whose selfishness cost him so much wear of mind. Once he said, 'Sitting here, where all the avenues to public patronage seem to come together in a knot, it does seem to me that our people are fast approaching the point where it can be said that seven eights of them are trying to find how to live at the expense of the other eighth."

A year or more before Mr. Lincoln's death, a delegation of clergymen waited upon him in reference to the appointment of the army chaplains. The delegation consisted of a Presbyterian, a Baptist, and an Episcopal clergyman. They stated that the character of many of the chaplains was notoriously bad, and they had come to urge upon the President the necessity of more discretion in these appointments. "But, gentlemen," said the President, "that is a matter which the Government has nothing to do with; the chaplains are chosen by the regiments." Not satisfied with this, the clergymen pressed, in turn, a change in the system. Mr. Lincoln heard them through without remark, and then said. "Without any disrespect, gentlemen, I will tell you a 'little story.' Once, in Springfield, I was going off on a short journey, and reached the depot a little ahead of time. Leaning against the fence just outside the depot was a little darkey boy, whom I knew, named 'Dick,' busily digging with his toe in a mud-paddle. As I came up, I said, '"Dick," what are you about?' 'Making a "*church*,"' said he. 'A church?' said I; 'what do you mean?' 'Why, yes,' said 'Dick,' pointing with his toe, 'don't you see? there is the shape of it; there's the "steps" and "front-door"—here the "pews," where the folks set—and there's the "pulpit,"' 'Yes, I see,' said I, 'but why don't you make a "minister?"' 'Laws,' answered 'Dick,' with a grin, 'I hain't got *mud* enough!'"

Mr. Lincoln had a dread of people who could not appreciate humor. He once instanced a member of his own cabinet, of whom he quoted the saying of Sydney Smith, that "it required a surgical operation to get a joke into his head." The light trifles of conversation diverted his mind, or, as he said of his theatregoing, gave him "a refuge from himself and his weariness."

One of the last stories I heard from Mr. Lincoln was concerning John Tyler, for whom it was to be expected, as an old Henry Clay Whig, he would entertain no great respect. "A year or two after Tyler's accession to the Presidency," said he, "contemplating an excursion in some direction, his son went to order a special train of cars. It so happened that the railroad superintendent was a very strong Whig. On 'Bob's' making known his errand, that official bluntly informed him that his road did not run any special trains for the President. 'What!' said 'Bob,' 'did you not furnish a special train for the funeral of General Harrison?' 'Yes,' said the superintendent, stroking his whiskers; 'and if you will only bring your father here in *that* shape, you shall have the best train on the road.'

"Once—on what was called a 'public day,' when Mr. Lincoln received all applicants in their turn—the writer* was struck

---

*Colonel Charles G. Halpine, *New York Citizen*.

by observing, as he passed through the corridor, the heterogeneous crowd of men and women, representing all ranks and classes, who were gathered in the large waiting-room outside the Presidential suite of offices.

"Being ushered into the President's chamber by Major Hay, the first thing he saw was Mr. Lincoln bowing an elderly lady out of the door,—the President's remarks to her being, as she still lingered and appeared reluctant to go: 'I am really very sorry, madam; very sorry. But your own good sense must tell you that I am not here to collect small debts. You must appeal to the courts in regular order.'

"When she was gone, Mr. Lincoln sat down, crossed his legs, locked his hands over his knees, and commenced to laugh,—this being his favorite attitude when much amused.

"'What odd kinds of people come to see me,' he said; 'and what odd ideas they must have about my office! Would you believe it, Major, that old lady who has just left, came in here to get from me an order for stopping the pay of a treasury clerk, who owes her a board-bill of about seventy dollars?' And the President rocked himself backward and forward, and appeared intensely amused.

"'She may have come in here a loyal woman,' continued Mr. Lincoln; 'but I'll be bound she has gone away believing that the worst pictures of me in the Richmond press only lack truth in not being half black and bad enough.'

"This led to a somewhat general conversation, in which I expressed surprise that he did not adopt the plan in force at all military head-quarters, under which every applicant to see the general commanding had to be filtered through a sieve of officers,—assistant adjutant-generals, and so forth,—who allowed none in to take up the general's time save such as they were satisfied had business of sufficient importance, and which could be transacted in no other manner than by a personal interview.

"'Of every hundred people who come to see the general-in-chief daily,' I explained, 'not ten have any sufficient business with him, nor are they admitted. On being asked to explain for what purpose they desire to see him, and stating it, it is found, in nine cases out of ten, that the business properly belongs to some one or other of the subordinate bureaus. They are then referred, as the case may be, to the quartermaster, commissary, medical, adjutant-general, or other departments, with an assurance that even if they saw the general-in-chief he could do nothing more for them than give the same direction. With these points courteously explained,' I added, 'they go away quite content, although refused admittance.'

"'Ah, yes!' said Mr. Lincoln, gravely,—and his words on this matter are important as illustrating a rule of his action, and to some extent, perhaps, the essentially representative character of his mind and of his administration,—'ah, yes, such things do very well for you military people, with your arbitrary rule, and in your camps. But the office of President is essentially a civil one, and the affair is very different. For myself, I feel—though the tax on my time is heavy—that no hours of my day are better employed than those which thus bring me again within the direct contact and atmosphere of the average of our whole people. Men moving only in an official circle are apt to become merely official—not to say arbitrary—in their ideas, and are apter and apter, with each passing day, to forget that they only hold power in a representative capacity. Now this is all wrong. I go into these promiscuous receptions of all who claim to have business with me twice each week, and every applicant for audience has to take his turn, as if waiting to be shaved in a barber's shop. Many of the matters brought to my notice are utterly frivolous, but others are of more or less importance, and all serve to renew in me a clearer and more vivid image of that great popular assemblage out of which I sprung, and to which at the end of two years I must return. I tell you, Major,' he said,—appearing at this point to recollect I was in the room, for the former part of these remarks had been made with half-shut eyes, as if in soliloquy,—'I tell you that I call these receptions my "*public-opinion baths*;" for I have but little time to read the papers and gather public opinion that way; and though they may not be pleasant in all their particulars, the effect, as a whole, is renovating and invigorating to my perceptions of responsibility and duty.'"

No nobler reply ever fell from the lips of ruler, than that uttered by President Lincoln in response to the clergyman who ventured to say, in his presence, that he *hoped* "the LORD was on our side."

"I am not at all concerned about that," replied Mr. Lincoln, "for I know that the LORD is *always* on the side of the *right*. But it is my constant anxiety and prayer that *I* and *this nation* should be on the LORD's *side*."

In the midst of the despondency produced by the raid on Washington, in the summer of 1864, and the successful return of the Rebel force to Richmond, the President's Proclamation of July 18th appeared, calling for five hundred thousand more men.

In view of the impending presidential canvass, Mr. Lincoln's strongest friends looked upon this step, at this time, as calculated to utterly defeat his chances of reëlection. Commissioner Dole ventured to say as much upon the President's announcement to him of his contemplated purpose.

"It matters not what becomes of me," replied Mr. Lincoln; "we must have the men! If I go down, I intend to go like the *Cumberland*, with my colors flying!"

Upon Mr. Lincoln's return to Washington, after the capture of Richmond, a member of the Cabinet asked him if it would be proper to permit Jacob Thompson to slip through Maine in disguise, and embark from Portland. The President, as usual, was disposed to be merciful, and to permit the arch-rebel to pass unmolested, but the Secretary urged that he should be arrested as a traitor. "By permitting him to escape the penalties of treason," persistently remarked the Secretary, "you sanction it." "Well," replied Mr. Lincoln, "let me tell you a story. There was an Irish soldier here last summer, who wanted something to drink stronger than water, and stopped at a drug-shop, where he espied a soda-fountain. 'Mr. Doctor,' said he, 'give me, plase, a glass of soda-wather, an' if yees can put in a few drops of whiskey unbeknown to any one, I'll be obleeged.' Now," continued Mr. Lincoln, "if Jake Thompson is permitted to go through Maine unbeknown to any one, what's the harm? So don't have him arrested."

I asked the President, during the progress of the battles of the Wilderness, how General Grant personally impressed him as compared with other officers of the army, and especially those who had been in command.

"The great thing about Grant," said he, "I take it, is his perfect coolness and persistency of purpose. I judge he is not easily excited,—which is a great element in an officer,—and he has the *grit* of a bull-dog! Once let him get his 'teeth' *in*, and nothing can shake him off."

One of the latest of Mr. Lincoln's stories was told to a party of gentlemen, who, amid the tumbling ruins of the 'Confederacy,' anxiously asked "what he would do with 'Jeff. Davis'?"

"There was a boy in Springfield," rejoined Mr. Lincoln, "who saved up his money and bought a 'coon,' which, after the novelty wore off, became a great nuisance. He was one day leading him through the streets, and had his hands full to keep clear of the little vixen, who had torn his clothes half off of him. At length he sat down on the curb-stone, completely fagged out. A man passing was stopped by the lad's disconsolate appearance, and asked the matter. 'Oh,' was the reply, 'this coon is such a *trouble* to me!' 'Why don't you get rid of him, then?' said the gentleman. 'Hush!' said the boy; 'don't you see he is gnawing his rope off? I am going to let him do it, and then I will go home and tell the folks *that he got away from me?*'"

LXIX.

The last story told by Mr. Lincoln was drawn out by a circumstance which occurred just before the interview with Messrs. Colfax and Ashmun, on the evening of his assassination.

Marshall Lamon of Washington had called upon him with an application for the pardon of a soldier. After a brief hearing the President took the application, and when about to write his name upon the back of it, he looked up and said: "Lamon, have you ever heard how the Patagonians eat oysters? They open them and throw the shells out of the window until the pile gets higher than the house, and then they move;" adding: "I feel to-day like commencing a new pile of pardons, and I may as well begin it just here."

At the subsequent interview with Messrs. Colfax and Ashmun, Mr. Lincoln was in high spirits. The uneasiness felt by his friends during his visit to Richmond was dwelt upon, when he sportively replied that he "supposed he should have been uneasy also, had any other man been President and gone there; but as it was, he felt no apprehension of danger whatever." Turning to Speaker Colfax, he said: "Sumner has the 'gavel' of the Confederate Congress, which he got at Richmond, and intended to give to the Secretary of War, but I insisted he must give it to you, and you tell him from me to hand it over."

Mr. Ashmun, who was the presiding officer of the Chicago Convention in 1860, alluded to the "gavel" used on that occasion, saying he had preserved it as a valuable memento.

Mr. Ashmun then referred to a matter of business connected with a cotton claim, preferred by a client of his, and said that he desired to have a "commission" appointed to examine and decide upon the merits of the case. Mr. Lincoln replied, with considerable warmth of manner, "I have done with 'commissions.' I believe they are contrivances to *cheat* the Government out of every pound of cotton they can lay their hands on." Mr. Ashmun's face flushed, and he replied that he hoped the President meant no personal imputation.

Mr. Lincoln saw that he had wounded his friend, and he instantly replied: "You did not understand me, Ashmun. I did not mean what you inferred. I take it all back." Subsequently he said: "I apologize to you, Ashmun."

He then engaged to see Mr. Ashmun early the next morning, and taking a card, he wrote:

"Allow Mr. Ashmun and friend to come in at 9 A.M. to-morrow.   A. Lincoln."

These were his last written words. Turning to Mr. Colfax he said: "You will accompany Mrs. Lincoln and me to the theatre, I hope?" Mr. Colfax pleaded other engagements,— expecting to start on his Pacific trip the next morning. The party passed out on the portico together, the President saying at the very last, "Colfax, don't forget to tell the people of the mining regions what I told you this morning about the development when peace comes;" then shaking hands with both gentlemen, he followed Mrs. Lincoln into the carriage, leaning forward, at the last moment, to say as they were driven off, "I will telegraph you, Colfax, at San Francisco,"—passing thus forth for the last time from under that roof into the creeping shadows which were to settle before another dawn into a funeral pall upon the orphaned heart of the nation.

*   *   *   *   *   *   *   *

LXX.

"On the Monday before the assassination,[*] when the President was on his return from Richmond, he stopped at City Point. Calling upon the head surgeon at that place, Mr. Lincoln told him that he wished to visit all the hospitals under his charge, and shake hands with every soldier. The surgeon asked if he knew what he was undertaking, there being five or six thousand soldiers at that place, and it would be quite a tax upon his strength to visit all the wards and shake hands with every soldier. Mr. Lincoln answered with a smile, he 'guessed he was equal to the task; at any rate he would try, and go as far as he could; he should never, probably, see the boys again, and he wanted them to know that he appreciated what they had done for their country.'

"Finding it useless to try to dissuade him, the surgeon began his rounds with the President, who walked from bed to bed, extending his hand to all, saying a few words of sympathy to some, making kind inquiries of others, and welcomed by all with the heartiest cordiality.

"As they passed along, they came to a ward in which lay a Rebel who had been wounded and was a prisoner. As the tall figure of the kindly visitor appeared in sight he was recognized

---

[*]Correspondence of the *N.Y. Independent*.

by the Rebel soldier, who, raising himself on his elbow in bed, watched Mr. Lincoln as he approached, and extending his hand exclaimed, while tears ran down his cheeks: 'Mr. Lincoln, I have long wanted to see you, to ask your forgiveness for ever raising my hand against the old flag.' Mr. Lincoln was moved to tears. He heartily shook the hand of the repentant Rebel, and assured him of his good-will, and with a few words of kind advice passed on.

"After some hours the tour of the various hospitals was made, and Mr. Lincoln returned with the surgeon to his office. They had scarcely entered, however, when a messenger came saying that one ward had been omitted, and 'the boys' wanted to see the President. The surgeon, who was thoroughly tired, and knew Mr. Lincoln must be, tried to dissuade him from going; but the good man said he must go back; he would not knowingly omit one, 'the boys' would be so disappointed. So he went with the messenger, accompanied by the surgeon, and shook hands with the gratified soldiers, and then returned again to the office.

"The surgeon expressed the fear that the President's arm would be lamed with so much handshaking, saying that it certainly must ache. Mr. Lincoln smiled, and saying something about his 'strong muscles,' stepped out at the open door, took up a very large, heavy axe which lay there by a log of wood, and chopped vigorously for a few moments, sending the chips flying in all directions; and then, pausing, he extended his right arm to its full length, holding the axe out horizontally, without its even quivering as he held it. Strong men who looked on—men accustomed to manual labor—could not hold the same axe in that position for a moment. Returning to the office, he took a glass of lemonade, for he would take no stronger beverage; and while he was within, the chips he had chopped were gathered up and safely cared for by a hospital steward, because they were 'the chips that Father Abraham chopped.' In a few hours more the beloved President was at home in Washington; in a few days more he had passed away and a bereaved nation was in mourning."

LXXI.

Mr. Lincoln returned from Richmond with a heart-full purpose to issue immediately a proclamation for a day of National Thanksgiving. "Babylon" had fallen, and with his own eyes, as from another Pisgah, he had looked over into the promised land of Peace,— a land which, like his great prototype, his feet were not to tread!

During his absence from Washington, Secretary Seward met with the serious accident by which his arm and jaw were broken. Mr. Lincoln's first visit was to the house of the Secretary, who was confined to his bed by his injuries. After a few words of sympathy and condolence, with a countenance beaming with joy and satisfaction, he entered upon an account of his visit to Richmond, and the glorious success of Grant,—throwing himself, in his almost boyish exultation, at full length across the bed, supporting his head upon one hand, and in this manner reciting the story of the collapse of the Rebellion. Concluding, he lifted himself up and said: "And now for a day of Thanksgiving!" Mr. Seward entered fully into his feelings, but observed, with characteristic caution, that the issue between Sherman and Johnston had not yet been decided, and a premature celebration might have the effect to nerve the remaining army of the Confederacy to greater desperation. He advised, therefore, no official designation of a day "until the result of Sherman's combinations was known." Admitting the force of the Secretary's view, Mr. Lincoln reluctantly gave up the purpose, and three days later suffered in his own person the last, most atrocious, but culminating act of the most wicked of all rebellions recorded on the pages of history! It was the last interview on earth between the President and his Secretary of State.

This incident, related by Mr. Seward to a friend* while slowly recovering from the murderous attack upon himself, was followed by an interesting account of his personal relations with Mr. Lincoln. "No knife was ever sharp enough to divide us upon any question of public policy," said the Secretary; "though we frequently arrived at the same conclusion through different

---

*J. C. Derby, Esq., of New York.

processes of thought." "Once only," he continued, musingly, "did we disagree in sentiment." Mr. D. inquired the subject of dissent. "His 'colonization' scheme," was the reply, "which I opposed on the self evident principle that all *natives* of a country have an *equal* right in its soil."

The knowledge of the terrible calamity which had befallen the nation was rigidly withheld from Mr. Seward at the time, his physician fearing that the shock would be too great for him to bear. The Sunday following, he had his bed wheeled around so that he could see the tops of the trees in the park opposite his residence,—just putting on their spring foliage,—when his eyes caught sight of the Stars and Stripes at half-mast on the War Department, on which he gazed awhile, then turning to his attendant, said: "The President is dead!" The confused attendant stammered as he tried to say nay; but the Secretary could not be deceived. "If he had been alive, he would have been the first to call on me," he continued; "but he has not been here, nor has he sent to know how I am; and there is the flag at half-mast." The statesman's inductive reason had discerned the truth, and in silence the great tears coursed down his gashed cheeks, as it sank into his heart.

LXXII.

At the Cabinet meeting held the morning of the day of the assassination, it was afterward remembered, a remarkable circumstance occurred. General Grant was present, and during a lull in the discussion the President turned to him and asked if he had heard from General Sherman. General Grant replied that he had not, but was in hourly expectation of receiving despatches from him announcing the surrender of Johnston.

"Well," said the President, "you will hear very soon now, and the news will be important."

"Why do you think so?" said the General.

"Because," said Mr. Lincoln, "I had a dream last night; and ever since the war began, I have invariably had the same dream before any important military event occurred." He then instanced Bull Run, Antietam, Gettysburg, etc., and said that before each of these events, he had had the same dream; and turning to Secretary Welles, said: "It is in your line, too, Mr. Welles. The dream is, that I saw a ship sailing very rapidly; and I am sure that it portends some important national event."

Later in the day, dismissing all business, the carriage was ordered for a drive. When asked by Mrs. Lincoln if he would like any one to accompany them, he replied, "No; I prefer to ride by ourselves to-day." Mrs. Lincoln subsequently said that she never saw him seem so supremely happy as on this occasion. In reply to a remark to this effect, the President said: "And well I may feel so, Mary, for I consider this day the war has come to a close." And then added: "We must both be more cheerful in the future; between the war and the loss of our darling Willie, we have been very miserable."

*   *   *   *   *   *   *   *

Little "Tad's" frantic grief upon being told that his father had been shot was alluded to in the Washington correspondence of the time. For twenty-four hours the little fellow was perfectly inconsolable. Sunday morning, however, the sun rose in unclouded splendor, and in his simplicity he looked upon this as a token that his father was happy. "Do you think my father has gone to heaven?" he asked of a gentleman who had called upon Mrs. Lincoln. "I have not a doubt of it," was the reply. "Then," he exclaimed, in his broken way, "I am glad he has gone there, for he never was happy after he came here. This was not a good place for him!"

LXXIII.

"President Lincoln," says the Hon. W. D. Keely,* "was a large and many-sided man, and yet so simple that no one, not even a child, could approach him without feeling that he had found in him a sympathizing friend. I remember that I apprised him of the fact that a lad, the son of one of my townsmen, had

---

*Address in Philadelphia upon the death of Mr. Lincoln.

served a year on board the gunboat *Ottawa*, and had been in two important engagements; in the first as a powder-monkey, when he had conducted himself with such coolness that he had been chosen as captain's messenger in the second; and I suggested to the President that it was in his power to send to the Naval School, annually, three boys who had served at least a year in the navy.

"He at once wrote on the back of a letter from the commander of the *Ottawa*, which I had handed him, to the Secretary of the Navy: 'If the appointments for this year have not been made, let this boy be appointed.' The appointment had not been made, and I brought it home with me. It directed the lad to report for examination at the school in July. Just as he was ready to start, his father, looking over the law, discovered that he could not report until he was fourteen years of age, which he would not be until September following. The poor child sat down and wept. He feared that he was not to go to the Naval School. He was, however, soon consoled by being told that 'the President could make it right.' It was my fortune to meet him the next morning at the door of the Executive Chamber with his father.

"Taking by the hand the little fellow,—short for his age, dressed in the sailor's blue pants and shirt,—I advanced with him to the President, who sat in his usual seat, and said: 'Mr. President, my young friend, Willie Bladen, finds a difficulty about his appointment. You have directed him to appear at the school in July; but he is not yet fourteen years of age.' But before I got half of this out, Mr. Lincoln, laying down his spectacles, rose and said: 'Bless me! is that the boy who did so gallantly in those two great battles? Why, I feel that I should bow to him, and not he to me.'

"The little fellow had made his graceful bow. The President took the papers at once, and as soon as he learned that a postponement till September would suffice, made the order that the lad should report in that month. Then putting his hand on Willie's head, he said: 'Now, my boy, go home and have good fun during the two months, for they are about the last holiday you will get.' The little fellow bowed himself out, feeling that the President of the United States, though a very great man, was one that he would nevertheless like to have a game of romps with."

There was not unfrequently a curious mingling of humor and pathos exhibited in Mr. Lincoln's exercise of the pardoning power. Lieutenant-Governor Ford, of Ohio, had an appointment with him one evening at six o'clock. As he entered the vestibule of the White House his attention was attracted by a poorly clad young woman who was violently sobbing. He asked her the cause of her distress. She said the she had been ordered away by the servants, after vainly waiting many hours to see the President about her only brother, who had been condemned to death. Her story was this: She and her brother were foreigners, and orphans. They had been in this country several years. Her brother enlisted in the army, but, through bad influences, was induced to desert. He was captured, tried, and sentenced to be shot—the old story. The poor girl had obtained the signatures of some persons who had formerly known him to a petition for a pardon, and, alone, had come to Washington to lay the case before the President. Thronged as the waiting-rooms always were, she had passed the long hours of two days trying in vain to get an audience, and had at length been ordered away.

Mr. Ford's sympathies were at once enlisted. He said that he had come to see the President, but did not know as *he* should succeed. He told her, however, to follow him up-stairs, and he would see what could be done. Just before reaching the door, Mr. Lincoln came out, and meeting his friend, said good-humoredly, "are you not ahead of time?" Mr. Ford showed his watch, with the pointers upon the hour of six. "Well," replied Mr. Lincoln, "I have been so busy to-day that I have not had time to get a lunch. Go in and sit down; I will be back directly."

Mr. Ford made the young woman accompany him into the office, and when they were seated, said to her: "Now, my good girl, I want you to muster all the courage you have in the world. When the President comes back he will sit down in that arm-chair. I shall get up to speak to him, and as I do so you must force yourself between us, and insist upon his examination of

your papers, telling him it is a case of life and death, and admits
of no delay." These instructions were carried out to the letter.
Mr. Lincoln was at first somewhat surprised at the apparent
forwardness of the young woman, but observing her distressed
appearance, he ceased conversation with his friend, and commenced an examination of the document she had placed in his
hands. Glancing from it to the face of the petitioner, whose
tears had broken forth afresh, he studied its expression for a
moment, and then his eye fell upon her scanty but neat dress.
Instantly his face lighted up. "My poor girl," said he, "you have
come here with no governor, or senator, or member of congress, to plead your cause. You seem honest and truthful; and"—
with much emphasis—"you don't wear '*hoops;* and I will be
whipped but I will pardon your brother!"

Among the applicants received on another occasion by the
President, was a woman who had also met with considerable
difficulty and delay in getting admission to him. She said that
her husband had been arrested some months before and sent
to the "Old Capitol" prison; that he had not been "tried," and
could not learn as he was likely to be; and she appealed to the
President as a husband and father to interfere and order an
immediate trial. Mr. Lincoln said he was sorry this could not
be done,—adding that such cases were much like the different
sacks of grain at a country grist-mill, all "waiting their turn to
be ground," and that it would be unfair for the "*miller*" to show

any "partiality." The woman left, but the next day appeared again before him. Recognizing her, Mr. Lincoln asked if anything "new" had happened. "No," replied the woman; "but I have been thinking, sir, about what you said concerning the 'grists,' and I am afraid *mine* will get 'mouldy' and 'spoil' before its turn comes around, so I have come to ask, Mr. President, that it may be taken to some other 'mill' to be ground."

Mr. Lincoln was so much amused at the wit and shrewdness of the request, that he instantly gave the woman an unconditional discharge for her husband.

LXXIV.

"Good morning, Abe!" was the greeting addressed to the President, as we sat together in his office one morning,—he absorbed at his desk, and I with my pencil. I looked up in astonishment at the unaccustomed familiarity.

"Why, Dennis," returned Mr. Lincoln, "is this you?"

"Yes, Abe," was the rejoinder; "I made up my mind I must come down and see you once while you were President, anyhow. So here I am, all the way from Sangamon."

Sitting down, side by side, it would have been difficult for one unfamiliar with democratic institutions to tell, by the appearance or conversation, which was the President and which the back-countryman, save that from time to time I overheard the man addressed as "Dennis" refer to family trials and hardships, and intimate that one object of his journey so far, was to see if his old friend "could not do something for one of his boys?"

The response to this was: "Now, Dennis, sit down and write out what you want, so that I can have it before me, and I will see what can be done."

I have always supposed that this was "Dennis Hanks," the early companion and friend of Mr. Lincoln; but my attention at the time being diverted, the matter passed out of my mind, and I neglected subsequently to inquire.

About this period—it may have been the following evening—the house was thrown into an uproar by a performance of little "Tad's." I was sitting in Mr. Nicolay's room, about ten o'clock when Robert Lincoln came in with a flushed face. "Well," said he, "I have just had a great row with the President of the United States!"

"What?" said I.

"Yes," he replied, "and very good cause there is for it, too. Do you know," he continued, "'Tad' went over to the War Department to-day, and Stanton, for the fun of the thing,—putting him a peg above the 'little corporal' of the French Government,—commissioned him 'lieutenant.' On the strength of this, what does 'Tad' do but go off and order a quantity of muskets sent to the house! Tonight he had the audacity to discharge the guard, and he then mustered all the gardeners and servants, gave them the guns, drilled them, and put them on duty in their place. I found it out an hour ago," continued Robert, "and thinking it a great shame, as the men had been hard at work all day, I went to father with it; but instead of punishing 'Tad,' as I think he ought, he evidently looks upon it as a good joke, and won't do anything about it!"

"Tad," however, presently went to bed, and then the men were quietly discharged. And so it happened that the presidential mansion was unguarded one night, at least, during the war!

The second week in July the whole country, and Washington in particular, was thrown into a fever of anxiety by the rebel raid upon that city under Early and Breckinridge. The night of Sunday, the 10th, I have always believed the city might have been captured had the enemy followed up his advantage. The defences were weak, and there were comparatively but few troops in the city or vicinity. All day Monday the excitement was at the highest pitch. At the White House the cannonading at Fort Stevens was distinctly heard throughout the day. During Sunday, Monday, and Tuesday, the President visited the forts and outworks, part of the time accompanied by Mrs. Lincoln. While at Fort Stevens on Monday, both were imprudently exposed,—rifle-balls coming, in several instances, alarmingly near!

The almost defenceless condition of the city was the occasion of much censure. Some blamed General Halleck; others

General Augur, the commander of the Department; others the Secretary of War; and still others the President.

Subsequently the rebel force returned to Richmond almost unharmed. I saw no one who appeared to take this more to heart than Mrs. Lincoln, who was inclined to lay the responsibility at the door of the Secretary of War.

Two or three weeks later, when tranquility was perfectly restored, it was said that Stanton called upon the President and Mrs. Lincoln one evening at the "Soldiers' Home." In the course of conversation the Secretary said, playfully, "Mrs. Lincoln, I intend to have a full-length portrait of you painted, standing on the ramparts at Fort Stevens overlooking the fight!"

"That is very well," returned Mrs. Lincoln, very promptly; "and I can assure you of one thing, Mr. Secretary, if I had a few *ladies* with me the Rebels would not have been permitted to get away as they did!"

LXXV.

It was not generally known before the publication of Dr. Holland's biography of Mr. Lincoln, that he was once engaged in a "duel," although a version of the affair had been published previous to his biographer's account of it, which, however, the few who saw it were disposed to regard as a fabrication.

One evening, at the rooms of the Hon. I. N. Arnold, of Illinois, I met Dr. Henry, of Oregon, an early and intimate friend of Mr. Lincoln's. Mr. Arnold asked me in the course of conversation if I had ever heard of the President's "duel" with General Shields? I replied that I might have seen a statement of the kind, but did not suppose it to be true. "Well," said Mr. Arnold, "we were all young folks together at the time in Springfield. In some way a difficulty occurred between Shields and Lincoln, resulting in a challenge from Shields, which was at length accepted, Mr. Lincoln naming '*broadswords*' for weapons, and the two opposite banks of the Mississippi, where the river was about a *mile* wide, for the '*ground*.'"

Dr. Henry, who had listened quietly to this, here broke in, "That will do for a 'story,' Arnold," said he, "but it will hardly pass with me, for I happened to be Lincoln's '*second*' on the occasion. The facts are these. You will bear me witness that there was never a more spirited circle of young folks in one town than lived in Springfield at that period. Shields, you remember, was a great '*beau*.' For a bit of amusement one of the young ladies wrote some verses, taking him off sarcastically, which were abstracted from her writing-desk by a mischievous friend, and published in the local newspaper. Shields, greatly irritated, posted at once to the printing-office and demanded the name of the author. Much frightened, the editor requested a day or two to consider the matter, and upon getting rid of Shields went directly to Mr. Lincoln with his trouble.

"'Tell Shields,' was the chivalric rejoinder, 'that I hold myself responsible for the verses.' The next day Mr. Lincoln left for a distant section to attend court. Shields, boiling over with wrath, followed and 'challenged' him. Scarcely knowing what he did, Mr. Lincoln accepted the challenge, seeing no alternative. The choice of weapons being left to him, he named 'broadswords,' intending to act only on the defensive, and thinking his long arms would enable him to keep clear of his antagonist.

"I was then a young surgeon," continued Dr. Henry, "and Mr. Lincoln desired me accompany him to the point chosen for the contest,—'Bloody Island,' in the Mississippi, near St. Louis,—as his 'second.' To this I at length consented, hoping to prevent bloodshed. On our way to the ground we met Colonel Hardin, a friend of both parties, and a cousin of the lady who was the real offender. Suspecting something wrong, Hardin subsequently followed us, coming in upon the party just as Lincoln was clearing up the underbrush which covered the ground. Entering heartily upon an attempt at pacification, he at length succeeded in mollifying Shields, and the whole party returned harmoniously to Springfield, and thus the matter ended."

This version of the affair coming from an eye-witness in undoubtedly in all respects correct. It subsequently came in my way to know that Mr. Lincoln himself regarded the circumstance with much regret and mortification, and hoped it might be forgotten. In February preceding his death a distinguished officer of the army called at the White House, and was entertained by the President and Mrs. Lincoln for an hour in the parlor. During the conversation the gentleman said, turning to Mrs. Lincoln, "Is it true, Mr. President, as I have heard, that you once went out to fight a 'duel' for the sake of the lady by your side?"

"I do not deny it," replied Mr. Lincoln, with a flushed face; "but if you desire my friendship you will never mention the circumstance again!"

LXXVI.

In August following the rebel raid, Judge J. T. Mills, of Wisconsin, in company with ex-Governor Randall, of that State, called upon the President at the "Soldiers' Home."

Judge Mills subsequently published the following account of the interview, in the "Gray County (Wisconsin) Herald":—

*   *   *   *   *   *   *   *

"The Governor addressed him: 'Mr. President, this is my friend and your friend Mills, from Wisconsin.'

"'I am glad to see my friends from Wisconsin; they are the hearty friends of the Union.'

"'I could not leave the city, Mr. President, without hearing words of cheer from your own lips. Upon you, as the representative of the loyal people, depend, as we believe, the existence of our government and the future of America.'

"'Mr. President,' said Governor Randall, 'why can't you seek seclusion, and play hermit for a fortnight? it would reinvigorate you.'

"'Aye,' said the President, 'two or three weeks would do me good, but I cannot fly from my thoughts; my solicitude for this great country follows me wherever I go. I don't think it is personal vanity or ambition, though I am not free from these infirmities, but I cannot but feel that the weal or woe of this great nation will be decided in November. There is no programme offered by any wing of the Democratic party but that must result in the permanent destruction of the Union.'

"'But Mr. President, General McClellan is in favor of crushing out the rebellion by force. He will be the Chicago candidate.'

"'Sir,' said the President, 'the slightest knowledge of arithmetic will prove to any man that the rebel armies cannot be destroyed by democratic strategy. It would sacrifice all the white men of the North to do it. There are now in the service of the United States near two hundred thousand able-bodied colored men, most of them under arms, defending and acquiring Union territory. The democratic strategy demands that these forces should be disbanded, and that the masters be conciliated by restoring them to slavery. The black men who now assist Union prisoners to escape are to be converted into our enemies, in the vain hope of gaining the good-will of their masters. We shall have to fight two nations instead of one.

"'You cannot conciliate the South if you guarantee to them ultimate success; and the experience of the present war proves their success is inevitable if you fling the compulsory labor of millions of black men into their side of the scale. Will you give our enemies such military advantages as insure success, and then depend on coaxing, flattery, and concession, to get them back into the Union? Abandon all the posts now garrisoned by black men; take two hundred thousand men from our side and put them in the battle-field or cornfield against us, and we would be compelled to abandon the war in three weeks.

"'We have to hold territory in inclement and sickly places; where are the Democrats to do this? It was a free fight, and the field was open to the War Democrats to put down this rebellion by fighting against both master and slave long before the present policy was inaugurated.

"'There have been men base enough to propose to me to return to slavery the black warriors of Port Hudson and Olustee, and thus win the respect of the masters they fought. Should I do so, I should deserve to be damned in time and eternity. Come what will, I will keep my faith with friend and foe. My enemies pretend I am now carrying on this war for the sole purpose of Abolition. So long as I am President, it shall be carried on for the sole purpose of restoring the Union. But no human power can subdue this rebellion without the use of the emancipation policy, and every other policy calculated to weaken the moral and physical forces of the rebellion.

"'Freedom has given us two hundred thousand men raised on Southern soil. It will give us more yet. Just so much it has subtracted from the enemy, and instead of alienating the South, there are now evidences of a fraternal feeling growing up between our men and the rank and file of the rebel soldiers. Let my enemies prove to the country that the destruction of slavery is not necessary to a restoration of the Union. I will abide the issue.'

"I saw that the President was a man of deep convictions, of abiding faith in justice, truth, and Providence. His voice was pleasant, his manner earnest and emphatic. As he warmed with his theme, his mind grew to the magnitude of his body. I felt I was in the presence of the great guiding intellect of the age, and that those 'huge Atlantean shoulders were fit to bear the weight of mightiest monarchies.' His transparent honesty, republican simplicity, his gushing sympathy for those who offered their lives for their country, his utter forgetfulness of self in his concern for its welfare, could not but inspire me with confidence that he was Heaven's instrument to conduct his people through this sea of blood to a Canaan of peace and freedom."

LXXVII.

No reminiscence of the late President has been given to the public more thoroughly valuable and characteristic than a sketch which appeared in the New York "Independent" of September 1st, 1864, from the pen of the Rev. J. P. Gulliver, of Norwich, Connecticut:—

"It was just after his controversy with Douglas, and some months before the meeting of the Chicago Convention of 1860, that Mr. Lincoln came to Norwich to make a political speech. It was in substance the famous speech delivered in New York, commencing with the noble words: 'There is but one political question before the people of this country, which is this, *Is slavery right, or is it wrong?*' and ending with the yet nobler words: 'Gentlemen, it has been said of the world's history hitherto that "might makes right;" it is for us and for our times to reverse the maxim, and to show that *right makes might!*'

"The next morning I met him at the railroad station, where he was conversing with our Mayor, every few minutes looking up the track and inquiring, half impatiently and half quizzically, 'Where's that 'wagon' of yours? Why don't the 'wagon' come along?' On being introduced to him, he fixed his eyes upon me, and said: 'I have seen you before, sir!' 'I think not,' I replied; 'you must mistake me for some other person.' 'No, I don't; I saw you at the Town Hall, last evening.' 'Is it possible, Mr. Lincoln, that you could observe individuals so closely in such a crowd?' 'Oh, yes!' he replied, laughing; 'that is my way. I don't forget faces. Were you not there?' 'I was, sir, and I was well paid for going;' adding, somewhat in the vein of pleasantry he had started, 'I consider it one of the most extraordinary speeches I ever head.'

"As we entered the cars, he beckoned me to take a seat with him, and said, in a most agreeably frank way, 'Were you sincere in what you said about my speech just now?' 'I meant every word of it, Mr. Lincoln. Why, an old dyed-in-the-wool Democrat, who sat near me, applauded you repeatedly; and, when rallied upon his conversion to sound principles, answered, "I don't believe a word he says, but I can't help clapping him, he is so *pat!*" That I call the triumph of oratory,—

"When you convince a man against his will,
Though he is of the same opinion still."

Indeed, sir, I learned more of the art of public speaking last evening than I could from a whole course of lectures on Rhetoric.'

"'Ah! that reminds me,' said he, 'of a most extraordinary circumstance which occurred in New Haven the other day. They told me that the Professor of Rhetoric in Yale College,—

a very learned man, isn't he?'

"'Yes, sir, and a fine critic too.'

"'Well, I suppose so; he ought to be, at any rate,—they told me that he came to hear me, and took notes of my speech, and gave a lecture on it to his class the next day; and, not satisfied with that, he followed me up to Meriden the next evening, and heard me again for the same purpose. Now, if this is so, it is to my mind very extraordinary. I have been sufficiently astonished at my success in the West. It has been most unexpected. But I had no thought of any marked success at the East, and least of all that I should draw out such commendations from literary and learned men. Now,' he continued, 'I should like very much to know what it was in my speech you thought so remarkable, and what you suppose interested my friend, the Professor, so much.'

"'The clearness of your statements, Mr. Lincoln; the unanswerable style of your reasoning, and especially your illustrations, which were romance and pathos, and fun and logic all welded together. That story about the snakes, for example, which set the hands and feet of your Democratic hearers in such vigorous motion, was at once queer and comical, and tragic and argumentative. It broke through all the barriers of a man's previous opinions and prejudices at a crash, and blew up the very citadel of his false theories before he could know what had hurt him.'

"'Can you remember any other illustrations,' said he, 'of this peculiarity of my style?'

"I gave him others of the same sort, occupying some half-hour in the critique, when he said: 'I am much obliged to you for this. I have been wishing for a long time to find some one who would make this analysis for me. It throws light on a subject which has been dark to me. I can understand very readily how such a power as you have ascribed to me will account for the effect which seems to be produced by my speeches. I hope you have not been too flattering in your estimate. Certainly, I have had a most wonderful success, for a man of my limited education.'

"'That suggests, Mr. Lincoln, an inquiry which has several times been upon my lips during this conversation. I want very much to know how you got this unusual power of "putting things." It must have been a matter of education. No man has it by nature alone. What has your education been?'

"'Well, as to education, the newspapers are correct; I never went to school more than six months in my life. But, as you say, this must be a product of culture in some form. I have been putting the question you ask me to myself, while you have been talking. I can say this, that among my earliest recollections I remember how, when a mere child, I used to get irritated when any body talked to me in a way I could not understand. I don't think I ever got angry at anything else in my life. But that always disturbed my temper, and has ever since. I can remember going to my little bedroom, after hearing the neighbors talk of an evening with my father, and spending no small part of the night walking up and down, and trying to make out what was the exact meaning of some of their, to me, dark sayings. I could not sleep, though I often tried to, when I got on such a hunt after an idea, until I had caught it; and when I thought I had got it, I was not satisfied until I had repeated it over and over, until I had put it in language plain enough, as I thought, for any boy I knew to comprehend. This was a kind of passion with me, and it has stuck by me; for I am never easy now, when I am handling a thought, till I have bounded it North, and bounded it South, and bounded it East, and bounded it West. Perhaps that accounts for the characteristic you observe in my speeches, though I never put the two things together before.'

"'Mr. Lincoln, I thank you for this. It is the most splendid educational fact I ever happened upon. This is *genius*, with all its impulsive, inspiring, dominating power over the mind of its possessor, developed by education into *talent*, with its uniformity, its permanence, and its disciplined strength,—always ready, always available, never capricious,—the highest possession of the human intellect. But, let me ask, did you prepare for your profession?'

"'Oh, yes! I "read law," as the phrase is that is, I became a lawyer's clerk in Springfield, and copied tedious documents, and picked up what I could of law in the intervals of other work. But your question reminds me of a bit of education I had, which I am bound in honesty to mention. In the course of my law-reading, I constantly came upon the word *demonstrate*. I thought at first that I understood its meaning, but soon became satisfied that I did not. I said to myself, "What do I mean when I *demonstrate* more than when I *reason* or *prove*? How does *demonstration* differ from any other proof?" I consulted Webster's Dictionary. That told of "certain proof," "proof beyond the possibility of doubt;" but I could form no idea what sort of proof that was. I thought a great many things were proved beyond a possibility of doubt, without recourse to any such extraordinary process of reasoning as I understood "demonstration" to be. I consulted all the dictionaries and books of reference I could find, but with no better results. You might as well have defined *blue* to a blind man. At last I said, "Lincoln, you can never make a lawyer if you do not understand what *demonstrate* means;" and I left my situation in Springfield, went home to my father's house, and stayed there till I could give any proposition in the six books of Euclid at sight. I then found out what "demonstrate" means, and went back to my law-studies.'

"I could not refrain from saying, in my admiration at such a development of character and genius combined: 'Mr. Lincoln, your success is no longer a marvel. It is the legitimate result of adequate causes. You deserve it all, and a great deal more. If you will permit me, I would like to use this fact publicly. It will be most valuable in inciting our young men to that patient classical and mathematical culture which most minds absolutely require. No man can talk well unless he is able first of all to define to himself what he is talking about. Euclid, well studied, would free the world of half its calamities, by banishing half the nonsense which now deludes and curses it. I have often thought that Euclid would be one of the best books to put on the catalogue of the Tract Society, if they could only get people to read it. It would be a means of grace.'

"'I think so,' said he, laughing; 'I vote for Euclid.'

"Just then a gentleman entered the car who was well known as a very ardent friend of Douglas. Being a little curious to see how Mr. Lincoln would meet him, I introduced him after this fashion:—'Mr. Lincoln, allow me to introduce Mr. L——, a very particular friend of your particular friend, Mr. Douglas.' He at once took his hand in a most cordial manner, saying: 'I have no doubt you think you are right, sir.' This hearty tribute to the honesty of a political opponent, with the manner of doing it, struck me as a beautiful exhibition of a large-hearted charity, of which we see far too little in this debating, fermenting world.

"As we neared the end of our journey, Mr. Lincoln turned to me very pleasantly, and said: 'I want to thank you for this conversation. I have enjoyed it very much.' I replied, referring to some stalwart denunciations he had just been uttering of the demoralizing influences of Washington upon Northern politicians in respect to the slavery question, 'Mr. Lincoln, may I say one thing to you before we separate?'

"'Certainly, anything you please.'

"'You have just spoken of the tendency of political life in Washington to debase the moral convictions of our representatives there by the admixture of considerations of mere political expediency. You have become, by the controversy with Mr. Douglas, one of our leaders in this great struggle with slavery, which is undoubtedly *the* struggle of the nation and the age. What I would like to say is this, and I say it with a full heart, *Be true to your principles and we will be true to you, and God will be true to us all!*' His homely face lighted up instantly with a beaming expression, and taking my hand warmly in both of his, he said: 'I say *Amen* to that—AMEN to that!'

"There is a deep excavation in the rock shown to visitors, among the White Mountains, into which one of the purest of the mountain streams pours itself, known as 'The Pool.' As you stand by its side at an ordinary time you look down upon a mass of impenetrable green, lying like a rich emerald in a setting of granite upon the bosom of the mountain. But occasionally the noon-day sun darts through it a vertical ray which penetrates to its very bottom, and shows every configuration of the varied interior. I felt at that moment that a ray had darted down to the bottom of Abraham Lincoln's heart, and that I could see the whole. It seemed to me as beautiful as that emerald pool, and as pure. I have never forgotten that glimpse. When the strange revocation came of the most rational and reasonable proclamation of Fremont,—'The slaves of Rebels shall be set free,'—I remembered that hearty '*Amen*,' and stifled my rising apprehensions. I remembered it in those dark days when McClellan, Nero-like, was fiddling on James River, and Pope was being routed before Washington, and the report came that a prominent Cabinet Minister had boasted that he had succeeded in preventing the issue of the Emancipation Proclamation; I said: 'Abraham Lincoln will prove true yet.' *And he has!* God bless him! *he has.* Slow, if you please, but *true*. Unimpassioned, if you please, but *true*. Jocose, trifling, if you please, but *true*. Reluctant to part with unworthy official advisers, but *true* himself— *true as steel!* I could wish him less a man of facts, and more a man of ideas. I could wish him more stern and more vigorous: but every man has his faults, and still I say: *Amen to Abraham Lincoln!*"*

LXXVIII.

The Hon. Orlando Kellogg, of New York, was sitting in his

---

*This article was written and first published some months previous to Mr. Lincoln's reëlection, during the depression of the public mind following the "raid" on Washington.

room at his boarding-house one evening, when one of his constituents appeared,—a white-headed old man,—who had come to Washington in great trouble, to seek the aid of his representative in behalf of his son. His story was this: "The young man had formerly been very dissipated. During an absence from home a year or two previous to the war, he enlisted in the regular army, and, after serving six months, deserted. Returning to his father, who knew nothing of this, he reformed his habits, and when the war broke out, entered heart and soul into the object of raising a regiment in his native county, and was subsequently elected one of its officers. He had proved an efficient officer, distinguishing himself particularly on one occasion, in a charge across a bridge, when he was severely wounded,—his colonel being killed by his side. Shortly after this, he came in contact with one of his old companions in the 'regular' service, who recognized him, and declared his purpose of informing against him. Overwhelmed with mortification, the young man procured a furlough and returned home, revealing the matter to his father, and declaring his purpose never to submit to an arrest,—'he would die first.'" In broken tones the old man finished his statement, saying: "Can you do anything for us, Judge?—it is a hard, hard case!" "I will see about that," replied the representative, putting on his hat; "wait here until I return." He went immediately to the White House, and fortunately finding Mr. Lincoln alone, they sat down together, and he repeated the old man's story. The President made no demonstration of particular interest until the Judge reached the description of the charge across the bridge, and the wound received. "Do you say," he interrupted, "that the young man was wounded?" "Yes," replied the congressman, "badly." "Then he has shed his blood for his country," responded Mr. Lincoln, musingly. "Kellogg," he continued, brightening up, "isn't there something in Scripture about the 'shedding of blood' being 'the remission of sins?'" "Guess you are about right there," replied the Judge. "It is a good 'point,' and there is no going behind it," rejoined the President; and taking up his pen, another "pardon"—this time without "oath," condition, or reserve—was added to the records of the War Office.

"Among a large number of persons waiting in the room to speak with Mr. Lincoln, on a certain day in November, '64, was a small, pale, delicate-looking boy about thirteen years old. The President saw him standing, looking feeble and faint, and said: 'Come here, my boy, and tell me what you want.' The boy advanced, placed his hand on the arm of the President's chair, and with bowed head and timid accents said: 'Mr. President, I have been a drummer in a regiment for two years, and my colonel got angry with me and turned me off. I was taken sick, and have been a long time in hospital. This is the first time I have been out, and I came to see if you could not do something for me.'

The President looked at him kindly and tenderly, and asked him where he lived. 'I have no home,' answered the boy. 'Where is your father?' 'He died in the army,' was the reply. 'Where is your mother?' continued the President. 'My mother is dead also. I have no mother, no father, no brothers, no sisters, and,' bursting into tears, 'no friends—nobody cares for me.' Mr. Lincoln's eyes filled with tears, and he said to him, 'Can't you sell newspapers?' 'No,' said the boy, 'I am too weak; and the surgeon of the hospital told me I must leave, and I have no money, and no place to go to.' The scene was wonderfully affecting. The President drew forth a card, and addressing on it certain officials to whom his request was law, gave special directions 'to care for this poor boy.' The wan face of the little drummer lit up with a happy smile as he received the paper, and he went away convinced that he had one good and true friend, at least, in the person of the President."*

No incident of this character related of the late President, is more profoundly touching in its tenderness and simplicity than that given to me the last evening I passed at the White House, in the office of the private secretary, by a resident of Washington,* who witnessed the scene.

"I was waiting my turn to speak to the President one day,

---

*Rev. Mr. Henderson, Louisville, Ky.

*Mr. Murtagh, of the *Washington Republican*.

some three or four weeks since," said Mr. M——, "when my attention was attracted by the sad patient face of a woman advanced in life, who in a faded hood and shawl was among the applicants for an interview."

"Presently Mr. Lincoln turned to her, saying in his accustomed manner, 'Well, my good woman, what can I do for you this morning?' 'Mr. President,' said she, 'my husband and three sons all went into the army. My husband was killed in the fight at——. I get along very badly since then, living all alone, and I thought I would come and ask you to release to me my oldest son.' Mr. Lincoln looked into her face a moment, and in his kindest accents responded, 'Certainly! Certainly! If you have given us *all*, and your prop has been taken away, you are justly entitled to one of your boys!' He immediately made out an order discharging the young man, which the woman took, and thanking him gratefully, went away.

"I had forgotten the circumstance," continued M——, "till last week, when happening to be here again, who should come in but the same woman. It appeared that she had gone herself to the front, with the President's order, and found the son she was in search of had been mortally wounded in a recent engagement, and taken to a hospital. She found the hospital, but the boy was dead, or died while she was there. The surgeon in charge made a memorandum of the facts upon the back of the President's order, and almost broken-hearted, the poor woman had found her way again into Mr. Lincoln's presence. He was much affected by her appearance and story, and said: 'I know what you wish me to do now, and I shall do it without your asking; I shall release to you your second son.' Upon this, he took up his pen and commenced writing the order. While he was writing the poor woman stood by his side, the tears running down her face, and passed her hand softly over his head, stroking his rough hair, as I have seen a fond mother caress a son. By the time he had finished writing, his own heart and eyes were full. He handed her the paper: 'Now,' said he, '*you* have one and *I* one of the other two left: that is no more than right.' She took the paper, and reverently placing her hand again upon his head, the tears still upon her cheeks, said: 'The Lord bless you, Mr. Lincoln. May you live a thousand years, and may you always be the head of this great nation!'"

LXXIX.

The Hon. W. H. Herndon, of Springfield, Illinois, for more than twenty years the law-partner of Mr. Lincoln, delivered an address in that city, December 12th, 1865, upon the life and character of the lamented President, which, for masterly analysis, has scarcely an equal in the annals of biographical literature. Quaint and original in style and construction, this description— an imperfect abstract of which I subjoin—is in singular harmony with the character it depicts. To those who knew Mr. Lincoln personally, so thorough a dissection of his nature and traits will need no indorsement; while to the multitude who knew him not, it may be commended as probably more complete and exhaustive in its treatment of the subject, than anything which has been given to the world.

"Abraham Lincoln was born in Hardin County, Kentucky, February 12th, 1809. He moved to Indiana in 1816; came to Illinois in March, 1830; to old Sangamon County in 1831, settling in New Salem, and from this last place to this city in April, 1837: coming as a rude, uncultivated boy, without polish or education, and having no friends. He was about six feet four inches high, and when he left this city was fifty-one years old, having good health and no gray hairs, or but few on his head. He was thin, wiry, sinewy, raw-boned; thin through the breast to the back, and narrow across the shoulders; standing, he leaned forward—was what may be called stoop-shouldered, inclining to the consumptive by build. His usual weight was one hundred and sixty pounds. His organization—rather his structure and functions—worked slowly. His blood had to run a long distance from his heart to the extremities of his frame, and his nerve-force had to travel through dry ground a long distance before his muscles were obedient to his will. His structure was loose and leathery; his body was shrunk and shrivelled, having dark skin, dark hair,—looking woe-struck. The whole man, body and mind, worked slowly, creakingly, as if it needed oiling. Physically, he was a very powerful man, lifting with ease four hundred or six hundred pounds. His mind was like his body, and worked slowly but strongly. When he walked, he moved cautiously but firmly, his long arms and hands on them, hanging like giant's hands, swung down by his side. He walked with even tread, the inner sides of his feet being parallel. He put the whole foot flat down on the ground at once, not landing on the heel; he likewise lifted his foot all at once, not rising from the toe, and hence he had no spring to his walk. He had economy of fall and lift of foot, though he had no spring or apparent ease of motion in his tread. He walked undulatory, up and down, catching and pocketing tire, weariness, and pain, all up and down his person, preventing them from locating. The first opinion of a stranger, or a man who did not observe closely, was that his walk implied shrewdness, cunning,—a tricky man; but his was the walk of caution and firmness. In sitting down on a common chair he was no taller than ordinary men. His legs and arms were, abnormally, unnaturally long, and in undue proportion to the balance of his body. It was only when he stood up that he loomed above other men.

"Mr. Lincoln's head was long and tall from the base of the brain and from the eyebrows. His head ran backwards, his forehead rising as it ran back at a low angle, like Clay's, and, unlike Webster's, almost perpendicular. The size of his hat, measured at the hatter's block, was 7⅛, his head being, from ear to ear, 6½ inches, and from the front to the back of the brain 8 inches. Thus measured, it was not below the medium size. His forehead was narrow but high; his hair was dark, almost black, and lay floating where his fingers or the winds left it, piled up at random. His cheek-bones were high, sharp, and prominent; his eyebrows heavy and prominent; his jaws were long, upcurved, and heavy; his nose was large, long, and blunt, a little awry towards the right eye; his chin was long, sharp, and upcurved; his eyebrows cropped out like a huge rock on the brow of a hill; his face was long, sallow, and cadaverous, shrunk, shrivelled, wrinkled, and dry, having here and there a hair on the surface; his cheeks were leathery; his ears were large, and ran out almost at right angles from his head, caused partly by heavy hats and partly by nature; his lower lip was thick, hanging, and undercurved, while his chin reached for the lip upcurved; his neck was neat and trim, his head being well balanced on it; there was the lone mole on the right cheek, and Adam's apple on his throat.

"Thus stood, walked, acted, and looked Abraham Lincoln. He was not a pretty man by any means, nor was he an ugly one; he was a homely man, careless of his looks, plain-looking and plain-acting. He had no pomp, display, or dignity, so-called. He appeared simple in his carriage and bearing. He was a sad-looking man; his melancholy dripped from him as he walked. His apparent gloom impressed his friends, and created a sympathy for him,—one means of his great success. He was gloomy, abstracted, and joyous,—rather humorous,—by turns. I do not think he knew what real joy was for many years.

"Mr. Lincoln sometimes walked our streets cheerily,— good-humoredly, perhaps joyously,—and then it was, on meeting a friend, he cried 'How d'y?' clasping one of his friend's hands in both of his, giving a good hearty soul-welcome. Of a winter's morning, he might be seen stalking and stilting it towards the market-house, basket on arm, his old gray shawl wrapped around his neck, his little Willie or Tad running along at his heels, asking a thousand little quick questions, which his father heard not, not even then knowing that little Willie or Tad was there, so abstracted was he. When he thus met a friend, he said that something put him in mind of a story which he heard in Indiana or elsewhere, and tell it he would, and there was no alternative but to listen.

"Thus, I say, stood and walked and looked this singular man. He was odd, but when that gray eye and face and every feature were lit up by the inward soul in fires of emotion, *then* it was that all these apparently ugly features sprang into organs of beauty, or sunk themselves into a sea of inspiration that sometimes flooded his face. Sometimes it appeared to me that Lincoln's soul was just fresh from the presence of its Creator.

*   *   *   *   *   *   *   *

"I have asked the friends and foes of Mr. Lincoln alike, what they thought of his perceptions. One gentleman of undoubted ability and free from all partiality or prejudice, said, 'Mr. Lincoln's perceptions are slow, a little perverted, if not somewhat distorted and diseased.' If the meaning of this is that Mr. Lincoln saw things from a peculiar angle of his being, and from this was susceptible to Nature's impulses, and that he so expressed himself, then I have no objection to what is said. Otherwise, I dissent. Mr. Lincoln's perceptions were slow, cold, precise, and exact. Everything came to him in its precise shape and color. To some men the world of matter and of man comes ornamented with beauty, life, and action, and hence more or less false and inexact. No lurking illusion or other error, false in itself, and clad for the moment in robes of splendor, ever passed undetected or unchallenged over the threshold of his mind,—that point that divides vision from the realm and home of thought. Names to him were nothing, and titles naught,—assumption always standing back abashed at his cold, intellectual glare. Neither his perceptions nor intellectual vision were perverted, distorted, or diseased. He saw all things through a perfect mental lens. There was no diffraction or refraction there. He was not impulsive, fanciful, or imaginative, but cold, calm, precise, and exact. He threw his whole mental light around the object, and in time, substance, and quality stood apart; from and color took their appropriate places, and all was clear and exact in his mind. His fault, if any, was that he saw things less than they really were; less beautiful and more frigid. In his mental view he crushed the unreal, the inexact, the hollow, and the sham. He saw things in rigidity rather than in vital action. Here was his fault. He saw what no man could dispute; but he failed to see what might have been seen. To some minds the world is all life, a soul beneath the material; but to Mr. Lincoln no life was individual or universal that did not manifest itself to him. His mind was his standard. His perceptions were cool, persistent, pitiless in pursuit of the truth. No error went undetected, and no falsehood unexposed, if he once was aroused in search of truth. If his perceptions were perverted, distorted, and diseased, would to Heaven that more minds were so.

* * * * * * * *

"The true peculiarity of Mr. Lincoln has not been seen by his various biographers; or, if seen, they have failed woefully to give it that prominence which it deserves. It is said that Newton saw an apple fall to the ground from a tree, and beheld the law of the universe in that fall; Shakspeare saw human nature in the laugh of a man; Professor Owen saw the animal in its claw;

and Spencer saw the evolution of the universe in the growth of a seed. Nature was suggestive to all these men. Mr. Lincoln no less saw philosophy in a story, and a schoolmaster in a joke. No man, no men, saw nature, fact, thing, or man from his standpoint. His was a new and original position, which was always suggesting, hinting something to him. Nature, insinuations, hints, and suggestions were new, fresh, original, and odd to him. The world, fact, man, principle, all had their powers of suggestion to his susceptible soul. They continually put him in mind of something. He was odd, fresh, new, original, and peculiar for this reason, that he was a new, odd, and original creation and fact. He had keen susceptibilities to the hints and suggestions of nature, which always put him in mind of something known or unknown. Hence his power and tenacity of what is called association of ideas must have been great. His memory was tenacious and strong. His susceptibility to all suggestions and hints enabled him at will to call up readily the associated and classified fact and idea.

"As an evidence of this, especially peculiar to Mr. Lincoln, let me ask one question. Were Mr. Lincoln's expression and language odd and original, standing out peculiar from those of all other men? What does this imply? Oddity and originality of *vision* as well as expression; and what is expression in words and human language, but a telling of what we see, defining the idea arising from and created by vision and view in us. Words and language are but the counterparts of the idea,—the other half of the idea; they are but the stinging, hot, heavy, leaden bullets that drop from the mould; and what are they in a rifle with powder stuffed behind them and fire applied, but an embodied force pursuing their object. So are words an embodied power feeling for comprehension in other minds. Mr. Lincoln was often perplexed to give expression to his ideas: first, because he was not master of the English language; and, secondly, because there were no words in it containing the coloring, shape, exactness, power, and gravity of his ideas. He was frequently at a loss for a word, and hence was compelled to resort to stories, maxims, and jokes to embody his idea, that it might be comprehended. So true was this peculiar mental vision of his, that though mankind has been gathering, arranging, and classifying facts for thousands of years, Lincoln's peculiar stand-point could give him no advantage of other men's labor. Hence he tore up to the deep foundations all arrangements of facts, and coined and arranged new plans to govern himself. He was compelled, from his peculiar mental organization, to do this. His labor was great, continuous, patient, and all-enduring.

"The truth about this whole matter is that Mr. Lincoln read *less* and thought *more* than any man in his sphere in America. No man can put his finger on any great book written in the last or present century that he read. When young he read the Bible, and when of age he read Shakspeare. This latter book was scarcely ever out of his mind. Mr. Lincoln is acknowledged to have been a great man, but the question is what made him great. I repeat, that he read less and thought more than any man of his standing in America, if not in the world. He possessed originality and power of thought in an eminent degree. He was cautious, cool, concentrated, with continuity of reflection; was patient and enduring. These are some of the grounds of his wonderful success.

"Not only was nature, man, fact, and principle suggestive to Mr. Lincoln, not only had he accurate and exact perceptions, but he was causative, *i.e.*, his mind ran back behind all facts, things, and principles to their origin, history, and first cause,— to that point where forces act at once as effect and cause. He would stop and stand in the street and analyze a machine. He would whittle things to a point, and then count the numberless inclined planes, and their pitch, making the point. Mastering and defining this, he would then cut that point back, and get a broad transverse section of his pine stick, and peel and define that. Clocks, omnibuses, and language, paddle-wheels, and idioms, never escaped his observation and analysis. Before he could form any idea of anything, before he would express his opinion on any subject, he must know it in origin and history, in substance and quality, in magnitude and gravity. He must know his subject inside and outside, upside and downside. He searched his own mind and nature thoroughly, as I have often heard him say. He must analyze a sensation, an idea, and words, and run them back to their origin, history, purpose, and destiny. He was most emphatically a remorseless analyzer of facts, things, and principles. When all these processes had been well and thoroughly gone through, he could form an opinion and express it, but no sooner. He had no faith. "Say so's" he had no respect for, coming though they might from tradition, power, or authority.

"All things, facts, and principles had to run through his crucible and be tested by the fires of his analytic mind; and hence, when he did speak his utterances rang out gold-like, quick, keen, and current upon the counters of the understanding. He reasoned logically, through analogy and comparison. All opponents dreaded him in his originality of idea, condensation, definition, and force of expression, and woe be to the man who hugged to his bosom a secret error if Mr. Lincoln got on the chase of it. I say, woe to him! Time could hide the error in no nook or corner of space in which he would not detect and expose it.

* * * * * * * *

"Though Mr. Lincoln had accurate perceptions, though nature was extremely suggestive to him, though he was a profound thinker as well as analyzer, still his judgments and opinions formed upon minor matters were often childish. I have sometimes asked prominent, talented, and honest men in this and other States for their manly opinion of Mr. Lincoln's judgments. I did this to confirm or overthrow my own opinions on this point. Their answers were that his judgments were poor. But now what do we understand by the word 'judgments?' It is not reason, it is not will, nor is it understanding; but it is the judging faculty,—that capacity or power that forms opinions and decides on the fitness, beauty, harmony, and appropriateness of things under all circumstances and surroundings, quickly, wisely, accurately. Had Mr. Lincoln this quality of mind? I think not. His mind was like his body, and worked slowly.

* * * * * * * *

"One portion of mankind maintained that Mr. Lincoln was weak-minded, and they look at him only from the stand-point of his judgments. Another class maintain that he was a great, deep, profound man in his judgments. Do these two classes understand themselves? Both views cannot be correct. Mr. Lincoln's mind was slow, angular, and ponderous, rather than quick and finely discriminating, and *in time* his great powers of reason on cause and effect, on creation and relation, on substance and on truth, would form a proposition, an opinion wisely and well,—*that* no human being can deny. When his mind could not grasp premises from which to argue he was weaker than a child, because he had none of the child's intuitions,—the soul's quick, bright flash over scattered and unarranged facts.

"Mr. Lincoln was a peculiar man, having a peculiar mind; he was gifted with a peculiarity, namely, a new lookout on nature. Everything had to be newly created for him,—facts newly gathered, newly arranged, and newly classed. He had no faith, as already expressed. In order to believe he must see and feel, and thrust his hand into the place. He must taste, smell, and handle before he had faith, *i.e.*, belief. Such a mind as this must act slowly,—must have its time. His forte and power lay in his love of digging out for himself and hunting up for his own mind its own food, to be assimilated unto itself; and then in time he could and would form opinions and conclusions that no human power could overthrow. They were as irresistible as iron thunder, as powerful as logic embodied in mathematics.

"I have watched men closely in reference to their approaches to Mr. Lincoln. Those who approached him on his judgment side treated him tenderly—sometimes respectfully, but always as a weak-minded man. This class of men take the judgment as the standard of the mind. I have seen another class approach him on his reason-side, and they always crouched low down and truckled, as much as to say, 'great,' 'grand,' 'omnipotent.' Both these classes were correct. One took judgment as the standard of the man, and the other took reason. Yet both classes were wrong in this,—they sunk out of view one side of Mr. Lincoln. A third class knew him well, and always treated him with human respect: not that awe and reverence with which we regard the Supreme Being; not that supercilious haughtiness which greatness shows to littleness. Each will please to examine itself, and then judge of what I say. I have approached Mr. Lincoln on all sides, and treated him according to the angle approached.

*   *   *   *   *   *   *   *

"An additional question naturally suggests itself here, and it is this: Had Mr. Lincoln great, good common sense? Different persons, of equal capacity and honesty, hold different views on this question,—one class answering in the affirmative, and the other in the negative.

These various opinions necessarily spring out of the question just discussed. If the true test is that a man shall quickly, wisely, and well judge the rapid rush and whirl of human transactions, as accurately as though indefinite time and proper conditions were at his disposal, then I am compelled to follow the logic of things, and say that Mr. Lincoln had no more than ordinary common sense. The world, men and their actions, must be judged as they rush and pass along. They will not wait on us; will not stay for our logic and analysis; they must be seized as they run. We all our life act on the moment. Mr. Lincoln knew himself, and never trusted his dollar or his fame on his casual opinions; he never acted hastily on great matters.

*   *   *   *   *   *   *   *

"Mr. Lincoln very well knew that the great leading law of human nature was *motive*. He reasoned all ideas of a disinterested action from my mind. I used to hold that an action could be pure, disinterested, and holy, free from all selfishness, but he divested me of that delusion. His idea was that all human actions were caused by *motives*, and that at the bottom of those motives was *self*. He defied me to act without a motive and unselfishly; and when I did the act and told him of it, he analyzed and sifted it, and demonstrated beyond the possibility of controversy that it was altogether selfish. Though he was a profound analyzer of the laws of human nature, still he had no idea of the peculiar motives of the particular individual. He could not well discriminate in human nature. He knew but little of the play of the features as seen in 'the human face divine.' He could not distinguish between the paleness of anger and the crimson tint of modesty. He could not determine what each play of the features indicated.

*　*　*　*　*　*　*　*

"The great predominating elements of Mr. Lincoln's peculiar character, were: First, his great capacity and *power of reason;*
secondly, his excellent *understanding;* thirdly, an exalted idea of
the sense of *right and equity;* and, fourthly, his intense venera-
tion of what was *true and good.* His reason ruled despotically all
other faculties and qualities of his mind. His conscience and
heart were ruled by it. His conscience was ruled by one faculty—reason. His heart was ruled by two faculties—reason and
conscience. I know it is generally believed that Mr. Lincoln's
heart, his love and kindness, his tenderness and benevolence,
were his ruling qualities; but this opinion is erroneous in every
particular. First, as to his *reason.* He dwelt in the mind, not in
the conscience, and not in the heart. He lived and breathed and
acted from his reason,—the throne of logic and the home of
principle, the realm of Deity in man. It is from this point that
Mr. Lincoln must be viewed. His views were correct and original. He was cautious not to be deceived; he was patient and enduring. He had concentration and great continuity of thought;
he had a profound analytic power; his visions were clear, and he
was emphatically the master of statement. His pursuit of the
truth was indefatigable, terrible. He reasoned from his well-
chosen principles with such clearness, force, and compactness,

that the tallest intellects in the land bowed to him with respect. He was the strongest man I ever saw, looking at him from the stand-point of his reason,—the throne of his logic. He came down from that height with an irresistible and crushing force. His printed speeches will prove this; but his speeches before courts, especially before the Supreme Courts of the State and Nation, would demonstrate it: unfortunately none of them have been preserved. Here he demanded time to think and prepare. The office of reason is to determine the truth. Truth is the power of reason—the child of reason. He loved and idolized truth for its own sake. It was reason's food.

"Conscience, the second great quality and forte of Mr. Lincoln's character, is that faculty which loves the just: its office is justice; right and equity are its correlatives. It decides upon all acts of all people at all times. Mr. Lincoln had a deep, broad, living conscience. His great reason told him what was true, good, and bad, right, wrong, just or unjust, and his conscience echoed back its decision; and it was from this point that he acted and spoke and wove his character and fame among us. His conscience ruled his heart; he was always just before he was gracious. This was his motto, his glory: and this is as it should be. It cannot be truthfully said of any mortal man that he was always just. Mr. Lincoln was not always just; but his great general life was. It follows that if Mr. Lincoln had great reason and great conscience, he was an honest man. His great and general life was honest, and he was justly and rightfully entitled to the appellation, 'Honest Abe.' Honesty was his great polar star.

"Mr. Lincoln had also a good understanding; that is, the faculty that understands and comprehends the exact state of things, their near and remote relation. The understanding does not necessarily inquire for the reason of things. I must here repeat that Mr. Lincoln was an odd and original man; he lived by himself and out of himself. He could not absorb. He was a very sensitive man, unobtrusive and gentlemanly, and often hid himself in the common mass of men, in order to prevent the discovery of his individuality. He had no insulting egotism, and no pompous pride; no haughtiness, and no aristocracy. He was not indifferent, however, to approbation and public opinion. He was not an upstart, and had no insolence. He was a meek, quiet, unobtrusive gentleman. These qualities of his nature merged somewhat his identities. Read Mr. Lincoln's speeches, letters, messages, and proclamations, read his whole record in his actual life, and you cannot fail to perceive that he had good understanding. He understood and fully comprehended himself, and what he did and why he did it, better than most living men.

*   *   *   *   *   *   *   *

"There are contradictory opinions in reference to Mr. Lincoln's *heart and humanity*. One opinion is that he was cold and obdurate, and the other opinion is that he was warm and affectionate. I have shown you that Mr. Lincoln first lived and breathed upon the world from his head and conscience. I have attempted to show you that he lived and breathed upon the world through the tender side of his heart, subject at all times and places to the logic of his reason, and to his exalted sense of right and equity, namely, his conscience. He always held his conscience subject to his head; he held his heart always subject to his head and conscience. His heart was the lowest organ, the weakest of the three. Some men would reverse this order, and declare that his heart was his ruling organ; that always manifested itself with love, regardless of truth and justice, right and equity. The question still is, was Mr. Lincoln a cold, heartless man, or a warm, affectionate man? Can a man be a warm-hearted man who is all head and conscience, or nearly so? What, in the first place, do we mean by a warm-hearted man? It is one who goes out of himself and reaches for others spontaneously, because of a deep love of humanity, apart from equity and truth, and does what it does for love's sake? If so, Mr. Lincoln was a cold man. Or, do we mean that when a human being, man or child, approached him in behalf of a matter of right, and that the prayer of such an one was granted, that this is an evidence of his love? The African was enslaved, his rights were violated, and a principle was violated in them. Rights imply obligations as well as duties. Mr. Lincoln was President; he was in a position that made it his duty through his sense of right, his love of principle, his constitutional obligations imposed upon him by oath of office, to strike the blow against slavery. But did he do it for love? He himself has answered the question: 'I would not free the slaves if I could preserve the Union without it.' I use this argument against his too enthusiastic friends. If you mean that this is love for love's sake, then Mr. Lincoln was a warm-hearted man—not otherwise. To use a general expression, his general life was cold. He had, however, a strong latent capacity to love; but the object must first come as principle, second as right, and third as lovely. He loved abstract humanity when it was oppressed. This was an abstract love, not concrete in the individual, as said by some. He rarely used the term love, yet was he tender and gentle. He gave the key-note to his own character, when he said, 'with malice toward none, and with charity for all,' he did what he did. He had no intense loves, and hence no hates and no malice. He had a broad charity for imperfect man, and let us imitate his great life in this.

"'But was not Mr. Lincoln a man of great humanity?' asks a friend at my elbow, a little angrily; to which I reply, 'Has not that question been answered already?' Let us suppose that it has not. We must understand each other. What do you mean by humanity? Do you mean that he had much of human nature in him? If so, I will grant that he was a man of humanity. Do you mean, if the above definition is unsatisfactory, that Mr. Lincoln was tender and kind? Then I agree with you. But if you mean to say that he so loved a man that he would sacrifice truth and right for him, for love's sake, then he was not a man of humanity. Do you mean to say that he so loved man, for love's sake, that his heart led him out of himself, and compelled him to go in search of the objects of his love, for their sake? He never, to my knowledge, manifested this side of his character. Such is the law of human nature, that it cannot be all head, all conscience, and all heart at one and the same time in one and the same person. Our Maker made it so, and where God through reason blazed the path, walk therein boldly. Mr. Lincoln's glory and power lay in the just combination of head, conscience, and heart, and it is here that his fame must rest, or not at all.

"Not only were Mr. Lincoln's perceptions good; not only was nature suggestive to him; not only was he original and strong; not only had he great reason, good understanding; not only did he love the true and good—the eternal *right*; not only was he tender and kind,—but, in due proportion and in legitimate subordination, had he a glorious combination of them all. Through his perceptions,—the suggestiveness of nature, his originality and strength; through his magnificent reason, his understanding, his conscience, his tenderness, and kindness, his heart, rather than love,—he approximated as nearly as most human beings in this imperfect state to an embodiment of the great moral principle, 'Do unto others as ye would they should do unto you.'

*　*　*　*　*　*　*　*

"There are two opinions—radically different opinions—expressed about Mr. Lincoln's will, by men of equal and much capacity. One opinion is, that he had *no* will; and the other is, that he was *all* will—omnipotently so. These two opinions are loudly and honestly affirmed. Mr. Lincoln's mind loved the true, the right, and good, all the great truths and principles in the mind of man. He loved the true, first; the right, second; and the good, the least. His mind struggled for truths and his soul for substances. Neither in his head nor in his soul did he care for forms, methods, ways,—the *non*-substantial facts or things. He could not, by his very structure and formation in mind and body, care anything about them. He did not intensely or much care for particular individual man,—the dollar, property, rank, order, manners, or such like things. He had no avarice in his nature, or other like vice. He despised, somewhat, all technical rules in law and theology and other sciences,—mere forms everywhere,—because they were, as a general rule, founded on arbitrary thoughts and ideas, and not on reason, truth, right, and the good. These things were without substance, and he disregarded them because they cramped his original nature. What suited a little, narrow, critical mind did not suit Mr. Lincoln's, any more than a child's clothes did his body. Generally, Mr. Lincoln could not take any interest in little local elections—town meetings. He attended no gatherings that pertained to local or other such interests, saving general political ones. He did not care (because he could not, in his nature) who succeeded to the presidency of this or that Christian Association or Railroad Convention; who made the most money; who was going to Philadelphia, when and for what, and what were the costs of such a trip. He could not care who, among friends, got this office or that—who got to be street inspector or alley commissioner. No principle of goodness, of truth, or right was here. How could he be moved by such things as these? He could not understand why men struggled for such things. He made this remark to me one day, I think at Washington, 'if ever this free people—if this Government itself is ever utterly demoralized, it will come from this human wriggle and struggle for office—a way to live without work; from which nature I am not free myself.' It puzzled him a good deal, at Washington, to know and to get at the root of this dread desire,—this contagious disease of national robbery in the nation's death-struggle.

"Because Mr. Lincoln could not feel any interest in such little things as I have spoken of, nor feel any particular interest in the success of those who were thus struggling and wriggling, he was called indifferent—nay, ungrateful—to his friends.

Especially is this the case with men who have aided Mr. Lincoln all their life. Mr. Lincoln always and everywhere wished his friends well; he loved his friends and clung to them tenaciously, like iron to iron welded; yet he could not be actively and energetically aroused to the true sense of his friends' particularly strong feelings of anxiety for office. From this fact Mr. Lincoln has been called ungrateful. He was not an ungrateful man by any means. He may have been a cool man—a passive man in his general life; yet he was not ungrateful. Ingratitude is too positive a word—it does not convey the truth. Mr. Lincoln may not have measured his friendly duties by the applicant's hot desire; I admit this. He was not a selfish man,—if by selfishness is meant that Mr. Lincoln would do any act, even to promote himself to the Presidency, if by that act any human being was wronged. If it is said that Abraham Lincoln preferred Abraham Lincoln to any one else, in the pursuit of his ambitions, and that, because of this, he was a selfish man, then I can see no objections to such an idea, for this is universal human nature.

"It must be remembered that Mr. Lincoln's mind acted logically, cautiously, and slowly. Now, having stated the above facts, the question of his will and its power is easily solved. Be it remembered that Mr. Lincoln cared nothing for simple facts, manners, modes, ways, and such like things. Be it remembered that he *did* care for truth, right, for principle, for all that pertains to the good. In relation to simple facts, unrelated to substance, forms, rules, methods, ways, manners, he cared nothing; and if he could be aroused, he would do anything for any body at any time, as well foe as friend. As a politician he would courteously grant all facts and forms—all non-essential things—to his opponent. He did so because he did not care for them; they were rubbish, husks, trash. On the question of substance, he hung and clung with all his might. On questions of truth, justice, right, the good, on principle his will was as firm as steel and as tenacious as iron. It was as firm, solid, real, vital, and tenacious as an idea on which the world hinges or hangs. Ask Mr. Lincoln to do a wrong thing, and he would scorn the request; ask him to do an unjust thing, and he would cry, 'Begone!' ask him to sacrifice his convictions of the truth, and his soul would indignantly exclaim, 'The world perish first!'

"Such was Mr. Lincoln's will. On manners and such like things, he was pliable. On questions of right and substance, he was as firm as a rock. One of these classes of men look at Mr. Lincoln from the stand-point of things non-essential, and the other looks at him from the stand-point of substance, rejecting forms. Hence the difference. Mr. Lincoln was a man of firm, unyielding will, when, in human transactions, it was necessary to be so, and *not* otherwise. At one moment Mr. Lincoln was as pliable and expansive as gentle air, and at the next moment he was as biting, firm, tenacious, and unyielding as gravity itself.

"Thus I have traced Mr. Lincoln through his perceptions, his suggestiveness, his judgments, and his four great predominant qualities, namely,—his powers of reason, his great understanding, his conscience, and his heart. I assert that Mr. Lincoln lived in the head. He loved the truth; he loved the eternal right and the good,—never yielding the fundamental conceptions of these to any man for any end.

"All the follies and wrong Mr. Lincoln ever fell into, or committed, sprang or came out of his weak points, namely, his want of quick, sagacious, intuitive judgment,—his want of quick, sagacious, intuitive knowledge of the play and meaning of the features of men as written on the face,—his tenderness and mercy, and, lastly, his utterly unsuspecting nature. He was deeply and seriously honest himself, and assumed that others were so organized. He never suspected men. These, with other defects of his nature, caused all his follies and wrongs, if he ever had any of either.

"All the wise and good things Mr. Lincoln ever did, sprang or came out of his great reason, his conscience, his understanding, and his heart, his love of truth, right, and the good. I am speaking now of his particular and individual faculties and qualities, *not their combination*, nor the result of wise or unwise combinations. Each man and woman must form his or her own estimate of the man in the mind. Run out these facts, qualities, and faculties, and see what they must produce. For instance, a tender heart; a wise, strong reason; a good understanding, an exalted conscience, a love of the good, must, in such combination, practically applied, produce a man of great humanity.

"Take another illustration in the combination of his faculties and qualities. Mr. Lincoln's eloquence lay, 1st, in the strength of his logical faculty, his supreme power of reasoning, his great understanding, and his love of principle; 2d, in his clear, exact, and very accurate vision; 3d, in his cool and masterly statement of his principles, around which the issues gather; in the statement of those issues, and the grouping of the facts that are to carry conviction, aided by his logic, to the minds of men of every grade of intelligence. He was so clear that he could not be misunderstood nor misrepresented. He stood square and bolt upright to his convictions, and formed by them his thoughts and utterances. Mr. Lincoln's mind was not a wide, deep, broad, generalizing, and comprehensive mind, nor versatile quick, bounding here and there, as emergencies demanded it. His mind was deep, enduring, and strong, running in deep iron grooves, with flanges on its wheels. His mind was not keen, sharp, and subtile; it was deep, exact, and strong.

"Whatever of life, vigor, force, and power of eloquence the whole of the above qualities, or a wise combination will give; whatever there is in a fair, manly, honest, and impartial administration of justice, under law, to all men at all times,—through these qualities and capabilities given, never deviating; whatever there is in a strong will in the right, governed by tenderness and mercy; whatever there is in toil and a sublime patience; whatever there is in particular faculties, or a wise combination of them,—not forgetting his weak points,—working wisely, sagaciously, and honestly, openly and fairly;—I say, whatever there is in these, or a combination of them, that Mr. Lincoln is justly entitled to in all the walks of life. These limit, bound, and define him as statesman, orator, as an executive of the nation, as a man of humanity, a good man, and a gentleman. These limit, bound, and define him every way, in all the ways and walks of life. He is under his law and his nature, and he never can get out of it.

"This man, this long, bony, wiry, sad man, floated into our county in 1831, in a frail canoe, down the north fork of the Sangamon River, friendless, pennyless, powerless, and alone,—begging for work in this city,—ragged, struggling for the common necessaries of life. This man, this peculiar man, left us in 1861, the President of the United States, backed by friends and power, by fame, and all human force; and it is well to inquire *how*.

"To sum up, let us say, here is a sensitive, diffident, unobtrusive, natural-made gentleman. His mind was strong and deep, sincere and honest, patient and enduring; having no vices, and having only negative defects, with many positive virtues. His is a strong, honest, sagacious, manly, noble life. He stands in the foremost rank of men in all ages,—their equal,— one of the best types of this Christian civilization."

LXXX.

At the end of six months' incessant labor, my task at the White House drew near completion. On the 22d of July, the President and Cabinet, at the close of the regular session, adjourned in a body to the State Dining-room, to view the work, at last in a condition to receive criticism. Sitting in the midst of the group, the President expressed his "unschooled" opinion, as he called it, of the result, in terms which could not but have afforded the deepest gratification to any artist.

The curiosity of the public to see the picture was so great that during the last two days of my stay in Washington, by the kind permission of the President, it was placed in the East Room, and thrown open to the public. During this time the house was thronged with visitors, the porters estimating their number each day at several thousands.

Towards the close of the second day's exhibition, intending to have the canvas taken down and rolled up during the night for transportation to New York, I watched for an opportunity to say a last word to Mr. Lincoln previous to his leaving for the

Soldiers' Home, where the family were then staying, At four o'clock the carriage drove up to the door, accompanied by the "Black-Horse Cavalry" escort. Knowing the President would soon appear, I stepped out under the portico to wait for him. Presently I caught sight of his unmistakable figure standing half-way between the portico and the gateway leading to the War Department leaning against the iron fence,—one arm thrown over the railing, and one foot on the stone coping which supports it, evidently having been intercepted, on his way in from the War Department, by a plain-looking man, who was giving him, very diffidently, an account of a difficulty which he had been unable to have rectified. While waiting, I walked out leisurely to the President's side. He said very little to the man, but was intently studying the expression of his face while he was narrating his trouble. When he had finished, Mr. Lincoln said to him, "Have you a blank card?" The man searched his pockets, but finding none, a gentleman standing near, who had overheard the question, came forward and said, "Here is one, Mr. President." Several persons had in the mean time gathered around. Taking the card and a pencil, Mr. Lincoln sat down upon the low stone coping, presenting almost the appearance of sitting upon the pavement itself, and wrote an order upon the card to the proper official to "examine this man's case." While writing this, I observed several persons passing down the promenade smiling, at what I presume they thought the undignified appearance of the head of the nation, who, however, seemed utterly unconscious, either of any impropriety in the action, or of attracting any attention. To me it was not only another picture of the native goodness of the man, but of true nobility of character, exemplified not so much by a disregard of conventionalities, as in unconsciousness that there *could* be any breach of etiquette or dignity in the manner of an honest attempt to serve or secure justice to a citizen of the Republic, however humble he might be. Rising to his feet he handed the man the card, with a word of direction, and then turning to me said: "Well C——, I must go in and take one more look at the picture before you leave us." So saying, he accompanied me to the East Room, and sitting down in front of it, remained for some time in silence. I said that I had at length worked out my idea, as he expressed it at our first interview, and would now be glad to hear his final suggestions and criticism.

"There is little to find fault with," he replied; "the portraiture is the main thing, and that seems to me absolutely perfect."

I then called his attention afresh to the accessories of the picture, stating that these had been selected from the objects in the Cabinet chamber with reference solely to their bearing upon the subject. "Yes," said he, "there are the war-maps, the portfolios, the *slave*-map, and all; but the book in the corner, leaning against the chair-leg,—you have changed the title of that, I see." "Yes," I replied; "at the last moment I learned that you frequently consulted, during the period you were preparing the Proclamation, Solicitor Whiting's work on the 'War Powers of the President,' and as Emancipation was the result in fact of a military necessity, the book seemed to me just the thing to go in there; so I simply changed the title, leaving the old sheepskin cover as it was." "Now," said he, "Whiting's book is not a regular law-book. It is all very well that it should be there; but I would suggest that as you have changed the title, you change also the character of the binding. It now looks like an old volume of United States Statutes." I thanked him for this criticism, and then said: "Is there anything else that you would like changed or added?" "No," he replied, and then repeated very emphatically the expression he used when the design was first sketched upon the canvas: "It is as good as it can be made."

I then referred at some length, to the enthusiasm in which the picture was conceived and had been executed, concluding with an expression of my profound appreciation of the very unusual opportunities afforded me in the prosecution of the work, and his unvarying kindness and consideration through the many weeks of our intercourse.

He listened pensively,—almost passively, to me,—his eyes fastened upon the picture. As I finished he turned, and in his simple-hearted, earnest way, said: "C——, I believe I am about as glad over the success of this work as you are." And with these words in my ear, and a cordial "goodbye" grasp of the hand,

President and painter separated: the one to gather into and around himself more and more the affections of a mighty people, till in the culmination and attainment of all his heart's desires he should be called from "glory to glory;" the other, in his humble sphere, to garner as a precious legacy to him and his these fragments of leaves from the daily life of one whose name and fame—inseparably bound up with devotion to freedom and reverence for law, fragrant with the tender memories and sweet humanities of life—are to grow brighter and stronger with God's eternal years, as men learn to appreciate and emulate a true Christian manhood.

INDEX